I WILL GIVE THEM A NEW HEART

I Will Give Them a New Heart

*Reflections on the Priesthood
and the Renewal of the Church*

CONRAD W. BAARS, M.D.

Edited by
Suzanne M. Baars, M.A. and
Bonnie N. Shayne, M.A.

ST PAULS

In accord with canon 830 §3 of the Code of Canon Law, I hereby grant my permission to publish *I Will Give Them a New Heart: Reflections on the Priesthood and the Renewal of the Church* [*Crisis in the Priesthood: Essays on the Priesthood and Religious Life*] by Conrad W. Baars, M.D.

Most Reverend José H. Gomez, S.T.D.
Archbishop of San Antonio
Chancery Office, San Antonio
December 12, 2006

Library of Congress Cataloging-in-Publication Data

Baars, Conrad W.
   I will give them a new heart : reflections on the priesthood and the renewal of the church / by Conrad W. Baars ; edited by Suzanne M. Baars and Bonnie N. Shayne.
      p. cm.
   ISBN 978-0-8189-1245-0
   1. Encouragement—Religious aspects—Christianity. 2. Clergy—Conduct of life. 3. Priesthood. 4. Church renewal. 5. Christian leadership.   I. Baars, Suzanne M.   II. Shayne, Bonnie N.   III. Title.

BV4647.E53B33 2007
253'.2—dc22
                                             2007005348

Produced and designed in the United States of America by the Fathers and Brothers of the Society of St. Paul, 2187 Victory Boulevard, Staten Island, New York 10314-6603 as part of their communications apostolate.

ISBN 13: 978-0-8189-1245-0
ISBN 10: 0-8189-1245-6

Printing Information:

Current Printing - first digit	1	2	3	4	5	6	7	8	9	10

Year of Current Printing - first year shown

2008	2009	2010	2011	2012	2013	2014	2015	2016	2017

Table of Contents

Foreword vii

Introduction ix

A Short Biography of Conrad W. Baars, M.D. xxxi

   I. How to Treat and Prevent the Crisis in the Priesthood 1

   II. Whatever Happened to Religious Life?
      "I Will Give Them a New Heart" 27

   III. The Secret of Affirmation 51

   IV. The Affirming Power of Love 65

   V. Morality and the Christian Anthropology
      of Thomas Aquinas 73

   VI. Philosophy as Intellectual Affirmation of the Seminarian 87

   VII. Mature and Affirming Bishops 97

   VIII. Psychological Aspects of Obedience 105

   IX. A Priest for All Seasons: Masculine and Celibate 145

   X. The Homosexual's Search for Happiness 183

   XI. The Alcoholic Priest 205

   XII. Anger and Forgiveness 215

Appendix A: The Essays of Conrad W. Baars, M.D. in
        Chronological Order 247

Appendix B: Acknowledgments 249

Glossary 251

Bibliography 255

Index 261

About the Editors

Suzanne M. Baars, M.A., LPC, IMFT, is a licensed professional counselor and marriage and family therapist in Texas where she has practiced since 1986. She holds a Master's Degree in Mental Health Counseling. Suzanne has appeared on EWTN's "Living His Life Abundantly" show with Johnette Benkovic and presented the work of her late father, Dr. Conrad Baars, in areas such as treating scrupulosity, Obsessive-Compulsive Disorder, depression and Emotional Deprivation Disorder. In addition to her private practice in Dallas, Texas, she continues the work of her late father as an accomplished and sought after lecturer. She has recorded numerous lectures to better aid both the layperson and professional alike to understand the psychology based on that of St. Thomas Aquinas, which truly integrates a Christian concept of the human person and sound psychological principles: *The Abode of Love: Developing the Heart, Emotional Maturity and the Spiritual Life,* and *Made in His Image: Healing and Wholeness for Living the Affirmed Life.*

Bonnie N. Shayne, M.A., inspired by Dr. Baars' compelling words of compassion and healing for individuals and humanity, has studied his work at length for many years. She is currently working with Suzanne Baars to edit and revise a number of Dr. Baars' books and monographs for publication, both those he authored or co-authored with his mentor, Dr. Anna A. Terruwe, M.D., including *Healing the Unaffirmed, Feeling & Healing Your Emotions* and *Psychic Wholeness and Healing.* She holds a Bachelor's Degree in Psychology and a Master's Degree in Counseling. She maintains the Conrad W. Baars, M.D. website, lectures, and moderates several educational and supportive e-mail discussion groups involving this profound work. She is currently living in San Antonio.

Foreword

Anyone in the Catholic Church familiar with the difficulties she has experienced in the past four decades is concerned with her pastors, their formation and their influence on her flock. My late father, psychiatrist Conrad Baars, M.D., lived out his belief that if we have a healthy and holy clergy, we will have a healthy and holy Church. What he offered was a unique integration of the valid developments of modern psychology and the anthropology of St. Thomas Aquinas which he had discovered in the work of his colleague Anna A. Terruwe, M.D., a fellow Catholic psychiatrist. He worked tirelessly on behalf of priests and religious within the scope of his own psychiatric practice, his writings, and the many lectures he delivered. His concern was not limited to the intellectual and spiritual formation of the clergy in the integration of faith and psychology, but his focus went further, to include mature emotional and psychological development. One could identify many priests and religious who know the faith well yet lack the concomitant psychological maturity and strength to proclaim it assertively and joyfully.

It is for this reason that we recognized the great need to compile my father's monographs related to this important topic in order to offer a more complete presentation of his thought as well as to contribute to the new springtime of evangelization announced by the late Holy Father Pope John Paul II.

I want to thank Bonnie Shayne, M.A., Mary Shayne, B.A.,

Phil Sutton, Ph.D. and W.D.V., S.T.D., for their tireless efforts to make this compilation possible. My gratitude also goes to Father Edmund Lane for his willingness to publish these works.

It is my sincere prayer that the Church and all of her sons and daughters who serve her so selflessly and faithfully may benefit in a profound way from this work of a Catholic psychiatrist who also devoted his own life to serving Christ and the Church.

Suzanne M. Baars, M.A.
May 2007
www.conradbaars.com

Introduction

The purpose of publishing these essays of Conrad W. Baars, M.D., is to make available a psychological doctrine applying the principle of affirming love to topics related to Christian life, particularly as it relates to the priestly heart in Christ.

The essays are a sample but not a systematic exposition of a psychology, based on Thomistic philosophy, which especially treats of the passions — emotions — and their role in our moral and spiritual perfection. As a psychotherapy, this includes healing of human "imperfection" in the emotional weaknesses we suffer as disordering wounds within human nature due to the effects of Original Sin. Among the effects of Original Sin there is a disordering of all the human faculties or powers, that is, a wounding or weakening of the Intellect, the Will, the two sets of emotions, and the body, as well as a disordering of their inter-relations, their hierarchical order, and their principles of function. Of the many efforts to explain these wounds the doctrine of Dr. Baars and his colleague Dr. Terruwe is one of the best interpretations of St. Thomas Aquinas' anthropology as it relates to the modern diagnosis of psychological disorders. This book of essays is a contribution to that doctrine and an application of the project to integrate Faith and psychology. It is a sign of the work of the Holy Spirit renewing the face of the earth in the human heart.

In the beginning God beheld his creation and affirmed

it: "God saw that it was good." After sin, God became man in Christ Jesus to heal us of the wounds that hindered us from being an image of God. As a Catholic psychiatrist, Dr. Baars saw his role to help restore that image of God by continuing the redemptive work of Christ, in particular the healing ministry of Jesus as an affirmer of wounded persons. To this end, Baars introduced into North America a psychotherapeutic approach developed by a Catholic psychiatrist from the Netherlands, Anna A.A. Terruwe, M.D. He introduced into psychological literature in English her concept of *"bevestigen,"* translated as "affirmation" and "affirming living" — terms that refer to the *nature of love* as an affective capacity to be moved by the good of the other, which normally precedes and enriches the effective activity of lovingly doing what is good for the other.

Such an approach is based on the Thomistic metaphysics of love which describes the causality of the good as moving us to love. This beautifully complements the Franciscan emphasis on the Will and affectivity as the human heart. Baars and Terruwe's approach to the healing art of affirming the person balances the roles of mind and heart, and the affective and effective aspects of our nature. There is an *ordo amoris*: St. John the Evangelist tells us "God is love"; St. Paul tells us that charity is the greatest of the theological virtues. Associated with the Charismatic Renewal in the Church, Dr. Baars regarded the Holy Spirit of love to be the source of fruitfulness in his life and ministry of healing through affirming love. In St. Francis — the seraphic doctor pierced with burning love — Baars saw an exemplar of the humanly and Divinely affirmed person who was able to affirm the goodness of God's creation in humanity and in the natural world.

In an insight into what is required to affirm the other person, Dr. Terruwe integrated doctrine on emotional love with the doctrine of Christian charity — *agape*, unselfish love — in the form of the notion: *amor sese retinere* — "love holding itself back." Such a love restrains its outward expressions and gratification to adapt to the needs and capacity of the other to receive. Terruwe and Baars call this *"self-restraining love,"* the charity that takes into account the true good of the other in an unselfish and even self-sacrificial way in regard to one's own passions and needs. This self-restraint is distinct from suppression or repression of one's emotions. By self-restraining love, Intellect and Will respectfully direct one's passions to subside for the sake of a greater good in the service of love. This, St. Thomas teaches, is in accord with the passions whose true nature is to obey reason — under a "political" rather than tyrannical exercise of authority over one's passions. Thus Terruwe integrated her insights with the theological perspective of Christian Faith, seeing in God's love in Christ Jesus the ultimate affirming love that heals human wounds and patiently awaits our graced response.

This self-restraining love finds a particular form in priestly life and celibacy. Most of the essays in this book apply the doctrine of affirming love to priestly ministry: the key essay is "A Priest for all Seasons: Masculine and Celibate." Here Dr. Baars gives us a portrait of the mature man who is called as a priest to be a spiritual father, ready and able to affirm the family of God. In this portrait Baars anticipates what Pope John Paul II, in *Pastores Dabo Vobis,* would refer to as the "human formation" of priestly candidates. In contrast to cultural confusion about male identity, Baars affirms that the male psychology is to be a fighter — not violent, but courageous in defense of the good. Baars recognizes that it is the truly masculine priest who serves the Church *in persona Christi,* in the person of Christ in relation to the Church. In his sacramental role the priest represents Christ precisely as the groom who loves and sacrifices himself for His Bride the Church. This sacrifice is exemplified in priestly celibacy. Baars treats of the human foundations for priestly celibacy on which grace builds to make a man free for commitment of all his energies for the sake of the Kingdom of God. The masculine priest who relates maturely to women appreciates the roles of man and woman in the Church. Baars cites the philosopher and pro-life author, Mary Joyce, who describes the complementary qualities of man and woman. She has a felicitous phrase about the collaboration of the Church's "masculine Magisterium and feminine intuition." Like our Mother Mary, the Church treasures the mysteries of Faith in her heart. The Church relies on the Magisterium exercised in the ministry of Holy Orders to articulate these truths.

In their prophetic office of teacher, priests are called to affirm the truths of Catholic doctrine and morals. Anticipating *Pastores Dabo Vobis*, Dr. Baars calls for a restoration of sound philosophy in the seminary curriculum in his essay, "Philosophy as Intellectual Affirmation of the Seminarian." By this he meant especially, though not exclusively, Thomistic philosophy. He cites the largely Thomistic philosophy curriculum of Polish seminaries, which produces priests who were able to defend the Faith against Communist propaganda. Without intellectual affirmation of the seminarian by truth, he is weakened and less able to teach his flock with the truths that strengthen them in Faith and Morals. Unfortunately, the Church in the West was weakened when sound philosophy, which can rationally present the Faith, was removed from the seminary curriculum. Consequently, priests became less able to nourish the flock with a rational exposition of the truths of the Faith. But in Poland, the intellectual affirmation of seminarians produces courageous clergy such as Karol Wojtyla — Pope John II.

Archbishop Wojtyla of Krakow was in Rome during the 1971 Synod on the Priesthood, and joined bishops gathered informally by Cardinal Wright (as Prefect of the Vatican Congregation for Clergy) to hear Drs. Terruwe and Baars give a talk on the causes of an emerging crisis among priests. This talk is reproduced here. Wojtyla stayed after their presentation to discuss in depth with them the nation of affirmation. They found that he appreciated this doctrine, and was himself a fully affirmed man, capable of affirming the Church and the world by the firm and warm loving manner in which he preached the truth to all, beginning with his first words as pope: "Be not afraid." In his person he exemplified the priestly mind and heart that this book is dedicated to foster.

A Thomistic Approach to Emotional Disorders

The work of Anna Terruwe and Conrad Baars is part of the renewal of the Church as it is served by a revival of Thomism, which is an ongoing development of the search for truth that stems from a doctor of the Church, St. Thomas Aquinas. Dr. Baars studied Thomism at Oxford University in England with Fr. Martin D'Arcy. After World War II, Baars came to the United States and met and married his wife, Mary Jean. They settled briefly near Chicago, Illinois, where he later became acquainted with the local Dominican school of philosophy in River Forest.

This school of thought, called "Aristotelian-Thomism," had a direct influence on Baars even though he was not formally a member of the "Albertus Magnus Lyceum." The leading exponent of this project is Fr. Benedict Ashley, O.P., who summarizes it in his metaphysics book, *The Way Toward Wisdom*.[1] The aim was to interface Aristotelian-Thomism with contemporary science in an approach to God's creation as revealed in the "book of nature" as well as in Revelation. At that time Baars

---

[1] Benedict M. Ashley, *The Way Toward Wisdom: An Interdisciplinary and Intercultural Introduction to Metaphysics,* University of Notre Dame Press, Notre Dame, IN, 2006.

met and became friends with Herbert Ratner, M.D., a member
of the Lyceum and colleague in the Catholic Physicians Guild
(now the Catholic Medical Association). Many years later when
Baars was giving a talk at their annual convention, Ratner was a
guest at the Baars' home a week before Conrad died. Dr. Ratner
is noted for his emphasis on the *respect for nature*, which is the
hallmark of this school of thought. Dr. Baars was fully aware of
this attitude, and of the principle of the proper autonomy of the
social sciences which study human nature. He was careful to
give a priority to Faith and theology, yet not to over-spiritualize
psychological matters. Dr. Ratner cautions against a tendency
to be "...recalcitrant to the teachings God the Father has revealed to us in nature, even though we know by faith that God
authored both the Book of Nature and the Book of Scriptures.
[we]... ignore nature and tend to replace it with sacraments, as
if once grace is possessed, nature is irrelevant."[2] Another friend
Dr. Baars met at the Lyceum was Fr. Jordan Aumann, O.P., who
promoted Baars' translations of Terruwe, wrote comments on
the moral aspects of their psychotherapy, and introduced the
doctrine on affirmation as it pertains to mystical theology in
his courses at the "Angelicum" — the Pontifical University of
St. Thomas in Rome, Italy.

Dr. Baars had originally tried to practice secular psychiatric theory and found it inadequate on many counts. He was
searching for a way to relate psychotherapy and Thomistic
psychology. While visiting relatives in Holland, by Divine
Providence, a cousin and Benedictine monk gave him Terruwe's
book. Baars was convinced her theory offered a way to integrate
psychiatry and the truths about human nature elucidated by St.
Thomas Aquinas. He then deepened his knowledge of Thomism
by study with Fr. Robert Brennan, O.P., who wrote *Thomistic*

---

[2] "Natural Institution of the Family," *Child & Family*, vol. 20, no. 2, 1988.

Psychology.[3] Baars also returned to Holland a number of times and began many years of fruitful collaboration with Anna Terruwe. This included translating her writings into English; indeed some essays in this collection are in part based on her writings as adapted by Baars.

Baars translated Terruwe's major work under the title *The Neurosis in the Light of Rational Psychology* (1960),[4] later revised as *Loving and Curing the Neurotic* (1972).[5] They then divided this into two books, each treating of separate emotional illnesses along the lines of St. Thomas Aquinas' division of the passions into two groups. Thus, the neurotic deprivation of the "concupiscible" emotions — called here "the Pleasure Appetite" — is treated in *Healing the Unaffirmed* (1976).[6] And repression by "irascible" emotions — called here "the Assertive Drive" — is treated in *Psychic Wholeness and Healing* (1981).[7] Much of the Terruwe-Baars doctrine is found in question and answer form in a popular presentation in his *Feeling and Healing Your Emotions* (1979),[8] in which Dr. Baars relates this doctrine to Biblical insights from a Christian perspective.

The classification of emotional disorders according to the involvement of one or both of the two groups of primary emotions is based on Aquinas' anthropology in the treatise on human passions, in his *Summa Theologica*, section Ia IIae, qq.

---

[3] Robert E. Brennan, *Thomistic Psychology: A Philosophic Analysis of the Nature of Man,* Macmillan, New York, 1941.

[4] Anna A. Terruwe, *The Neurosis in the Light of Rational Psychology.* Trans. by Conrad W. Baars, New York: P.J. Kenedy & Sons, 1960.

[5] Anna A. Terruwe and Conrad W. Baars, *Loving and Curing the Neurotic: A New Look at Emotional Illness,* Arlington House, New Rochelle, NY, 1972.

[6] Conrad W. Baars and Anna A. Terruwe, *Healing the Unaffirmed: Recognizing Emotional Deprivation Disorder.* Rev. ed., Suzanne M. Baars and Bonnie N. Shayne, eds., ST PAULS/Alba House, Staten Island, NY, 2002.

[7] Anna A. Terruwe and Conrad W. Baars, *Psychic Wholeness and Healing: Using All the Powers of the Human Psyche,* Alba House, Staten Island, NY, 1981.

[8] Conrad W. Baars, *Feeling and Healing Your Emotions,* Rev. ed., Suzanne M. Baars and Bonnie N. Shayne, eds., Bridge-Logos, Gainesville, FL, 2003.

22-48.[9] The *Summa* is a theological text organized as a threefold study which includes the creation of humans by God, the human moral act, and the saving act of Christ whereby He enables humans to participate by grace in a return to God. In the section on the human act, Aquinas treats of its sources: the Intellect, the Will *and the emotions* as embodied. Aquinas' treatise on the passions is unsurpassed today as a basis for philosophical psychology.

The idea of utilizing the Thomistic doctrine on the passions to interpret mental illnesses as these were being newly identified by emerging psychological science and psychotherapeutic practice originated from Fr. Willem A. Duynstee, C.Ss.R., a professor at the Catholic University in Nijmegen, the Netherlands. In 1936, he offered to Dutch Catholic psychiatrists, who were dissatisfied with the moral implications of the Freudian approach, an alternative approach based on Thomism: "The Theory of Repression Judged from a Thomistic Standpoint." Fr. Duynstee hypothesized that while Freud's observations might be accurate, his theory and therapy have flaws. Freud "blamed" what he called repression on the "Superego" — his version of the conscience. We speak imprecisely of "repression" as it is a concept yet to be scientifically clarified. In popular culture Freud's ideas were absorbed into modern society by Freudianism, which caricatured the moral conscience as the source of neuroses. This reinforced a general rejection of moral absolutes and promoted moral relativism. The effect of such tendencies in Western society has been a decline of morality, the spread of permissiveness, and an ensuing social decadence. It has led to a "therapeutic mentality" which displaces sin with sickness, morality with psychology, and fosters narcissism.

---

[9] *Summa Theo.*, Ia IIae, qq. 22-48 (*Summa Theologica: St. Thomas Aquinas,* translated by the Fathers of the English Dominican Province, Westminster, MD: Christian Classics, 1981).

The alternative direction was taken by Duynstee, Terruwe, and Baars who respect the different domains of psychology and religion. These three scholars cautiously reinterpreted the findings of Freud and others regarding newly developing concepts about emotional illness and related them to Thomistic philosophical psychology. Their foundation has yet to be fully explored. As Baars was in private practice, not teaching at a university, he had no academic disciples to disseminate the doctrine. Though he wrote and lectured, the Terruwe-Baars theory and terms have yet to be "mainstreamed" into contemporary psychology.

The Deprivation of Love and the Importance of Affirmation

The essays in this book often speak of the disorder of "emotional deprivation" or in lesser degree in the "unaffirmed state." The Terruwe-Baars "deprivation neurosis" is broader than, but approximates to some degree, several categories found in the *Diagnostic and Statistical Manual of Mental Disorders* of the American Psychiatric Association[10] including some of the Axis II personality disorders. To help in classification and terminological issues, Dr. Baars' daughter, Suzanne Baars, herself a practicing psychotherapist, adapted his terms to current usage. Hence, the illness of the Pleasure Appetite is now called "Emotional Deprivation Disorder." There is yet no like term for "repressive" illnesses of the Assertive Drive, referred to by Terruwe and Baars as "fear neurosis," "energy neurosis," and "fear neurosis camouflaged by energy." This is in part due to the unresolved meaning of repression, as mentioned above. In this text we refer to the irascible passions under the term "as-

---

[10] American Psychiatric Association: *Diagnostic and Statistical Manual of Mental Disorders*, Fourth Edition, Text Revision. Washington, DC, American Psychiatric Association, 2000.

sertive emotions" as preferable to earlier editions which used the term "utility emotions." This is based on the idea behind the Latin usage of St. Thomas, who collectively named this set of emotions from anger — from *ira* for *irascible* — to signify that these passions draw on the force of anger to overcome difficulty and danger. This terminology relates to Dr. Baars' original development of the doctrine on anger as assertiveness (not unprovoked aggressiveness), and the proper way to address anger in forgiveness. Because these are relevant on the priestly ministry of reconciliation, we include an essay on this topic.

At the time Terruwe began her psychiatric work, psychiatry focused on repression as the cause of neuroses. To her credit, Terruwe thought "outside the box" — prompted by a physical therapist, Franz Veldman, to whom she referred her patients. Veldman would later develop a doctrine and establish a discipline of Haptonomy, based on the power of affectivity, manifested through touch. Terruwe was open to Veldman's clinical observations regarding patients who did not have symptoms of repression. Having the perspective of the Thomistic distinction of two sets of primary emotions — the Pleasure Appetite and the Assertive Drive — *Terruwe was able to conceptualize that there are illnesses proper to each set of human emotions.* Hence: repression involves the Assertive Drive as it relates to the Pleasure Appetite; the other is an emotional illness related solely to the Pleasure Appetite itself. Terruwe at first called this the "frustration neurosis" to indicate that a lack of being loved causes a frustration of the human need for happiness and joy. She later termed this the "deprivation neurosis." In light of current usage, Suzanne Baars has adapted this into "Emotional Deprivation Disorder." The sub-clinical but widely seen form of deprivation in lesser degrees is called the "unaffirmed state."

Terruwe's great discovery was to psychologically identify this wound to the human heart, its cause in the denial of affirming love, and its healing by an affirming other. Terruwe also recognized that not only professional psychotherapists but emotionally mature persons can do much to heal unaffirmed persons, provided they understand what is needed and unselfishly will the good of the other person.

Terruwe's discoveries of truths about the psychological aspects of human love, the wounds it suffers, and the way to truly heal the human heart, were acknowledged in 1969 in a private audience with *Pope Paul VI; he affirmed her healing ministry as "a gift to the Church."* Yet no one has appreciated Anna Terruwe's gift more than Conrad Baars who faithfully developed and transmitted it. These two colleagues have taught us much about love and healing; we tenderly speak of them as "doctors of the heart."

Moral Aspects of Therapy for Repression

It is imperative at this juncture in Church history, when a new generation seeks to protect the Faith in response to a half century of crisis in the Church, that we reassure the faithful regarding the Terruwe-Baars doctrine and psychotherapeutic method as it relates to religious truth and morals. Dr. Baars belonged to the Fellowship of Catholic Scholars and was aware of the issues facing theology and the social sciences during this era. To help address this situation, we have cited an extended passage from *The Peasant of the Garonne* by Jacques Maritain.[11] This passage is relevant as a context for responding to a few concerns which have been raised about the Terruwe-Baars doctrine and practice in relation to the tenets of the Catholic Faith. Maritain's perspective on the pre- and post-Vatican II Church provides a

---

[11] Jacques Maritain, *The Peasant of the Garonne: An Old Layman Questions Himself About the Present Time,* translated by Michael Cuddihy and Elizabeth Hughes. Holt, Rinehart and Winston, New York, 1968.

wider context for issues in the relation of faith and psychology. For this reason it is part of the background to the essays in this book on the priesthood. Priests encounter these issues in their ministry as confessors and spiritual counselors when this relates to persons in psychotherapy. This is treated at length in Terruwe and Baars' *Psychic Wholeness and Healing*, which is about repressive disorders and the moral issues involved.

This section will touch on moral theology and its related discipline of ascetical theology *as these pertain to the problems of persons which obsessive-compulsive and other repressive neuroses. It does not pertain to discussions about normal persons.* This caveat must not be forgotten, because what applies in the case of the emotionally ill person is not identical to what applies to the psychologically healthy person. Pope John Paul II teaches that there are not different degrees of obligation to the moral law. All are equally obliged to respect the objective moral order and norms. But also the pope acknowledges that there can be different degrees of moral readiness and culpability. We are referring to this degree of gradual readiness when we speak of the moral aspects of the area under treatment in patients during psychotherapy. Bishop Sheen, who studied under the Catholic philosopher of psychology, Cardinal Mercier, once stated that "the denial of guilt is the cause of all neuroses." We can offer two interpretations of his remark. He could have referred to the fact that *not* to take responsibility for sin can be a cause of psychological afflictions as well as of moral disorder. The normal person who denies his or her guilt can become emotionally disordered precisely because such denial is a form of suppression of the moral truth, and that is unhealthy because it redounds to the psychological dimension. But Sheen certainly could not have meant that every neurotic person needs to become more preoccupied with guilt in order to be healed.

At the intersection of moral theology and psychology is

the question of Free Will. One aim of psychotherapy is to restore normal functioning of the emotions so that the person is better able to subordinate the passions to the guidance of Intellect and Will. Our Will and its freedom are at the core of our being and our capacity for moral action and responsibility. By this power we direct our lives and, as it were, fashion who we are by our choices and actions. God Himself never forces our Will and never permits the devil to rob us of this power. Only we can enslave ourselves to sin. However, due to the effects of sin, our Will has been weakened. This wound to the Will and its relation to the passions in persons suffering from obsessive-compulsive disorders and other emotional illnesses can diminish their readiness for moral freedom and culpability in the areas of repression. Drs. Terruwe and Baars spent their professional lives with this mystery of how the effects of Original Sin wound the emotional dimension of the person and how this affects the freedom of the Will. It is a complex matter: those who have not been engaged in this problem in depth should not be too quick to evaluate the moral aspects of therapy. That is why we have cautioned that the problems and remedies considered below are always within the context of what applies to the emotionally afflicted person, *not* to the normal person.

In a topic involving such delicate moral matters, it is to be expected that a few concerns have been raised by sincere persons whom we do not name so as to focus on the merits of the point itself. The first occurred in the pre-Vatican II era when Terruwe's therapy for repression was mistakenly associated with Freudianism as a disregard for the moral conscience, and as such reported to the Holy Office in Rome (the Congregation for the Doctrine of the Faith, which is responsible for protecting orthodoxy in faith and morals). This is ironic as her approach offers a "Catholic" alternative to Freudianism. Without any input from her, a *monitium* was issued by the Holy Office. Although not mentioning Terruwe by name, it warned clergy and seminarians not to consult women psychiatrists. Dr. Terruwe obediently respected this. Later, at Baars' urging, she wrote a defense, and with the help of Archbishop Alfrink of Utrecht who interceded in the Vatican, her therapeutic method was reconsidered. On April 9, 1965, in a missive released through Alfrink, the Holy Office expressed regret if Terruwe's good name had suffered. It also declared that the Holy Office is "...completely certain of her loyalty to the Catholic Faith, and convinced that her writings, based on sound and proper principles, could be of great help both to priests and to others."[12] Xavier Rynne notes that the public restoration of Dr. Terruwe's good name was at that time considered "unique in the annals of the Holy Office"; (on June 10th, 1965 at the Eucharistic Congress, Pope Paul VI made a similar gesture on behalf of Galileo, urging us "to imitate the faith of Galileo").

There are two other instances we know of when concerns were raised abut the moral aspects of the Terruwe-Baars doctrine. In response to Baars' talk, "Whatever Happened to Religious Life?" given to religious sisters in a 1978 gathering of *Consortium Perfectae Caritas* (now the Institute on Religious Life), a concern was raised if Baars was blaming the Church and asceticism for the crisis in religious life. It was also asked if Baars underestimated the effects of Original Sin and was too optimistic about the goodness of human emotions. More recently, a similar concern came from a scholar studying the causes of the clergy sex abuse scandal. A similar concern was raised in response to the text of the talk Terruwe and Baars had given in Rome, "How to Treat and Prevent the Crisis in the Priesthood." In this case, the concern was if Baars attributed

---

[12] *Herder Correspondence*, Sept-Oct 1965, p. 289, citing *Katholiek Archief*, 16 April, 1965; cf. also "Letter from Vatican City" by Xavier Rynne, *The New Yorker*, Sept. 11, 1965, p. 145.

the clergy crisis to asceticism — when instead, was it not the opposite — was the crisis due to a *lack* of clerical asceticism during the era of misconduct? A major neglect of ascetical practices occurred among Catholics in the permissive era, and this was a partial, but not the specific, cause of the clergy misconduct. Baars died before this scandal became widely publicized, so he did not comment on it directly. But both he and Terruwe, as psychiatrists who treated many clergy, were aware of a crisis in the priesthood which they prophetically warned the hierarchy about in their talk in Rome.

It is ironic that two psychiatrists explicitly dedicated to healing the disordering effect on emotions caused by Original Sin and all sin, are thought to deny Original Sin to the point of finding too much goodness in human emotions. Drs. Terruwe and Baars' optimism came from the promise and power of grace; it was not a Pelagian confidence in unaided natural powers. A favorite prayer of theirs was from the Roman Missal, the fourth week of Easter: "Father, in restoring human nature you have given us a greater dignity than we had in the beginning." Their view is that of St. Thomas Aquinas who affirms the goodness of human passions and their role as sources contributing to the perfection of the human moral act. This position is confirmed by the new *Catechism of the Catholic Church* (#1762-1775),[13] which teaches that emotions in themselves are morally neutral and become moral only as they are taken up into the virtues (or vices). Further, the *Catechism* makes its own a passage of St. Thomas that Baars often cites: "Moral perfection consists in man's being moved to the good not by his will alone, but also by his sensitive appetite, as in the words of the psalm, 'My heart and my flesh sing for joy to the living God'" (CCC, #1770, citing Aquinas

---

[13] *Catechism of the Catholic Church*, Washington, DC: United States Catholic Conference, 1994.

and Psalm 84). The authentic doctrine of Aquinas teaches that
the Virtues of Temperance and Fortitude are precisely the right
formation of the passions of the Pleasure Appetite and Assertive Drive.

Baars' essay, "Morality and the Christian Anthropology
of Thomas Aquinas," gives further background. He summarizes the research of scholars who studied the original texts of
Aquinas and found that his authentic doctrine on human nature was not always fully transmitted. In later centuries it was
corrupted into a rationalism that excluded the emotions from
the moral life, or replaced by a voluntarism that aimed to altogether extinguish the passions by exercise of sheer Will. Baars'
essay, "The Psychological Aspects of Obedience," based on Fr.
Willem Duynstee's writings on justice and law, is a critique of
the harmful effects of voluntarism. This is corroborated by Fr.
Servais Pinckaers, O.P. who has written of the deleterious effect
of voluntarism on moral theology. All this research suggests that
the crisis of the permissive era can be traced back to the pre-
ceding era of authoritarianism. Authoritarianism, legitimated
by a voluntarist mentality and involving repression, provoked
its opposite: an equally voluntaristic rebellious rejection of all
authority. Extremes provoke each other: *extrema se tanguent.*

Now let us to turn to the wisdom of Jacques Maritain
to provide a perspective on the crisis in terms of the mutual
causality of extremes. In *The Peasant of the Garonne*, Maritain
describes the crisis in the Church as a torrent that rages around
but does not shake the island of sanity which is the orthodox
teachings of Vatican Council II. The Council's sound teachings
must be distinguished from unorthodox influences that taint
the application of its teachings. This has come to the forefront
recently with a critique of the way Vatican II has been mis-
applied. Maritain points to a major source of the problem, an
infection which had persisted in the Church for centuries:

Manichean dualism. Dualism is the erroneous view that only the soul is good and important for salvation and the body is evil, or at most, morally indifferent. If the body is evil, then a person might regard it suitable to repress the passions to save their soul. Or, if the body and its passions are morally indifferent for the soul, a person might regard sensuality in a permissive way. This dualism has for centuries infected Christians' attitudes and practices even though it is contrary to the official doctrine of the Church. Maritain claims that the distorting influence of dualism is manifest in two extremes: "despising the world" which then provokes its opposite of "kneeling before the world." In psychological language, these are the repressive and permissive swings of the pendulum. Too much despising of the world, Maritain says, resulted in an "untenable psychic burden" — which Terruwe and Baars identify as the tension of repression. In the permissive era, dualism is manifest in a "kneeling before the world."

That there was an "untenable psychic burden" can be missed by younger scholars who experienced the ravages of the permissive era but have little first hand experience of the now mostly deceased generation of those who suffered repression. In the Church, one must distinguish a critique limited to causes of specific conditions afflicting the emotionally ill, from the liberal critique of tradition in general. One must also distinguish the non-neurotic effect of inordinate ascetical practices by a normal adult from the predisposing repressive effects of a premature pedagogy of fear in some children, which is then followed in religious or priestly formation by flawed ascetical practices done in blind obedience to voluntaristic authorities. In persons with predisposing early childhood factors, excessive and unbalanced ascetical practices and voluntaristic authoritarianism in adult life can become aggravating factors for repression. Terruwe and Baars identify this psychological burden and its associated moral tension.[14] These are due to the mistaken anthropology of dualism: it values only the spirit, not the body or the emotions. It aims to entirely extinguish the passions which are treated as a threat to morality. Hopefully, dualism has been finally rooted out by an authentic anthropology and moral theology attributed in good part to John Paul II's *Theology of the Body*.[15]

Our response to the concerns raised requires us to put them in a larger context by appealing to two distinctions clarified by Jacques Maritain. First, there is the distinction we have been explaining between *authentic Church teaching* and foreign elements that distort this *as it is applied in policies in the practical – prudential order.* Second, there is distinction between the *Church herself* and her *members.* Jacques Maritain explains this distinction in his book, *On the Church of Christ: The Person of the Church and Her Personnel.*[16] It is a distinction between the indefectible Church herself, and her members who are sinners. In historic crises it is *not the Magisterium* that is at fault, for it cannot be in error. Rather, problems occur because of the human element — *personnel who fail.* They might fail due to moral faults, a lack of knowledge of better practices, imprudent policies in the practical order, or due to a lack in their prayer life, which kept them from being open to guidance by the Holy Spirit in their practical decisions and actions. By distinguishing in the Church her Divine aspect from the imperfect human element, and combining this distinction with that between official teaching and practical attitudes and policies, one may legitimately "blame" personnel for their attitudes and practices, without faulting the Church herself or her official teachings. Baars legitimately at-

---

[14] See *Psychic Wholeness and Healing* for an in-depth discussion on this topic.

[15] John Paul II, *The Theology of the Body: Human Love in the Divine Plan*, Pauline Books & Media, Boston, 1997.

[16] Jacques Maritain, *On the Church of Christ: The Person of the Church and Her Personnel*, Trans. by Joseph W. Evans, University of Notre Dame Press, Notre Dame, IN, 1973.

tributes problems to the human element: to the attitudes and policies of personnel.

With these distinctions as background, we can make a more specific reply to the concern raised if Baars were "blaming the Church or asceticism for the crisis." That is not the case. Asceticism is self-discipline in renunciation of sin and vices, and even of earthly goods in service of greater freedom for holy excellence, for attachment to God. Terruwe and Baars rely on ideas about asceticism presented by Fr. Duynstee in his untranslated text, "The Significance of Neurosis for the Study of Asceticism." Duynstee recognized that in the past asceticism emphasized mortification of the Pleasure Appetite; this is quite understandable because our desires can be disordered by temptations. But Duynstee proposed that a *balanced asceticism* should mortify *both* the Pleasure Appetite (concupiscible emotions) *and* the Assertive Drive (irascible emotions). This latter is especially suited to our utilitarian times. Terruwe and Baars applied this approach in a psychotherapeutic regimen limited to treatment of repressive disorders, calling their method *"mortification therapy."* In their books they explain this therapy, and what they mean by the psychological effects of *flawed* ascetical practices, as distinguished from sound ones. The dualist attitude underlies *flawed* ascetical practices — not authentic ones. *This distinction between authentic and flawed asceticism is crucial for understanding the views of Terruwe and Baars.* Their critique is directed at flawed mortifications that aggravate emotional disorders, so these can be distinguished from sound mortifications necessary for emotional and moral growth. Terruwe and Baars' therapy does not aim to extinguish the sense of guilt or eliminate the conscience, but rather, it is nothing less than a moral re-education of the passions so they can be integrated under the guidance of Intellect and Will, and thus contribute to the perfection of the human moral act in the redeemed person.

Terruwe and Baars' insights contribute to knowledge of the psychological wounds due to Original Sin by specifying the particular emotional disorders in our wounded nature. They have done this by identifying the pathogenesis of the diseases. They have found that flawed ascetical practices can aggravate emotional wounds such as excessive fear. And they have developed ways to treat these illnesses, which include the use of specific mortifications as a necessary part of restoring both emotional health and moral freedom. In all of this, these psychiatrists have contributed to the Christian participation in Christ's work of redeeming human nature.

Conclusion

The doctrine of affirming love is an important prescription for healing the Church during this time of polarization, and hence a remedy to be used in priestly ministry. Baars called on brothers and sisters to love even those who disagree with them, not to love only those on their side: "for what merit is there in that, even the Pharisees do as much." We are called to affirm the other precisely in his otherness, seeing the good in his person and intentions, though we might at the same time have to disagree with their positions or even firmly oppose their errors. This is the import of Baars' essay on leadership, "Mature and Affirming Bishops" — which applies also to pastors in the parish as they seek to reconcile their flock in unity.

Affirmation can bridge the gap between polarized members of the Church. It not only reminds us to love our "enemy," but it helps us to know *how* to love them. This is according to *different types of affirmation*, which Dr. Baars distinguishes as: *emotional affirmation, intellectual affirmation, and moral affirmation*. We noted above the importance of sound philosophy in the seminary curriculum to affirm and prepare future priests. Without the distinction of different types of affirmation, we can fall into mistaken notions about affirmation, such as approval of everything in the name of "love." Such emotionalism pervades the permissive era. Genuine emotional affirmation delights in the good of the other. We accept the other's unique personhood by our affective power in the emotions of our Pleasure Appetite, as well as by our will for their good. But when persons are in error, or misbehave, all our faculties, including our Assertive Drive emotions must be activated along with our Intellect and Will to oppose their mistakes and misconduct. This is done through intellectual affirmation which presents the true and corrects mistaken ideas, and by moral affirmation, which directs us to the good and disciplines misconduct. The true and the good intellectually and morally affirm. And whatever strengthens a person on these levels redounds to also affirm their emotions. Untruth and moral misconduct cannot bear good fruit in the emotional dimension, for by denying the other person the truth or the good, we frustrate their person and hence their emotional life as well.

Baars warned about the harm done by erroneous teachings in sexual morality in his critique of the permissive approach found in the book, *Human Sexuality,*[17] which Baars labeled "psychotheological quicksand." He and Dr. Terruwe were early and strong proponents of *Humanae Vitae*. Terruwe went to Rome when it was issued in 1968 to show her support for Pope Paul VI. An application of their distinction between the emotional acceptance of a person, as distinguished from an intellectual opposition or moral correction of their position, is exemplified in Baars' essay "The Homosexual's Search for Happiness." Like his contemporary Fr. John Harvey who ministers to homosexuals, Baars too emphasizes affirmation of *the person* of the homosexual. It is Baars' thesis that homosexual persons have expe-

---

[17] Anthony Kosnik et al., *Human Sexuality — New Directions in American Catholic Thought: A Study commissioned by the Catholic Theological Society of America*, Paulist Press, New York, 1977.

rienced a lack of affirming love and even rejection. We should not further this feeling of alienation, but heal the emotional dimension of the person in this unaffirmed state. At the same time, we hold firmly to Church teaching about this orientation and the moral status of disordered sexual acts, for it affirms the person to communicate the truth which sets us free.

Dr. Baars worked with patients whose problems included alcoholism. Among them were clergy whom he treated at a center in Minnesota, Guest House, and at a program that he helped start, the House of Affirmation. Unfortunately, he soon departed from the latter program because it did not represent his approach or develop as he had hoped it would. His essay on "The Alcoholic Priest" shows us the way to approach addiction crises within the life of a priest as this might involve obsessive-compulsive disorders. Could the tragedy of clerical abuse of minors have been alleviated if there were a better grasp of its causes in the light of the Thomistic psychology of Terruwe-Baars which went unheeded at that time? In the face of the anguish felt by victims, it is helpful to read Baars' original contribution on the nature of anger and forgiveness, addressed in many of his talks which have been synthesized into the text "Anger and Forgiveness." If we respond to the anger of victims and the failings of clergy with this approach to forgiveness and mercy, we can with God's grace heal the victims, the clergy and the Church.

Dr. Baars saw his work of healing the wounded members of the Church as a way to overcome not only individual suffering but to heal the collective crisis in the Church. We hope the lessons in this book serve the Holy Spirit's renewal of the heart of the Church. As St. Francis was called by Christ "to rebuild my Church," so may the Holy Spirit form the heart of each priest so he may serve as a mature and affirming man "for all seasons."

© WDV

A Short Biography of Conrad W. Baars, M.D.

Conrad Walter Baars was born in 1919 in Rotterdam, the Netherlands, the second of six children of Walter Baars and Constance de Groot. Walter Baars was an international business lawyer and served as mayor of Rotterdam. Conrad was sent to England to Campion Hall, Oxford, where he was introduced to the thought of St. Thomas Aquinas by Father Martin D'Arcy. Conrad also studied chemical engineering in Holland at Delft University. Inspired by his uncle, Professor Marius Van Bouwdyk Baastianse, who was dean of Obstetrics and Gynecology at Amsterdam University Medical School, Conrad enrolled in medical school. The Nazi occupation led to a raid on the school; Conrad hid and escaped, and entered the underground resistance. He aided downed Allied flyers, for which he would later receive the Croix du Combattant de L'Europe. The Nazis captured and sent him to Buchenwald concentration camp, where he remained until it was liberated by the United States Army under General Patton.

Baars described his ordeal in Buchenwald as an "imprisonment within the prison" because the Communist prisoners took control of the other prisoners in a reign of terror which taught the young Conrad the crucial difference between the rhetoric and reality of Communism. He came to realize that not only political freedom, but also interior, spiritual freedom is needed for human dignity. The faith he had received as a child matured under the trials of prison existence. He deepened his love of Jesus in the Eucharist — Whom he could receive on the rare occasions when another prisoner who was a priest was able to secretly celebrate Mass.

Because of his medical profession, Conrad was assigned to the Buchenwald infirmary. The refusal of the Nazis to provide him with adequate food and medicine to treat his patients was a source of great frustration and anger which, along with other stresses of prison existence and his own malnourishment, may have predisposed Conrad to develop a cardiac condition which would later contribute to his early death. Though infuriated by his captors, he dared not express this anger lest that interfere with what good he could do for his suffering patients. He recognized that his anger had stimulated life-saving adrenaline, and later wrote that, "next to my faith in God, it was my anger at the Nazis for having deprived me of my liberty and their inhuman treatment of their prisoners, that motivated me to survive and to deny them the satisfaction of seeing me defeated and dead." Indeed, prisoners who gave in to despair became weak and sick. Of the one thousand prisoners sent to Buchenwald in the same transport with Conrad, only six survived the entire ordeal.

After World War II, Conrad emigrated to the United States, completing his residency at Loretto Hospital in Oak Park, Illinois. While in the Chicago area, he met Mary Jean Kennedy, and they were married in 1948. Conrad and Mary Jean later moved to Minnesota and had three children: Michael, Suzanne, and Eleanor. (Michael Baars works for a financial management group in Missouri and maintains an Internet based mail order business for his father's books and tapes, Suzanne Baars is a psychotherapist in private practice in Dallas, and Eleanor Baars Moser is married with five children in Dallas.) Conrad received his physician's license, and practiced psychiatry at Anoka State Hospital. During the Korean War he was at Camp Cooke, California where he treated soldiers suffering from psychological trauma. He then worked at Rochester State Hospital (Minnesota) before entering private psychiatric practice from 1960 to 1973. He became convinced that the accepted psychiatric theories and therapy were inadequate, and his quest for a deeper understanding of human nature led him to Thomistic Psychology and the work of Dr. Anna A. Terruwe. During this time, his association with priests and religious increased because he was a consultant for residents of Guest House, a treatment center for alcoholic clergy.

In 1973 he became a founding member of the first House of Affirmation, a therapeutic community for treating emotionally troubled priests and religious. Conrad had hoped that in this setting the discoveries of Fr. Willem Duynstee and Dr. Anna Terruwe could be implemented to heal and strengthen clergy and religious. Shortly thereafter, he came into sharp theoretical and practical conflict with the director. When Baars submitted his resignation in the hope that this would prompt an inquiry about the director, the Board of Directors instead notified Baars that he himself had been removed as an officer of the House of Affirmation. Only one board member, Fr. John C. Ford, S.J., the distinguished moral theologian who had made an extensive investigation into the matter, voted in Baars' favor. Immediately after that board meeting, Fr. Ford also resigned. He remained a friend and advisor to Conrad.

Dr. Baars had made great sacrifices to move his family and give up his private practice in order to come to Massachusetts to found the House of Affirmation; under these circumstances he had to leave the future of this therapeutic center in the hands of the director, Fr. Thomas Kane, whom he did not consider a proper interpreter of the authentic approach to affirmation. In the late 1980's, the crisis and scandal involving Fr. Kane's malfeasance at the House of Affirmation was vindication of Dr. Baars' position and convictions.

Dr. Baars also differed with those whose views dominated the American Psychiatric Association and eventually he resigned his membership there. He was pleased to join the newly founded Fellowship of Catholic Scholars and was a long-time member of the Catholic Physicians' Guild. Throughout his professional career, Dr. Baars was a strong advocate of the right to life of the unborn child. Conrad was a founding member of the Minnesota Citizens for Life; he was a Trustee in Alternatives to Abortion International, and a Director of the World Federation of Doctors Who Respect Human Life. Conrad was associated with Robert E. and Mary R. Joyce, pro-life philosophers whose ideas impressed him deeply.

In the last years of his life, Dr. Baars practiced psychiatry in San Antonio, Texas. There he was associated with the healing ministry, conducted by members of the charismatic prayer movement in the Church. Although not an active charismatic, Conrad was devoted to the Holy Spirit and gave seminars on healing.

Baars also participated in seminars for renewal of the clergy and religious, such as the programs held in St. Louis in 1978 by the Institute on Religious Life, and that at Seattle University in 1980 on Emotional Development in Religious Life.

In 1980 Conrad W. Baars was the recipient of the Christian Culture Award, bestowed annually by Assumption University in Canada, to "an outstanding lay exponent of Christian ideals." Other recipients of this award have been Sigrid Undset, Jacques Maritain, Dorothy Day, and Malcolm Muggeridge.

Dr. Baars made extensive lecture tours in the United States and Canada in order to explain what he called the "ecology of the emotions" — the nature of emotional integration, affectivity, and authentic affirmation. In November of 1980 he collapsed just as he was beginning a speech at a conference in Canada. His heart was ailing; he learned that there is a form of myocardial ischemia stimulated specifically by the stress of public speaking, which can cause traumatic myocardial infarction. Dr. Baars had to give up lecturing and saw fewer clients.

In the fall of 1981, at the Catholic Physician's Guild meeting in San Antonio, Dr. Baars gave what would be his last talk, addressing the emotionally healthy family. He and Mary Jean hosted a dinner at their home for their friends, noted family physician Herbert Ratner, and Charles Corcoran, O.P., specialist in philosophical psychology. A few weeks later, Conrad went into the hospital for emergency gall bladder surgery; while recovering, he suffered cardiac arrest. Conrad W. Baars, M.D., entered eternal life on October 18th, 1981, the Feast of St. Luke the Physician. We thank God for the legacy of life and love, ideas and work he gave his wife and children, his family, friends, and patients.

CHAPTER I

How to Treat and Prevent the Crisis in the Priesthood

Everyone agrees that a crisis exists in the priesthood. Not everyone realizes that this crisis, as the title of this paper suggests, amounts to an illness, severe in some, moderate to slight in others.

It is the purpose of this paper to go beyond some of the recent excellent sociological and psychological studies by priest-researchers and confirm their findings by exposing the root causes of this illness in the priesthood, and for that matter, also in our society. It will be shown that it is the Church herself, hierarchy and priests alike, who must be the primary physicians to heal the sick, prevent the illness, and check its contagion, assisted in various ways by medical experts in this particular area of pathology.

For reasons to be explained later, the Church cannot permit herself to be tardy in this matter and allow the secular sciences to assume a role that is uniquely the Church's. If ever, it is now that the Church must lead and guide, not passively wait and trail behind the sciences, which are just beginning to comprehend what in truth has been the Church's most precious possession from the beginning.

Throughout the ages, it has been not so much the Church as a whole, but rather a relatively few of her members, her most sainted, yet at the same time her most truly human members who, precisely because they were so human in the best sense of the word, were able to live the words of Christ, "I came to bring you life, that you may have it more abundantly" (John 10: 10). Francis of Assisi, Damien the Leper, John XXIII and Mother Teresa are some of those fully grown people capable of giving abundant life to others! In our day, however, the People of God, priests included, suffer so acutely in their need for identity, self-worth, self-love and being loved that the Church must learn the life-giving "secret" of a Francis, a Damien, a John and a Teresa, and share it with all. Now, not later!

In their study, "Some factors associated with voluntary withdrawal from the Catholic priesthood," Father Schallert and Miss Kelley state, "...the drop-out priest is not the only priest who feels strange or foreign in the Catholic Church today. Nor is his alienation qualitatively or quantitatively very much different from the 'stay-in' priest." They define the sense of alienation apparently experienced by a very large number of priests as "a sense of powerlessness, normlessness, meaningless, self-estrangement and isolation." They conclude their study: "Far more research is needed before the phenomenon of the clerical drop-out is completely understood."

In the summary report of the National Conference of Catholic Bishops[1] Ad Hoc Committee for the Study on Priestly Life and Ministry, one reads, "The underdeveloped, emotionally immature priests represent a large segment of American priests and... reflect the fact that a great many American males are also underdeveloped." The authors describe the manifestations of this incomplete personal development as, "distant, unrewarding relationships and uneasiness about intimacy with as result few close friends; difficulty with one's own personal identity; non-

---

[1] Editors' Note: now called the United States Conference of Catholic Bishops.

integrated psychosexual identity; and lack of self-confidence." Both studies confirm what my colleague from the Netherlands, Dr. Anna Terruwe, and I have observed in our clinical psychiatric practices of a combined total of forty years and approximately 15,000 patients — 10% of whom were priests and religious — and what we have been able to narrow down to one specific cause, namely, non-affirmation. This is not to say that all priests with psychological problems are non-affirmed. Some priests are afflicted with another type of emotional illness, a repressive disorder. In general, we estimate that 10-15% of all priests in Western Europe and North America are mature; 20-25% have serious psychiatric difficulties, especially in the form of neurotic disorders and chronic alcoholism, or a combination of both; and 60-70% suffer from a degree of emotional immaturity which does not prevent them from exercising their priestly function but precludes their being happy men and effective priests whose fundamental role is to bring people the joy of Christ's love and to be the appointed affirmers of all.

We have been advised by Vatican observers of the crisis in the entire World Church that there is a remarkable agreement between their statistics and our percentages. The latter also seem to correspond to the findings reported by the above-mentioned Ad Hoc Committee: "Developed men — small in number; developing men — sizable group; underdeveloped men — large segment; maldeveloped men — very few in number."

It is my intention to present the results of our clinical observations in respect to the causes, treatment and prevention of emotional immaturity and illness in priests, by reproducing in somewhat revised form the paper, "Human Growth in the Priesthood," which Dr. Terruwe and I had the privilege of presenting in Rome, Italy, at a meeting sponsored by members of the 1971 Synod of Bishops. We also discussed this paper in person with other members of the Synod who could not attend this presentation and had it distributed in English and French to every Synod participant. Since our paper was addressed to all the bishops of the World Church, through this present article we hope to bring it to the attention of all bishops, religious superiors, vocational directors, rectors of seminaries, moral theologians and all those concerned with the selection and formation of candidates for the priesthood and with the welfare of all priests now afflicted with mental and emotional problems.

At the end of this paper the reader will find an addendum of ten practical recommendations composed at the request of members of the Synod.

The Synod's discussion paper on "The Priestly Ministry" rightly objects to an uncritical acceptance of just any school of psychology. It is with this in mind that efforts to reconcile the faith and anthropology are to be made. Inasmuch as the *sensus fidei*, according to *Lumen Gentium*, no. 13,[2] includes the testimony of laypersons who, through their experience, have learned to give new interpretations of established facts, the discussion paper, in order to be an exhaustive study and inquiry, should not have been composed only by theologians. After all, the discussion paper deals with the ministry of the priest who is a man, and therefore should concern itself with the entire human person of the priest. The *bonum naturale* in the past, not always taken very seriously in ecclesiastical circles, deserves the fullest attention of the bishops who have the first and final word on the priestly ministry. "Secularization" should no longer be considered identical with "desacralization"! Moreover, it should be mentioned that His Holiness, Pope Paul VI, showed his deep personal interest in our scientific data by discussing them in person with Dr. Terruwe in the summer of 1969.

---

[2] Second Vatican Council, *Dogmatic Constitution on the Church (Lumen Gentium)*, 1964.

As psychiatrists sharing the bishops' concern with the happiness of priests and all of humanity, we shall present our views on the priest's loss of identity, his doubts about the value of the celibate state, his reasons for leaving the priesthood, and the advisability of the Church changing her approach and services to modern man — who phenomenologically has changed so much in the twentieth century, and whose emotional and spiritual growth to maturity have not kept pace with his physical and intellectual growth. We believe that his retarded and distorted emotional life is directly responsible for his spiritual aridity and indifference.

Repression and Frustration of the Emotional Life

Since Sigmund Freud's discovery that the repression of emotion leads to serious and disabling psychological illness, psychiatrists in Europe and North America, if not in other parts of the world, have reported a steady and alarming increase in the incidence of neurotic disorders. A neurosis is an illness of one's emotional life which develops in a young individual with an innately healthy and normal predisposition as the result of early exposure to mistaken notions and shortcomings on the part of parents and educators. These causative factors are twofold: First, a faulty attitude toward the significance of the entire emotional life for the overall well-being of the child, adolescent and adult; and Second, failure to affirm the growing child.

The first factor, a faulty attitude toward the role of the emotions, enhanced by the living example of parents and educators, leads the child to repress first the outward manifestations of his or her emotions and, sooner or later, also the very emotions themselves from the moment they are aroused. In time, the child develops the clinical signs of a repressive disorder involving soma, mind and spiritual life. In a person with this kind of neurotic disorder, the emotions are not subordinate to direction by reason and will, but they are "controlled" instead by one or two assertive emotions — emotions of the utility (irascible) appetite.[3] This "control" is an unnatural process, a pathological misdirection, called repression, which prevents the emotion involved from taking its natural course either toward the sense object as such, or toward the object insofar as it is (*prout substat rationi*). The repressed emotion is doomed to remain active in a state of abnormal tension in the subconscious until such a time — usually in psychotherapy — that the hypertrophied emotions of the utility appetite, the assertive emotions of fear or energy,[4] or both, have been taught to concern themselves solely with their proper objects — obstacles or danger — which do not include other emotions.

It should be mentioned that this particular interpretation of the repressive disorders was developed as early as 1935 by Professor Dr. Willem Duynstee of Nymegen, the Netherlands, who thus offered the Church the opportunity to refute Freud's theory that the repressing action is exercised by the superego which encompasses the conscience and the moral norms!

The second factor responsible for an undeveloped or partially developed emotional life is the failure on the part of parents or educators to provide the child's emotional life with its proper nourishment, namely unselfish emotional love. They may give the child food for its body, academic and moral

---

[3] Editors' Note: The utility appetite consists of the emotions of hope, despair, courage, fear and anger. These emotions are also called the *assertive emotions*. In contrast, the pleasure appetite consists of the emotions of love, hate, desire, aversion, joy and sadness. Please see *Psychic Wholeness and Healing* (Anna A. Terruwe, M.D. and Conrad W. Baars, M.D. Staten Island, NY: Alba House, 1981) for further information.

[4] Editors' Note: The authors use the term *energy* to denote a combination of the emotions of hope and courage.

training for its intelligence and character, even expressions of volitional or spiritual love to *tell* the child it is loved, but unless they also give the child emotional love, it will not *feel* loved (i.e., literally *sense* the parent's love), and will develop what we have called a frustration neurosis [now called *Emotional Deprivation Disorder*[5]]. This illness differs essentially from the repressive disorders and therefore requires a different therapy, but because of a growing existential fear, it also predisposes to the development of a repressive disorder. It is for this reason both types of neurotic disorders frequently co-exist in the same person.

Both types of disorders are extreme manifestations of an underdeveloped or distorted emotional life with clearly defined clinical symptoms. Although their incidence is enormous, even greater is the number of people with what may be called subclinical forms of these disorders, with symptoms and complaints which do not reach the intensity and scope of the full-blown neurotic disorders, yet cause much suffering through worry, tension, anxiety, restlessness, feelings of inferiority, inadequacy, loneliness and depression.

Excessive Irrational Fear and Striving

Before discussing the nature of Emotional Deprivation Disorder — the most urgent subject of study for the Church of our day — we must briefly mention the factors present in society as well as in the Church which tend to stimulate emotional fear and energy (our term for the emotions of hope and courage) to an unreasonable degree. They are:

---

[5] Editors' Note: Emotional Deprivation Disorder is explained in detail in *Healing the Unaffirmed: Recognizing Emotional Deprivation Disorder* (Conrad W. Baars, M.D. and Anna A. Terruwe, M.D., Rev. ed., Suzanne M. Baars and Bonnie N. Shayne, eds., Staten Island, NY: Alba House, 2002).

1. a more extensive and varied intellectual schooling with greater factual knowledge at an earlier age tends to stimulate fear and energy much more than the emotions of love, desire and joy which are aroused more by the stimulation of the senses and imagination.

2. a reduced world dimension through faster transportation and instant communication tends to threaten one's sense of security and belonging which once were inherent in a relatively small and stable community.

3. a more unstable family life as the result of working parents, corporation-induced changes of location, and the rise in the divorce rate have a similar effect and enhance anxiety.

4. the so-called hyperfunctionalism of the all-too-busy modern man or woman tends to reduce all his or her contacts to business-like, matter-of-fact encounters which do little to stimulate lasting friendships and the joy of love.

5. unparalleled scientific progress without a concomitant growth of one's philosophical and religious sense tends to evoke greater and greater attempts to protect oneself from danger, illness, misfortune and death. The idea of surrendering to an all-loving God is not likely to occur in a "God is dead" society.

6. space does not permit us to dwell on more specifically Catholic factors. We mention briefly: a suspicious and fearful attitude toward the emotional life, indicated for example by the pejorative connotation of the words *concupiscible* and *irascible*, and the inclusion of anger among the seven capital sins; premature stimulation of the fear of sin rather than emphasis on the love of God; training the "motor" of the will without utilizing to the fullest the "motor" of the emotions; reliance on authoritarianism and blind obedience in the establishment of order; and the overestimation of the human

person's own efforts and accomplishments in the matter of eternal salvation.

Asceticism of the Assertive Emotions

Suffice it to say that the Church is in dire need of a sound pastoral theology of the emotions of fear and energy, and of a keen awareness that the emotions of the pleasure appetite are not the only ones that have suffered the consequences of original sin. Fear and energy, too, must remain at all times under the direction of reason and will, and can never be allowed to grow to exaggerated proportions, not even for the purpose of avoiding sin, being virtuous, or attaining one's salvation. Not only must the Church teach a sound asceticism of the assertive emotions as she has done of old regarding the pleasure emotions, but she must also permit the latter to mature to its fullest extent if the human person is to experience the joy of love and happiness as ordained by the Creator.

Both appetites are to be directed by the will informed by reason rather than being "mortified," if that means "to be brought to death" by each other. A person with an undeveloped, atrophied or repressed emotional life has little or nothing to be directed by his or her reason and will. Such a person is forced to rely solely on the motor of the spiritual will, which indeed can attain much, but not the full joy for which he or she was made. This person is like the expert rider whose horse is weak, half-starved and crippled; the rider will get where he or she wants to go and will endure the hardships of the journey through sheer will power, but will be too exhausted to enjoy the beauty along the trail and the goodness of the goal.

Emotional Deprivation Disorder

We must spend even more time in discussing Emotional Deprivation Disorder and its sub-clinical form of the non-affirmed person, as they have an even greater bearing on the future of the Church. A thorough understanding of the repressive disorders on the part of the Church, as Dr. Terruwe and I understand and successfully treat them, is important for their prevention. Even more important than treatment of the repressive disorders through a correct teaching of the asceticism of the assertive emotions is the Church's understanding of Emotional Deprivation Disorder. This is important both for its prevention and treatment, save for the most severe and chronic cases, which require expert psychotherapy. People who have not been affirmed benefit greatly when significant others understand their condition and are themselves mature enough to come to their assistance and refrain from criticizing and denying them. Priests especially are called to play an important role in this regard, as we shall explain later on. First, however, it is necessary to describe the symptoms of this neurotic syndrome.

In contrast to the anxiety, fears, restlessness, tension, phobias, scrupulosity, obsessive thinking and compulsive acts of the person with a repressive disorder, the chief characteristics of Emotional Deprivation Disorder are: feelings of inferiority and inadequacy, inability to establish normal rapport with one's peers and form lasting friendships, feelings of loneliness and insecurity, doubts about one's self-worth and identity, fear of the adult world, and often deep depressions. Although the more energetic among them are able to succeed in business or profession, they fail in their personal lives. If married, they find it impossible to relate in a spontaneous and emotionally satisfying way with spouse and children. In matters of faith, dullness prevails as their feelings cannot participate in their spiritual life. Their religious experience is neither "a burden that is light," nor "a yoke that is sweet." Their psychosexual immaturity may express itself in various ways, for instance, in masturbation, pornography, homosexuality, sexual impotence or frigidity.

The syndrome of Emotional Deprivation Disorder, discovered in the late 1950's by Dr. Terruwe, has put into focus the significance of emotional love for one's growth as a unique person as well as for one's spiritual life. This is a decidedly different focus from that of the ascetical teachings of the Church, which in the past seemed to leave little or no room for the emotion of love as something worth cultivating for the sake of the spiritual life. The only love valued by the Church was volitional love, the love of the spiritual will prompting acts of love. Emotional love, affection, and simple human cordiality, if not considered evil, were looked upon with suspicion and thought potentially harmful to one's life in and with Christ. Spiritual books left one with the impression that intercourse with the Lord presupposed a breaking of all the natural ties one can have with other people, and that the mortification of human affections was ascetically laudable in the noble pursuit of solitude and withdrawal from others.

What we have learned in years of psychotherapeutic practice, namely that emotional love is absolutely necessary for each person, does not in any way imply — and we mention this explicitly — an accusation of a culpable shortcoming or neglect on the part of the doctors of the Church. These clinical discoveries are typically the proper object of the *scientiae humanae* which we are obliged and willing to submit to the Church. Their exploration and interpretation is fully in keeping with the spirit of Vatican II, which encourages the faithful to clarify to an ever greater degree the inter-relatedness of the natural and the supernatural.

Origin of Emotional Deprivation Disorder

At the root of Emotional Deprivation Disorder lies an absent or inadequate feeling of self-worth. The source of this feeling of self-worth is always another person — the "significant other" — who can either give or withhold it. The process whereby a person receives his or her feeling of self-worth from the "significant other" is for every human being a *bonum fundamentale*. In a very special relationship with the significant other, the person is seen and experienced by the other as good, worthwhile and lovable. The pleasure of the approving and loving other is perceived in such a manner that the person literally *feels* this throughout his or her entire being.

This emotionally felt experience of being good and lovable engenders an inner sense of goodness and worth, together with a deep feeling of peace and tranquility, and is the *conditio sine qua non* for the person's future self-love and self-esteem. It is the fundamental prerequisite for the child who enters life isolated and enclosed within himself, to open and grow toward what he is supposed to become, uniquely himself. What opens the child to the significant other is the fact that the child experiences the other as good, and that he may be what he is in the growing joy of the other's — and later their mutual — love and affection. It is only when a human being has been opened to a significant other that he or she can also be open to the good of all creation and to the Creator Himself. Only then can the person experience the world and the Creator with love and joy.

Affirmation and Self-Restraining Love

The process by which the significant other reveals me to myself as good, and thereby himself to me as good, is a unique manifestation of the fruitfulness of human love, inasmuch as both of us receive fulfillment, inner expansion and joy in giving being to the other. Its ultimate fruitfulness is in truth one's *psychic [psychological]*⁶ *incarnation.* One cannot fully understand this unless one has experienced for oneself this process which Dr. Terruwe has called affirmation, the essence and core of all mature, unselfish love. In this love, giving and receiving are only formally distinguishable because in essence they are both affirmation.

At times it happens that a person whom I would like to affirm cannot, or cannot as yet, for some reason or other, receive the expression of my love. It is then the noblest and purest form of love not to express my love outwardly, even when it has already grown into desire. Frequently this is the most tender and delicate form of affirmation, for the other person is allowed by me to be as he or she is — with his or her immaturity and shortcomings. I allow the other to be as is *in facto* in order that the other may become the person he or she is *in potentia.* Contrary to the person with a neurotic disorder who represses love out of fear, I restrain myself in certain expressions of my love for the sake of the other.

Affirmation as self-restraining love⁷ is precisely what adults must give to those still in the process of maturing; parents

---

⁶ Editors' Note: Dr. Baars used the words "psychic" and "psyche" in a much broader sense then strictly psychological. He included the emotions, the spiritual life, the intellectual life and the life of the will in this concept. Throughout this book, the term "psychic" is to be understood in that context and will be used interchangeably with the term "psychological."

⁷ or *amor sese retinens, amour qui se retient. Retinere* means "to hold back" as in *retinere lacrimas, retinere mercedem;* it also means "to protect" as in *retinere amicos, retinere aliquem in fide.*

and educators to children and pupils; the educated and wise to the uneducated; those in authority to their subjects.

Authentic affirmation is much more than speaking a word of encouragement or the giving of a compliment. *It focuses on the very being of the other, on his or her goodness as a unique human being.* It presupposes openness, confident expectation and uninterrupted attention to everything that happens in the other, to all the person is not able to express, and to all the anticipated good within the other, even though the other is still unsuspecting of that future good.

Denial

The very opposite of affirmation is denial. One denies the other by unnecessarily reminding the other of what is not yet good in him or her, by thoughtless criticism, or the giving of premature advice without first having really listened to the person. One denies the other by not "forgiving him for being other," as a Chinese sage wrote long ago. One denies a woman by counseling abortion when she does not want her child to be born because she is too immature to love and affirm it. One denies people in undeveloped countries by imposing one's own cultural and spiritual values on them. One denies the other by counseling the person to ignore a norm or law on the grounds that it is too difficult for him or her to obey.

Whereas authentic affirmation is truly life-giving, denial kills. Was it not Goethe's Mephistopheles who described himself so aptly with the words, "Ich bin der Geist der stets verneint!" — "I am the spirit who always denies!"

It is not without reason that Don Quixote's characterizations of human realities have received wide acclaim for centuries. His love for Aldonza, a woman of easy morals, made him see her in her veiled beauty, and he called her Noble Lady Dulcinea. It was because of the affirming love of Don Quixote that Aldonza could indeed become the Noble Lady he thought her to be. Don Quixote, like Aldonza, was amazed when he beheld the fruit of his love!

Neither words nor silence will be used lightly by the one who knows that a word can kill if spoken in an untimely or inappropriate manner, that a word can be life-giving if it is the spoken word of affirmation, that silence can kill if it is the unspoken word of the one who is called to give affirmation, and that silence can be life-giving if it is the discerning silence of a leader.

Is it not indeed affirmation of an entire people when bishops speak out against their country's occupation by a hostile, godless power and openly defy its threats in the name of God?[8] Is it not also denial of a people when a government allows a war to be endlessly protracted for fear of world opinion or threats by the enemy's sympathizers?

Phenomenology of the Modern Human Person

It seems to us that much of what afflicts the modern human person and society can be understood in greater depth in the light of what we have said so far about non-affirmation. One thinks of the increasing complaints of loneliness and abandonment and the mounting rate of suicide among children and young people. According to the World Medical Association's report on causes of death in forty-eight countries, suicide is

---

[8] One of the Cardinals of such a country told us that his clergy possessed a much greater degree of maturity than our percentages indicated for the clergy on this side of the Iron Curtain!

second among children between the ages of 5 to 13, both in
urban and rural communities.

One also thinks of the large number of people who voice
their uncertainty about their personal worth, their feeling of
identity, and of the desperate search for meaning in the use of
mind-altering drugs, especially among the younger generation.
One thinks of the daily reports of aggressive and destructive
outbursts even to the point of self-immolation, and, too, of the
crisis of authority, the revolt against authoritarianism, pater-
nalism, discrimination and manipulation, of children who run
away from home, and of young people who voice their protest
through anti-establishment life styles.

Could all this be a cry for affirmation? If so, is not this cry
being echoed by the priest?

Emotional Immaturity in Priests

More often than not the priest comes from a "fine Catholic
home," a strict one with little emotional love. Spurred on to
develop his character, train his will, and grow intellectually,
his emotional growth lags behind. Neither minor nor major
seminary were capable of closing this "maturity gap" through
authentic affirmation, and trained — the word is used delib-
erately — him to function without the benefit of the emotional
life. The consequences of this unbalanced formation have been
largely disastrous.

In our clinical practices we have seen many priests with
obvious identity problems. Priests who were uncertain in their
attitude toward life, felt unloved, lonely and depressed, and
whether they realized it or not, awkward in their interpersonal
relationships. Psychosexual immaturity expressed in hetero- or
homosexual activity was often encountered. Many experienced

difficulties in matters of faith, or suffered from severe scrupulosity, while a growing number of them seriously considered leaving the priesthood. Virtually all of these priests were non-affirmed men, suffering from severe to moderate Emotional Deprivation Disorder, with or without associated obsessive-compulsive repression,[9] scrupulosity or chronic alcoholism.

Happily, many of them responded to our therapy by gradually maturing emotionally, acquiring a feeling of personal worth and dignity, and becoming more sure of themselves in their interpersonal relationships. Their sexual problems gradually disappeared without analytic scrutiny. Their faith and religious sentiments also benefited from their growing emotional maturity, and in the course of a few years they became happy priests capable of bringing joy and happiness to those entrusted to their pastoral care.

Other priests who had married after leaving the priesthood sought help because of sexual impotence, depressive states and psychological conflicts and difficulties with their spouses. At times, both of them would have been only too happy if their marriage could have been dissolved. This is not surprising because in a non-affirmed priest, the search for affirmation is likely to express itself in an intense and virtually irresistible desire for tactile contacts, the very first expression of affirmation meaningful to his undeveloped emotional life. In choosing a partner he is therefore bound to make a serious mistake both in his thinking and in his feelings, and he will enter marriage devoid of the emotional capacity to establish a mutually meaningful and satisfying relationship.

Related to this is the fact that many former priests seem to

---

[9] Editors' Note: See *Psychic Wholeness and Healing* and *Feeling and Healing Your Emotions* (Conrad W. Baars, M.D., Rev. ed., Suzanne M. Baars and Bonnie N. Shayne, eds., Bridge-Logos: Gainesville, FL, 2003) for information about repression, including obsessive-compulsive repression and scrupulosity.

have found their partner among women either much older or younger than they, suggesting the possibility that either they enter into a relationship with an older woman in the hope that their need for affirmation will be gratified, or they prefer a younger woman with whom they can relate more comfortably on an equal level of relative emotional immaturity.

Our clinical observations over many years have convinced us that priests in general — and some to an extreme degree — possess an insufficiently developed or distorted emotional life, while at the same time they must be considered to belong to a group of men whom nature has endowed with superior intelligence and sensitivity. In some, the causes for their emotional underdevelopment go back to childhood and remain unrecognized during the seminary years. Others enjoyed a fairly normal childhood but became emotionally disturbed through misguided ascetical practices in the seminary. Whatever the causes, however, it is a fact that the majority of today's priests with psychological trouble suffer from some degree of non-affirmation. A smaller, but not insignificant number of priests are seriously incapacitated by obsessive-compulsive repression. Many show the symptoms of both types of disorder, often combined, at least in North America, with chronic alcoholism.

These findings also explain why the Church as a whole finds herself in a crisis. Because of the priest's special position as mediator between God and humankind, the effects of his non-affirmation on other people will be far more radical and widespread than in the case of the non-affirmed single or married layperson. A priest without identity, without a firm sense of self-worth, cannot reveal to others their personal worth. Because he cannot affirm, he cannot love others in a way which strengthens both them and the Church.

Moreover, as a non-affirmed priest depends for his sense of personal worth on the people around him, he lives in constant anticipation of what they expect from him, is fearful of displeasing them, afraid to assert himself or to defend the truths of his faith except on a purely intellectual level. Desirous of being loved by all, he may remain silent when it is his duty to point out the errors contained in other faiths, new schools of thought, popular movements or modern systems of education. Instead of being a source of strength and joy to the people he chose to serve, the non-affirmed priest may be said to be at the mercy — whether for good or evil — of all with whom he comes in contact.

Priests who remain happy in their work possess an innate sensitive appreciation of the sense goods of this world under the ready direction of intellect and will, and likewise, an emotional appreciation of spiritual goods. In other words, they are able to direct themselves quite easily at the *objectum prout substat rationi*. This necessary capacity to deny themselves certain sense goods without becoming unhappy does not seem to have been given sufficient consideration in the selection of candidates for the priesthood. In priests so disposed, the need for concrete goods will increasingly give way to a growing delight in the spiritual, with an ensuing greater expansion of mind and spirit and an ever growing happiness.

Observations on Celibacy

Marital life has a profound effect on the emotional life of the human person. For this reason, the ecclesiastical law of celibacy which represents essentially a theological view of the task of the priest and obliges him to chastity as a single man cannot be considered lightly. The obligation this law imposes is responsible for the priest's emotional life acquiring a structure entirely its own. Whereas it is the task of the Church to decide whether the advantage of this law outweighs its possible difficulties or problems for the priest, it is the duty of the *scientiae humanae* to study the psychological effects of the celibate life. Strictly speaking, celibacy demands nothing more than the renouncement of sexual intercourse and thus of all manifestations of love which lead, directly or indirectly, to sexual intercourse. It cannot demand the renouncement of love itself, as the Lord commands every one of us to love others without regard to gender. Admittedly this refers specifically, as all commandments concerning love do, to volitional love, but certainly not to the exclusion of emotional love. Like every other person, the priest who chooses the celibate life for the Lord's sake is required to direct his feelings of love by volitional love informed by reason. Of all men, the priest must do this in the most perfect way by a deep love of restraint, for the wealth of the joy of love is never determined by an abundance of expression, but only by the measure of unselfish openness to the other. In this manner, the emotionally mature priest's freely chosen celibate state makes his love of men and women more beautiful and intense and immeasurably enriches the fruits of his ministry. Our clinical observations have demonstrated this beyond doubt.

The claim has also been refuted, in today's attempts at renewal, that one's feelings of love must be freely expressed and experienced if one is to find one's fulfillment and identity. We can have sympathetic understanding for this claim if it is founded in the desire to be done forever with neurotic repression and its consequences. This does not change the fact, however, that there is a world of difference between the pathological repression of emotions and the rational direction of feelings, whether for example, in the periodic continence required in marriage, or in the permanent continence in the celibate priesthood. Here, too, the Church has a most important task in teaching that all emotions are good and have an innate need to be directed by the will informed by reason, so that the emotions may run their proper course without causing psychological harm and enlarge one's capacity for joy and happiness. Failure by the Church to do so would condemn the emotionally immature priest to a life of continued repression or tempt him to seek fulfillment — and vainly so — in emotional abandon and force the mature priest to carry an unnecessarily heavy burden, instead of a yoke that is sweet.

In our experience, priests who find the celibate life burdensome are either emotionally underdeveloped or they chose the priesthood less for spiritual and altruistic motives than for self-seeking ones, such as, for instance, the desire to get a college education or establish a career, the fear of alienating parents who want a priest in the family at all cost, or the need to make amends for past sexual sins, or the promise of affirmation not found at home.

Not only are there no valid psychological objections to the celibate life, it even may be said that the celibate life constitutes a positive good for the priest himself as well as for the Church. In the mature priest, it enhances his openness to others and God, and therefore enhances spiritual joy in which his feeling of joy will fully participate. In the Church, it promotes the priest's serviceability, both in depth and in time spent, to the people of God. So long as God's love has not been brought to the hearts of all people, the Church, it seems to us, cannot relax her efforts to fulfill this mission through her celibate priests, just as in an analogous sense it could be said that the suffering of the world's emotionally ill cannot be relieved without a similarly dedicated group of celibate psychotherapists!

Conclusion

In conclusion, we want to express our sincere hope that the Church will lose no time in recognizing the importance of the entire emotional life for each person's full growth to maturity and the enrichment of his or her spiritual life, in comprehending the significance of emotional love in bringing volitional love to its most fruitful expression, and in teaching the proper asceticism of the assertive emotions. We hope this for the sake of the countless millions whose fears, restless striving and lack of identity keep them from finding themselves and God in the love of Christ.

We hope that the Church, by using those scientific data which supplement and confirm — not contradict — the authentic writings of the Scholastics concerning the nature of the human person, will give candidates for the priesthood their personal identity through affirmation by their superiors, and their priestly identity through the Lord's affirmation in ordination.

A brief note of warning must be sounded. In view of the countless writings on the subject of love during the past several decades, one may be inclined to believe that the subject has been exhausted, just as one is generally inclined to think that all emotions must be expressed if one is to be fulfilled as a person and to escape the fate of an emotional illness. Neither belief is correct. The manner in which each and every emotion, including hate, anger and despair, is to be utilized, as well as the subjects of affirmation and self-restraining love deserve more than a passing glance by the Church of Love.

Finally, we respectfully submit the results of our professional observations in the form of ten practical recommendations for the purpose of lending our support to the Church's task of fulfilling the words of our Lord, "Abide in my love... that my joy may be in you, and that your joy may be made full" (John 15: 11).

Summary and Practical Recommendations

1. Rectors of seminaries are advised to admit only young men who have been affirmed by their parents. A priest with average intelligence coupled with a mature emotional life is a far greater asset to the Church than one with superior intelligence and a retarded or neurotically disturbed emotional life. Investigation of the candidate's background by a knowledgeable rector is superior to psychological testing. Some unfavorable home factors: working mothers of young children; "absent" fathers; passive, submissive fathers and domineering mothers; cold, unaffectionate parents; utilitarian attitudes toward life and family, etc.

2. Home and seminary must avoid attitudes and teachings which unduly stimulate the assertive emotions (the utility or irascible appetite) and the inevitable consequence of a retarded, underdeveloped pleasure (concupiscible) appetite. Fearful or excessively-driven priests who are not capable of finding joy in the sensory and spiritual goods of this life are obstacles to the Church's mission to bring Christ's love and joy to all people and to help them to love God in freedom and without fear.

3. Parents, educators, and Church authorities must possess a fully integrated emotional and volitional love capable of affirming individuals entrusted to their care. As volitional love and good deeds alone are insufficient to lead people to true maturity, the Church must teach the significance of the entire emotional life and of emotional love in particular, always integrated with and assimilated by the life of the intellect, will and spirit. Without this, priests cannot become adequate affirmers of all people as the Lord intended them to be.

4. A sound home and seminary life can only be founded on an intelligent grasp of a proper philosophy of life and of a correct psychology of the human person. The authentic writings of Scholastic writers, complemented by established facts in clinical psychiatry and psychology provide, in our opinion, the best sources of knowledge about normal and emotionally disturbed persons. The Church should also be particularly cognizant of the negative aspects of the voluntaristic philosophy[10] which has prevailed for centuries, of the largely untenable psychoanalytic views which have affected our culture to a considerable extent, and of the psychological reasons why the present-day overreactions against decades of neurotic repression — e.g., situation ethics, sensitivity training, mind-altering drugs, sexual abandon, the contraceptive mentality, anti-life movements — are detrimental to a healthy personality development.

5. Bishops, religious superiors, priests, rectors of seminaries, vocational directors and moral theologians should be fully instructed in the psychology of the normal human person and also have an adequate working knowledge of neurotic psychopathology. The Church is advised that as the result of the many diverse, if not opposing views in psychology and psychiatry, it cannot be safely assumed that every psychologist or psychiatrist is properly qualified to teach these important subjects. Too many widely-read psychiatrists and psychologists consider it the highest degree of maturity to have no need of God and to reject His love in favor of complete self-reliance.

6. Already existing neurotic disorders — with or without chronic alcoholism — in priests should be speedily diag-

---

[10] Editors' Note: The voluntaristic philosophers saw the will as the supreme force in the life of the person; the emotions were seen as threats to virtue.

nosed and treated in the shortest and most effective manner. Neither Emotional Deprivation Disorder and the less-severe non-affirmed states, nor obsessive-compulsive repression and scrupulosity lend themselves to cure by psychoanalysis. The former respond favorably to affirmation and self-restraining love as explained in this paper; obsessive-compulsive repression and scrupulosity respond well and lastingly to a psychotherapy based on the view that not Freud's superego, which encompasses the conscience, but rather an assertive emotion of the utility appetite such as fear or energy is the repressing factor in these disorders. For the purpose of preventing these neurotic disorders and scrupulosity the Church must teach the proper mortification of the assertive emotions, just as she teaches this regarding the emotions of the pleasure appetite.

7. Moral theologians are advised to make a special study of this particular therapy of obsessive-compulsive repression and scrupulosity, as their fully informed assurance of the intelligent priest-patient concerning the moral propriety of this therapy is of great significance in speeding his recovery. Moral theologians or confessors who approve, directly or indirectly, of certain immoral psychiatric treatment methods aimed at the freeing of the patient's emotional life, should be warned about the extremely harmful psychological consequences of their expressed or implied assent.

8. The formation of priests should be in the hands of men who not only are experts in the proper psychology of human nature and its aberrations and a Scholastically sound philosophy of life, but also possess an emotionally mature, open, warmly affectionate personality to whom the candidates will be drawn spontaneously. These same qualifications should also be the primary consideration in the appointment of pastors, religious superiors and bishops, who in their respective

positions must deal paternally and fraternally with large numbers of individuals. Their ready ability to affirm and practice the love of restraint should be the deciding factor in their appointments.

9. If abnormal tensions develop in celibate priests, this cannot be considered evidence that the celibate state is at fault; however, they do indicate that the priest either failed to achieve a complete integration between his emotional life and the life of intellect and will, or he chose the priesthood less for spiritual than self-seeking motives, or he possesses a normally developed emotional life, but his innate need to experience concrete sense goods is too strong for him to be happy in renouncing them when necessary. Such a man can be a good priest, but not a happy priest. In considering the pros and cons of laicization, one should remember that in no way can the married state be considered an effective form of therapy for the emotionally immature priest.

10. All young people, candidates for the priesthood included, require direction and help in the process of becoming independent and responsible adults. It is the task of the Church to provide this guidance and thus to affirm them in the intellectual and volitional order. Not to do so, to encourage intellectual floundering through abandonment of fundamental curricular requirements, and to allow them to behave as they please, amounts to pedagogical neglect, which presents virtually the same clinical picture as that of the emotionally neglected or frustrated person, namely fear, anxiety, insecurity, and feelings of inferiority and being abandoned.

CHAPTER II

Whatever Happened to Religious Life?
"I Will Give Them a New Heart"

PREFACE TO THE ESSAY ON THE CRISIS IN RELIGIOUS LIFE

Excerpts from *The Peasant of the Garonne*,[1]
by Jacques Maritain

[Note: the following lengthy excerpts from Maritain are background for the remarks made in the essay on the crisis in religious life. Jacques Maritain points to the fundamental ambivalence of the world when considered in its relation to the Kingdom of God, for the world is the domain at once of man, of God and of the devil. Christians respect the world as made by God; they also realize that the devil is the prince of this world. Christians renounce even what is good in the world, for a greater good. The attitude of Christians toward the world, observes Maritain, has swung like a pendulum from the one extreme of despising the world to another extreme of kneeling before the world. A balanced view is needed.]

[For] centuries... Christian homiletic teaching was busy teaching men (who naturally love created things, but not in the way saints do) that created

---

[1] Jacques Maritain, *The Peasant of the Garonne: An Old Layman Questions Himself About the Present Time,* translated by Michael Cuddihy and Elizabeth Hughes, New York: Holt, Rinehart and Winston, 1968.

things are worthless. The trouble was that by dint of repeating this commonplace, the ascetic writers and the preachers wound up extending St. Paul's "dung hill" to the whole of creation, no doubt in as much as it might tempt the human being, but also, finally, and without being aware of the distortion, even when the creation was taken in itself. Simply through inattention, a masked Manichaeism was thus superimposed on the Christian faith, though without ruining it.... Hence the creature was in itself a dung hill; the world was in itself nothing but corruption. Original sin had rotted everything in nature. A Catholic would certainly not have advanced such a position. But it often underlay in a more or less unconscious way his idea of fallen nature (p. 46).

And whereas St. Paul and all the saints (for whom the world in itself was not evil, but rather, if anything, too good) despised the world only by virtue of boundless love for the One who loved us first, ... the adulterated Christianity I have been describing, on the contrary, [left the divine love in a shadow and saw the world as] worth nothing in itself. Henceforth the practical formulas which it dispensed became mainly prohibitive, and caused the values of negation, refusal and fear to be in the forefront — as well as setting oneself to regard created things as enemies, and to stay away from them. Lower the eyes, turn away the head. Flee from dangerous contacts. The moral took precedence over the theological; the flight from sin over charity.... This description has no bearing whatsoever on the real life of the Church as it was actually carried on in the depths of her being; it has to do with that version of Christianity that reigned in the mind and affected the mores of the great mass, more or less badly instructed, of the people of God (p. 47).

It was in the nineteenth century, and still more in the first half of the twentieth, that everything took a decided turn for the worse. Then the virus penetrated into the substance. At the same time, the unconscious work which had for so long been carried on in secret took visible form. Men began to suffer seriously, at times cruelly, from a sort of invasion of practical Manichaeism, which chiefly affected educational procedures and piety... and imposed a negativist attitude toward the world — with all the more aggressiveness as the world itself was making its claims and promises heard on all sides. From that moment, for a good many interior souls, the current vocabulary, with its reprobation of nature and the world, which was hitherto accepted as a matter of course in this particular rhetoric, grew increasingly difficult to bear.... Other souls rebelled. The mass of people felt that a grave injustice, against which they were defenseless, was committed with respect to the world, as well as with respect to themselves, and was of a nature to lead to disaster.

This kind of invasion of practical Manichaeism, whose effects were felt in this way, did not present itself as a doctrinal error formulated by the intellect and pronounced externally. No, it was spread *inwardly*, in the form of purely moralistic prohibitions, injunctions to flight, habits of fear, disciplines of denial in which love had no part, and which led the soul to starvation and sickliness... (p. 48).

The hostility of a civilization in which Christianity

— and especially such a disfigured Christianity — was called to question on all sides, and where science was held to be the enemy of religion; the weakening of natural defenses due to modern psych-asthenia which was already so well kept going by psychiatrists, and the weakening of intellectual defenses due to a teaching extremely poor in matters of doctrine; the modernist crisis, with its first epidemic of itching ears and piously intended errors; and in the indispensable struggle against these errors, the almost exclusive recourse to disciplinary measures; the spiritual impoverishment of a Christian laity.… All this was going to build up, in the unconscious of many Christians, clerics and laymen, an enormous weight of frustration, disillusionment, repressed doubts, resentment, bitterness, healthy desires sacrificed, with all the anxieties and pent-up aspirations of the unhappy conscience (p. 49).

Comes the *aggiornamento*. Why be astonished that at the very announcement of a Council, then in the surroundings of it, and now after it, the enormous unconscious weight which I have just mentioned burst into the open in a kind of explosion that does no honor to the human intelligence? Thus, the Council appears as an island guarded by the Spirit of God in the middle of an ocean which is overturning everything, the true and the false, pell-mell.

[The teachings of Second Vatican Council are]… the final liquidation of that masked Manichaeism which I spoke of at such length, which had poisoned several centuries of history, until in our day it had created an untenable psychological situation, and provoked, in reaction, the most serious crisis.

As to the present crisis itself, with all the confusions, follies and denials it carries with it... it will only be liquidated in its turn by a great and patient work of revitalizing in the order of intelligence and the order of spirituality. [As far as the Church is concerned] ... she has, through the Council, put an end from now on to the misunderstanding from which Catholic thought has too long suffered as regards the things of the world.

But among a good many Christians the misunderstanding continues and grows worse (p. 53).

As far as the attitude of the Christian to the world is concerned, the pendulum was suddenly carried to the opposite extreme from the quay Manichean contempt for the world... [to a kneeling before the world]. This time, we no longer confront an aberration projected internally in forms that were somber and tormented, but an aberration which is projected externally, with all the glamour and happy arrogance of a reason maddened by frenzy for novelty. This is the second poisonous fruit, equally dangerous, if not more so than the first (on account of its intellectual character).... For when foolishness acquires such considerable dimensions among Christians, either it must be resorbed pretty quickly, or it will ultimately detach them from the Church. What foolishness? Kneeling before the world.... In other words, there is henceforth only the earth. A complete *temporalization of Christianity*.... What do we find at the origin of this kneeling? An insane mistake — the confusion between two completely different senses in which the same word "world" is being understood. [In one sense]... the world is fundamentally *good*... the world,

insofar as it accepts to be assumed into the kingdom,
is *saved*... [but in another sense] insofar as it refuses
the kingdom, and encloses itself in the lust of the
flesh, the lust of the eyes, and the pride of the spirit,
it is the adversary of Christ and his disciples, and
hates them (pp. 49, 50, 56, & 60).

Whatever Happened to Religious Life?
"I Will Give Them a New Heart"

What has happened to religious men and women that a
crisis of unprecedented proportions could occur? If one were to
reply that religious have failed to pray and courted temptation
by failing to practice self-denial and mortification, failed to
cooperate with the daily gift of Grace, and failed to carry the
cross with and for Christ, we must still try and answer the
question, "Why did they fail to do these things?" In considering
certain root causes for the upheaval in religious life, I hope to
make a constructive and practical contribution to the defense
of authentic religious life.

To reassure those of you who may have reservations about
the competence of a psychiatrist to speak authoritatively on this
sensitive subject, involving as it does the spiritual life, I want
to make it clear from the start that I shall not speak as a representative of the psychiatric profession as it is generally known
in our society. Its orientation and that of the human sciences of
our day are not geared to an understanding of human beings
on all levels of their existence. The supernatural order and the
laws of Grace are not considered in these secular sciences which
claim to study the whole human person.

I shall speak as a Christian psychiatrist who in the fifties
became disenchanted with certain aspects of his training and

whose sole reason for not leaving his specialty was the chance discovery of the pioneering work of a Redemptorist priest and a female psychiatrist in their native country. It was then that my education in authentic psychology and intelligible psychopathology truly began. The philosophical studies of Fr. Willem Duynstee and the clinical discoveries of Dr. Anna Terruwe, described in the sixties as a "gift to the Church" by His Holiness Pope Paul VI, are founded on the anthropology of Thomas Aquinas. Over the years they have proven scientifically sound and therapeutically beneficial to countless priests, brothers, sisters and Christian lay people who sought our help for serious afflictions of their emotional-spiritual lives.

We have been much encouraged in our clinical work by scholarly research of the original manuscripts of Aquinas. This revealed that much of what we were privileged to discover about the laws of the emotional life and the price one must pay when these laws are violated had already been known in some form or other to the Angelic Doctor. Unfortunately for the Church and the world of today, some scribal copyists of his texts or translators had deemed it advisable to omit part of his thoughts for fear that they would be too radical for his times.

Before presenting Aquinas' radical ideas concerning human emotional life and its significance for the spiritual life, I want to present a brief outline of certain historical developments, which in my opinion have culminated in the sad state of affairs in the religious life as well as in our society. This I shall do without attaching blame to the Church herself insofar as her faith and dogmas are concerned. However, insofar as the ideas and beliefs of Church leaders (such as superiors of religious orders) were influenced by a flawed theology or philosophical anthropology, these representatives of the Church may have implemented teachings and practices which contained the seeds for the present crisis.

If religious life is to endure as long as the Church of Christ will endure, that is until the end of the world, then we must have the courage to examine two basic questions. Was the religious life as we knew it authentic? If not, precisely what is authentic religious life — the kind of life that is as convincing, inviting and durable as the truths of the faith of our Catholic religion?

Roots of the Crisis in Faulty Theology and Philosophical Psychology

The life histories of thousands of educated Christians who sought our help and whom we treated as patients, lay as well as religious, all sincere and earnest in their striving to please God and their superiors in unquestioning obedience, have helped us in our understanding of the human person. They have made it clear to us that the fear and suspicion of human emotions and drives — attitudes which Christians have held for many generations — has had an adverse effect on our nature, already wounded by original sin, though not deprived of its original goodness. These faulty ideas have weakened the human psyche so insidiously that it has gone unrecognized except in the obvious cases of emotional disorders. It is certain that the ultimate breakdown in the form of the present crisis in religious life has been accelerated by the effect of Calvin's teaching on society — the teaching that human nature had been corrupted by original sin. This led to the Protestant work ethic with its pathologic fear of idleness, Victorian ethics and prudery, and Immanuel Kant's doctrine that all feelings are pathological.

It seems plausible that a faulty interpretation of the story of the Fall as recorded in Genesis has played an important role in the development of this fearful attitude among Christians. Because the forbidden fruit is described as appealing to our first parents, the sin may have been popularly interpreted as a temptation of our sensory appetite, and in particular a sin of lust. Their sudden awareness of their nakedness, and making themselves clothes after they had sinned, seems to reinforce the idea that their "lower nature" had been the primary cause of their downfall. Furthermore, the historic vulnerability and perversion of human sexuality would also seem to make it a candidate for the primordial sin. The overriding impression left by this kind of reading of the text is of human weakness for temptations of the senses and sexual desires. Of course, these interpretations have doctrinal flaws, but nonetheless may have influenced many religious and pedagogical practices.

This attitude of fear of our "lower nature," prevalent among both Protestant and Catholic Christians, led Church leaders to aim catechesis at establishing early in childhood a firm and ready submission of the drives and feelings of human nature to the will under the guidance of reason as enlightened by Faith. A glance at the old textbooks of morality used in the seminaries and at the customs and rules of daily living of many a religious order founded in Europe in the 19th century reveals an exaggerated and unhealthy intensity of efforts aimed at subduing and mortifying our "lower nature." The hoped for results of deeper spirituality and Christ-like living did not materialize, however. In its stead, the first symptoms of obsessive-compulsive repression began to make themselves felt, and these were to spread gradually among religious men and women, as well as among the laity who attended Catholic schools. In time, because of this development, psychoanalysis drew the mistaken conclusion that religion and moral laws themselves were responsible for most of the emotional ills afflicting our society to an ever greater degree.

We believe that this charge by psychoanalysis is false, and its recommended corrective measures are even more disastrous and destructive than past repressive training methods ever were.

Obsessive-Compulsive Disorder is an emotional illness which begins early in life and makes itself manifest later in life, first by an obsession with the very feelings, thoughts and fantasies which one has always striven to eliminate from one's conscious life, and next by a compulsion to do the very things one has never willed to do. The scrupulous person is motivated by fear, the person with an energy-based repressive disorder by the emotion of courage.[2] As both are engaged in a neurotic process that is contrary to nature, both sooner or later become the helpless victims of the very emotions or drives they have fought so conscientiously since childhood. The repressing emotions of fear or energy (our term for the emotion of courage) become so powerful that they make it impossible for the will to exercise its proper function in guiding and controlling the emotions.

Since these two types of repressive disorders develop primarily, if not solely, in children of superior intellect, of a serious and refined nature, and possessed of a profound desire to lead lives pleasing to God and His representatives on earth, it is not surprising that they occur especially in those called to the religious life. Once ordained or professed as priests, sisters, or teaching brothers, they will inflict their own neurotic disorder on their pupils and students in the seminary and novitiate by their attitude and training methods, just as the parents of similarly gifted children do on their children at home.

I have never ceased to admire these outstanding men and women for their willingness to act against their nature, to blame

---

[2] Editors' Note: See *Psychic Wholeness and Healing: Using All the Powers of the Human Psyche* (Anna A. Terruwe, M.D. and Conrad W. Baars, M.D., Alba House, Staten Island, NY, 1981) and *Feeling and Healing Your Emotions* (Conrad W. Baars, M.D., Rev. ed., Suzanne M. Baars and Bonnie N. Shayne, eds., Bridge-Logos: Gainesville, FL, 2003) for a discussion of the repressive disorders, including fear-based and energy-based repressive disorders.

only themselves if they experienced little joy and peace in their service of God, and to consider themselves weak-willed, while actually it was their superior, though misdirected will-power, that was responsible for their failure to "rise above their feelings" or to be victorious in their battle between the flesh and the spirit.

It is impossible not to feel pity and compassion for these men and women who silently and without complaining suffered their neurotic and psychosomatic illnesses, tragically man-made in the name of Christianity. Only with the realization that all this had been brought about unwittingly and unintentionally within the framework of Christian teachings has it been possible not to be scandalized and to continue in loving service to the Church of Christ.

At this point one could ask whether the current, more liberal, nonrepressive life style of so many religious represents the authentic religious life. The answer is no, not necessarily. There is still another disabling force at work in the lives of numerous religious and laity that must be eliminated if we are to be able to lead authentic human lives, whether in the married or celibate state.

Our discovery of Emotional Deprivation Disorder, an emotional illness not caused by repression of emotions, has clarified the nature of this disabling force. It often operates in what has been called the "typical good Catholic home," the primary source of religious vocations, the home in which the parents provide strict moral upbringing but without sufficient affection and emotional love. These parents themselves were the victims of the repressive philosophy discussed before which in trying to subdue a single feared emotion prevented all emotions, even and precisely the desirable emotions of love and joy, from developing.

From generation to generation parents became increasingly

incapacitated in affirming their children. Their unaffirmed children grew up to become either "people-pleasers," in their burning desire to be loved, or to become "self-pleasers," "self-affirmers" who manipulate others — determined to attain by their own efforts what they had not received as a gift from their parents. Either way both types of unaffirmed persons, in spite of their totally different adaptation to life, are equally lacking in psychic strength and the ability to affirm, to strengthen others. It is for this reason that these persons in large numbers inevitably sap the strength and hinder the growth of both Church and society today.

Someone has said that large scale social changes follow upon a change in the way reality is perceived by the members of society. This perception can be altered from without by exposure to different teachings. If the teachings are false, the changes will be for the worse, if truthful, for the better.

Changes for the worse can also occur when perception of reality is altered from within while what is taught remains the eternal, unchanging truth of God. This may happen when the human psyche is weakened by any number of factors. In the matter under discussion here, the weakening has been the result of chronic, neurotic repression and/or deprivation of the emotional life, resulting in fear of the adult world, and feelings of worthlessness and depression that demand change at any price and rob one of the courage to defend the good and oppose the evil.

I must add that the psychiatric profession as a whole has not yet recognized the syndrome of non-affirmation as a clinical category. Moreover, it persists in subscribing to Freud's mistaken notion that the superego of the human person — that strange concoction of conscience, moral standards and social mores — is the culprit in the repressive process. This persistent psychiatric myth is largely responsible for many regressive phenomena in our post-Freudian era. To mention a few: people's inability to distinguish between neurotic repression and rational restraint; their insistence on the need to gratify and express all emotions, especially sexual feelings; their readiness to ignore God and His commandments and to embrace situation ethics; their uncritical support of theologians' demythologizing of the Scriptures, particularly of the first sin; their defiance of the encyclical *Humanae Vitae* and their welcoming of such pastoral guidelines as presented in the book, *Human Sexuality*, which I have described in a recent review as "psycho-theological quicksand."

With this comprehensive review of some of the psychological factors responsible for, or contributing to, the crisis in religious life and society, factors which have affected all of us in various degrees, the best of us often more than others, we are ready to propose answers to the fundamental question: How do we establish unity and harmony between all of the faculties of our nature so that we are best prepared to carry the cross with Christ; to live the Little Way[3] of faith and surrender; to facilitate the perfection of our nature by Grace; to heal those who have been emotionally crippled and spiritually impoverished by past misconceptions; to safeguard future generations against suffering a like fate; and to lead authentic human lives as religious and lay persons?

The answer to this question is found in a new and positive attitude toward our emotional life, based on a thorough grasp of its proper function and relationship to our other faculties and to our spiritual life. Our Savior became man at the Incarnation and entered into His Paschal Mystery of dying and rising in order to become the first human affirmer, that He might reveal to us that our unique individual goodness, imperfect since the sin of Adam, can be transformed, restored, and healed by our

---

[3] Editors' Note: The "Little Way" of St. Thérèse of Lisieux.

mutual affirmation, rather than by training aimed at the suppression of what we have falsely believed to be the evil of our "lower nature." Jesus became one with us in order "that the Father might see and love in us what He sees and loves in Christ" (Eucharistic Preface).

Jesus, Perfect as Man, Perfect in His Way of Loving Us

There has been a tendency in recent interpretations of the Gospels and in recent Christology to emphasize the humanity of Jesus. In place of the Christology of the past, which is criticized for presenting an infant Jesus in the manger who could have carried on a rational conversation with Mary and Joseph (in other words, a Christology which emphasized the divinity of Christ), we have a new Christology today which speaks of Jesus' "limited knowledge" and His "faith struggle." This Christology believes that such an image of Jesus will help us identify with Him and emulate one who is like us. In fact, Jesus is true God and true man. Jesus possessed at each stage of this human growth toward manhood the perfection proper to each stage.

One motivation which may be operating behind the new Christology is the mentality of those with repressive disorders or Emotional Deprivation Disorder who complain that it would be unfair of God to expect us to imitate a perfect Jesus, because God did not give us the same advantages He gave His Son. It is true that Jesus was raised by gentle, loving parents; He had a superior intellect which amazed the scholars in the Temple; He was without sin and thus never plagued by guilt and shame; He had His ego boosted repeatedly by all who witnessed His miracles; and He received much strength through His direct contact with His heavenly Father. Since Jesus was never troubled by feeling inferior, insecure, unloved, worthless, and depressed, it is no wonder that He succeeded to make it in the end — or so the complaint goes. Thus the new Christology of the unaffirmed person would make Jesus "like us in all things" by distorting the truth about Him and making Him equally confused, troubled, tempted by disordered emotions, and so having our human qualities. This "human" Jesus is supposed to be easier for us to identify with, and more capable of empathizing with us.

My years as a Christian psychiatrist have taught me that wounded human beings need and do respond to the God-Man Jesus who was, and is, perfect as man; perfect in His way of loving, living and relating to people; perfect in His willingness and ability to devote all His energies to each of us. If the idea of working hard at one's own happiness and salvation appeals to the pride of "healthy" people (self-affirming persons and those with energy-based repressive disorders), it is a relief for wounded people (the weak and sinful) to discover that they are loved unconditionally, just the way they are ("while we were yet sinners..."), by a "Jesus Christ who is the same yesterday, today, and forever" (Hebrews 13:8).

Jesus always adjusts His perfect love to our imperfect state. His beautiful self-restraining love, which adapts to our readiness to receive, and His authentic affirming love are possible only in a man whose lack of imperfections enable him to be totally present to others. It is my hope that Christology will shed more light on the image of Jesus as the one who emptied Himself of His divine prerogatives (not of His Divinity), and who now invites us to share in this forgetfulness of self and unselfish love for others.

Let us remember that the sufferings of Jesus did not extend to those caused by physical, mental or emotional illness. Jesus did not preach a beatitude of illness. On the contrary, He always went out of His way to heal the sick, for He knew how sickness makes a person preoccupied with their pain. Sickness also can make us bitter and reluctant, if not unable to carry our crosses. Jesus did not say "blessed are the sick," but He did say blessed are they who suffer hate, insults, persecution and slander for His sake. We need every ounce of psychological strength to share joyfully in the sufferings of Jesus, and if Jesus wants us to share in His sufferings, is it not reasonable to assume that He also wants us to share as much as possible in the integrity of His human nature, and of His psychological and spiritual health? Did He not come to heal and restore our nature? Let us open ourselves to a Jesus who was never sick physically, emotionally or mentally, who does not want us to be sick either, and who will heal us when we pray with confidence for the healing power of Jesus' compassionate love. As a psychotherapist who prays with his patients, I observe this healing power operating daily.

The Sacred Heart of Jesus can become the symbol of the renewed human being. As the heart is the symbol of our feelings and emotions, the words of Ezekiel assume new meaning. "I will give you a new heart and put a new spirit within you, taking from your bodies your stony hearts and giving you natural hearts. I will put my spirit within you and make you live by my statutes, careful to observe my decrees" (Ezekiel 36:26-27). In my opinion, the stony heart stands for the underdeveloped, deprived, distorted emotional life that keeps us from being truly human and from being God's people. The new and natural heart, on the other hand, is our fully grown emotions in harmony with reason, supporting the will, and giving warmth and joy to the spiritual life. This affective heart arouses within us a liking, a desire, a real feeling for observing and carrying out God's law, and it is this heart that stimulates the will affectively to live according to God's statutes.

When will this exchange of hearts take place? I think the time is now. Now is the moment that the Church possesses the knowledge to become in truth the loving mother and wise teacher she is meant to be. It is now that laity and religious together must put into effect what Aquinas offered the Church over seven hundred years ago. Shall we have the faith and the courage to do so? Shall we really believe that it is Grace and not our own puny efforts that will perfect our nature when we surrender it without prejudice and manmade distortion in all humility to our Redeemer?

Authentic Christian Teaching About Human Nature

To answer these questions, let us take a look at the authentic anthropology of Thomas Aquinas, or at least, let me give you a glimpse of the heart of his doctrine.

Thomas taught that all emotions without a single exception are good and necessary if we are to be fully and authentically human. Moreover, every emotion has an inborn need to be guided by reason. This means that reason first of all acknowledges and respects the emotion when it is aroused. Second, that reason guides the emotion in its orientation toward the sense object, without extinguishing the emotion itself in the process. Only this guidance restores the emotional life to its original equilibrium.

Cultivation of the emotional life in its entirety, not its extinction or repression, is a prerequisite for harmony and cooperation between emotions and reason. Any theory that the emotions must be diminished or disappear, Thomas stated explicitly, would be inane, absurd. The emotions are not non-human, or infra-human, or animal. They are not to be battled by reason. To let the emotions do as they please against reason is morally wrong; but so is repressing or suppressing them.

According to Aquinas, reason and will are not the only principles of the human act. The emotions are positive principles which add moral value to the human act. Having a feeling, a liking for the good, definitely adds something to the moral value of the will-act. It is not only psychologically important to strive after the good with heart and soul, but also morally better.

The will, Thomas said, is not an absolute ruler. It is not the sole principle of human conduct. The will must respect and listen to the emotions and rule them democratically. It must do them justice in their tendency to strive for the rational good. "The will not only moves, it is moved itself.[4] The will must first be moved affectively" — in the sense that we use the word in, for example, a "moving experience" or "moved to tears." If at all possible, the good must please the will emotionally, and at the same time appeal to it via reason. To will, in the broader Thomistic concept, is first of all *affectivity*. Only secondly, and dependent on this affectivity, is the will an active mover — *effective*. Virtue, therefore, is not only in the will and reason, but also in the emotions.

This all too brief review of Aquinas' positive and optimistic outlook on human emotional life corresponds fully with the words of many of the prayers in the Missal: "O God, who established the nature of man in wondrous dignity, and still more admirably has restored it...." This attitude removes fear and suspicion of the human person's "lower nature." This healthy philosophy can only be lived by those who believe in the fundamental goodness of human nature and in God's Grace being sufficient to heal imperfections, in His unchanging desire to lead us into His happiness, even in this world. On the other hand, those who continue to insist that our nature is such that the evil holds a greater attraction for it than the good have no

---

[4] *Summa Theo.*, Ia IIae, q. 9, a. 2. (*Summa Theologica: St. Thomas Aquinas*, translated by the Fathers of the English Dominican Province, Westminster, MD: Christian Classics, 1981).

choice but to cling to old repressive techniques of childrearing and training of religious.

The authentic anthropology of Thomas Aquinas, updated and enlarged by our clinical studies of the past three decades holds a key to solving the present crisis in living. It provides the blueprint for the development of the virtues of fortitude and temperance; for the healing and prevention of scrupulosity; for an asceticism of the assertive drive that clears the way for a life of faith and surrender; for living the teaching of *Humanae Vitae*; for mature authority that invites gladly given obedience; for a joyous spiritual life; and for the formation of mature, dedicated religious men and women.

Most importantly, this non-fearful, respectful attitude toward the goodness of our emotions will enable us to imitate the God-man Jesus in living the authentic human life, and thus the authentic religious life. Because this life does not do violence to our nature, its imperfections are continuously open to God's healing Grace. Unlike the person who must direct all his or her energies to counteracting the inner turmoil caused by repression, deprivation, or both, the person educated according to sound anthropological principles is free to cooperate with Grace as long as his or her will is well-directed.

Religious Life as an Authentic Affirming Life

What is authentic human living? It is the affirming life lived by Jesus as the First Affirmer of humanity, and taught by Him in two ways. First, by means of parables and lessons to the multitudes. This often included asking questions of them, for questions were His perfect, loving way of showing His respect for their knowledge, adjusting to their mentality, and thus opening their minds to His teachings. Second, this was taught by the intimate sharing of Himself with a privileged few during the years of His public ministry. The Bible records in great detail what we must do, but only inferentially teaches what we must be and how we are to become what God wants us to be. This is so because this teaching must be lived rather than preached if it is to achieve its goal of giving the other person the gift of his or her own unique being. Preaching this aspect of the affirming life and laying down precise rules for it, exposes the hearer to the danger of applying it as a technique, instead of living it as a way of life. In that case it would lose its creative and life-giving effect. It is for this reason that the term "affirming living," which suggests a state of being, is much to be preferred to the word "affirmation," which suggests doing, action. In fact, this misinterpretation of the word "affirmation" has been the rule rather than the exception ever since I introduced it in the literature twenty years ago. Ever mindful of the possible misapprehension of this subject, let us now consider the nature of this way of living.

I lead the affirming life by being *continuously present* with the full attention of my whole being to everything that is; by being fully capable of being *moved emotionally* by all I encounter in the world around me; and by *allowing the delight and joy that I experience to be revealed* naturally and spontaneously so that the object of my delight can be moved too by his or her own goodness.

It is in this way of being present to another, prior to my doing anything, that the other is born psychologically, delivered from the prison of his loneliness and self-centeredness, is strengthened and made firm in the realization that he may be who he is and may become who he is meant to be in his own way and at his own pace. It is in this process that the other is gradually opened to the goodness of all creation and to God Himself.

The affirming response to others involves *doing* as well as *being*. First among the gifts of doing is the fulfillment of my obligation to gratify the other person's fundamental need (second only to the need to be loved), namely of possessing the truth. This I must do by constantly adjusting and timing my instructions, guidance and corrections to the other's level of development and his or her needs on that level, so that I do not discourage, frustrate or embarrass the other in his or her inability to receive or respond to what I offer.

It is through this delicately balanced process of being and doing, this intensely personal and sensitive communion and communication that the other attains the fulfillment of his or her being; and becomes the free, self-possessed man or woman who can love himself or herself, love others and God unselfishly without compulsion to be sexually active on the genital level; and ultimately becomes capable in turn of being a co-creator of all that is.

What are the requirements for my living this authentic affirming life, this state of continuously being open to all that is with respect and compassion?

First, that I myself have received the gift of myself from another, and am willing to lead the affirming life.

Second, that I constantly safeguard the center of my affirming life, my affective heart. This includes my senses and imagination, and my "humane emotions" ennobled by my intuitive or contemplative mind. In our modern world, these emotions are always in danger of being smothered by the utilitarian or assertive emotions under the over-stimulation of our ever-active *ratio* or thinking mind. The cultivation of my affectivity is done by leading a quieter, more unhurried life, with a minimum of distractions, idle talk and noise, with daily opportunities for contemplation in nature, the arts, and the Scriptures.

Third, that I am always open to the Holy Spirit who assists

me to discern the hidden and unique goodness in everyone I meet on my life journey.

While all men and women are called to live the affirming life, for the sake of their own happiness as well as that of others, religious men and women are called to live it in a special way.

How are women religious to live the affirming life? For the answer to this question, we must look at Mary who always accompanied Jesus during His life on earth. After God the Father, it was Mary who of all human beings affirmed the Lord most perfectly, first as His mother, and then as His companion in the work of redemption. Just as Mary fulfilled Jesus in His human nature most perfectly by receiving and thus returning the gift of His love, so religious women have the special vocation of affirming the person of the Lord, as brides of Christ, revealing to all people who the Lord truly is, and what His life is all about. They are to reveal Him as the First Affirmer by whom they themselves have been opened, and as the one who is for all of us the Way, the Truth and the Life. All this is revealed most perfectly in their living of the vows by which they say to Jesus, "I love you more than all human beings, more than a husband, more than children; I love you more than all material goods; I love you more than my own chosen manner of existence, whatever it may be."

In her affirming presence to others, the mature and affirmed religious woman gives and receives the joy of love, which makes her life and work, as well as those of others, fruitful and joyful, but she is also present to others in this authentic human way for the sake of her love of Jesus, with whom she desires to cooperate in His task of opening humanity to the Father. In her spiritual life she cooperates with Him by offering Him the joy of love that she receives when the other responds to her affirming presence. Because Jesus is then able to show His Father another human being who has become fulfilled by her affirming love, He has again succeeded in the task His Father has given Him.

The affirmed and affirming religious woman also cooperates with Jesus whenever she can offer Him the suffering of unrequited love when others choose not to respond to her affirming presence, refuse to return the gift of her love, or even deny her. Thus she shares in Jesus' suffering when, as St. John says, "To his own He came, yet His own did not accept Him." The same is true for her sharing with Jesus the lesser pains she encounters from time to time in loving: the pain of separation, of being misunderstood, of not being appreciated, and so on.

In reflecting on the foregoing, one begins to realize that the affirmed and affirming religious woman occupies a very special position in church and society as the representative of Mary as woman. Mary is not solely the Mother of Jesus, although she has been most commonly represented as such in art and church history throughout the centuries. In addition to being Jesus' companion in the work of redemption as mother, she is His companion as "bridalmother" — in the words of the theologian Matthias Sheeben.

I believe that at long last the Church is becoming sufficiently mature to understand the deepest meaning of what Mary "treasured and reflected on in her heart" and which she grew to understand to the fullest extent in deepest joy, but also in deepest pain, when Jesus addressed her for the second time as "woman" when she stood under the cross.

Just as Jesus led Mary very gradually and gently in His self-restraining love to the point where she was able to recognize and give her assent to the ultimate meaning of her vocation, the same moment when He was separated from her in death, so the teaching Church must lead all Christians to the recognition and acceptance of the special relationship between Jesus and Mary about which the early Church Fathers already spoke in terms of the second Adam and the second Eve, our spiritual parents who live in Heaven as King and Queen. I refer to Mary, the "pattern of the Church in its perfection," as the Bride of Christ. Thus in a special way do women religious embody the role of Mary when they affirm Christ as His brides.

It is of the utmost urgency for our troubled and divided Church and world that all Christians grow to the point of being able and willing to affirm Mary, i.e., to know, love and reveal her as she really is, not solely mother, but also the bride of Christ. Only by affirming her in her true role as the model of the Church as Bride of Christ, is it possible for the joy of love to come into the people of God, and thus for the peace and happiness for which we are created to enter into our hearts and minds. In my opinion, it is the affirmed and affirming religious woman who can most perfectly image this role of Mary, and as a co-affirmer with Christ, lead us and set the example of revealing His love.

Finally, in order to be wholly creative and strength-giving, the religious life must be lived in community of at least two persons. It will be solely in the polarity of affirming relationships that you will reveal the power of love. So it was with the apostles when Jesus sent them out ahead of Him in pairs, into the towns without walking staff, without traveling bags. Their authentic affirming presence to one another, shared with and in Jesus, nothing more, provided them with the power to work miracles and heal the afflicted.

CHAPTER III

The Secret of Affirmation

Interview of Conrad W. Baars, M.D. by Jack Wintz, O.F.M.

Psychiatrist Conrad Baars, M.D., tells a story about a true childhood experience of a friend. "At the age of five or six, my friend John was home alone with his mother one day when the pastor came to visit. Being shy, John hid under the table, but not entirely out of sight, while the pastor and his mother visited. Neither paid attention to him. When the pastor had left and John had come out from under the table, his mother stroked his hair and with a friendly smile said, 'Were you shy, Johnny?'"

Dr. Baars reports that his friend never forgot this incident and the wonderful feeling that "it was all right for him to be shy" and that he did not have to force himself into adulthood or change his character for the visitor.

"Johnny had been affirmed both by his mother and by her understanding visitor," points out Dr. Baars. They had allowed him to be who he was and to grow at his own pace into what he was to become. John felt that the affirmation and loving acceptance he had received in this instance helped cure or at least diminish his shyness.

What if his mother had scolded him and told him to speak up like a big boy? "That would be *denial*, the opposite of affirmation," answers Dr. Baars, "because it would say in effect:

'You should not be shy.' Actually the mother affirmed him by saying in effect, 'You may be a shy person, Johnny. You are just as lovable the way you are.' This gives him strength because at that particular age and under those particular circumstances, that's the only way he could feel."

To have told Johnny to come out from under the table and shake hands with the pastor and "don't be a baby," would have been clearly unaffirming and would have adversely affected his emotional development, according to Dr. Baars.

This story illustrates Dr. Baars' notion of affirmation. "What happens when you are affirmed," he explains, is that you receive the gift of yourself from another person. You receive it, accept it, possess it and now *you possess yourself* — and no one can disturb you anymore."

The late Dr. Conrad W. Baars, of San Antonio, Texas, was interviewed in Cincinnati, Ohio, by *St. Anthony Messenger.* He was born in the Netherlands and received his medical degree from the University of Amsterdam, having also attended Oxford University in England. During World War II, Dr. Baars served in the anti-Nazi underground in Belgium, France and Holland and spent two years in Buchenwald concentration camp imprisoned by the Nazis. He came to the United States in 1946 and became a psychiatrist. Among his books are *Healing the Unaffirmed*, co-authored with a colleague, the late Dr. Anna A. Terruwe, *Feeling and Healing Your Emotions,* and *Born Only Once: The Miracle of Affirmation.*

A key concept that Dr. Baars keeps coming back to is that "psychological health comes from living in the affirming orbit of another person who gives you to yourself, and you accept this gift of yourself and become self-possessed." As Dr. Baars points out in *Born Only Once,* "Every human being, no matter how many close friends he has, is also in the ultimate analysis *unique* and *alone.* He stands alone in his unique self either weakly, inadequately and unhappily — or firmly, strongly and happily.

"If he perceives himself to be good, worthwhile, desirable, lovable, he will possess himself strongly and firmly. For this sense of one's own *firm*-ness each human being is totally dependent on another human being's gift of af-*firm*-ation. The earlier in life he receives this gift, the sooner his growing firmness and strength enable him to cope with the world, to contribute to the world his own strength, and share his happiness with others."

Commenting on this in the interview, Dr. Baars states that "the unshakable realization of who one is — the result of having been affirmed — is what makes a person hold together or stand firm as a human being. Unaffirmed persons do not stand firm in their uniqueness and in accepting who they really are." Such people become "rattled," insecure and unglued, for example, when criticized by others for something they have said or done.

Examples of Denial

The word "denial" sums up the various ways we cause people to be unaffirmed and shaky about their identity. We deny and belittle people in many ways, refusing to let them be who they are. Dr. Baars uses the example of parents who thoughtlessly criticize their child for getting poor marks in school. "Why didn't you bring home better grades? When I was your age I was in the top 10 per cent of the class. You must improve!" By reacting in this way, stresses Dr. Baars, they are "denying the child" and causing him or her to have a low self-image. A more affirming approach, according to Dr. Baars, would be to say: "Cindy, you've worked hard this year. You've tried your best. Some teachers feel you can improve here or there. How can I help you develop your abilities and interests in certain areas?"

According to Dr. Baars, the following are typical ways we deny people instead of affirm them:

• **Denial by overprotection.** In effect, overprotective parents are saying to the child: "'I consider you weak and helpless, and so I must protect you.' They take away any chance the child may have to start believing in himself. They always wrap him up to protect him against the weather and catching colds, and he is not allowed to play with other kids because they may harm him. Such people are really saying to the child: 'I have no faith in you.' An affirming person has faith in the goodness of a child and in the strength of a child... even if he gets sick."

• **Denial by belittling others.** We can deny or belittle others, says Dr. Baars, by "ignoring" them, by "drawing attention to another's faults," and by "tactless criticism." Sometimes we belittle others by desperately trying to prove our own importance and comparing ourselves with them in ways that often make them feel inferior. "We try to build our own ego by besting the other, by boasting of our greater accomplishment, of our greater strengths and virtues." In effect we are denying the other.

• **Denial by possessive love.** "Possessive love is unaffirming by its very nature. It's not a love that lets the other person be. It's destructive. It seeks to possess the other, instead of allowing the other to be free — and who he or she is. Possessing means making you part of me. In reality, you're not part of me. Nobody's part of me — except when the person freely wants to give himself to me."

• **Denial by imposing behavior patterns on others.** "Jimmy comes home after getting hurt in a fight with another boy in front of his house. His father tells him, 'You sissy, go after him and get even with him. No son of mine is going to let himself be beaten up by anybody!'"

An affirming parent, says Dr. Baars, would have accepted his child the way he was instead of trying to hurry his development or correct him for not living up to his parent's value system. Dr. Baars feels there are too many *trainers* and not enough *sensitive educators*. "A *trainer* is interested in making a kid behave in a certain way while a *sensitive educator* follows the development of the child with respect" and encourages the child to develop according to his or her own pace and needs.

An affirming father would have "put his arm around the angry Jimmy and let him cry. And when Jimmy had calmed down he might have said, 'Does it hurt, Jimmy?' or, 'Are you sad, Jimmy?' or 'Do you want to tell me about it?'"

"By this tender acceptance of Jimmy in his grief and pain, the affirming parent discloses to him that he finds delight in Jimmy. And it is exactly and solely this tender, almost nonverbal disclosure of Jimmy's goodness and lovableness that is perfectly attuned to Jimmy's level of development."

• **Denial by pseudo-affirmation.** Examples of false forms of affirmation, according to Dr. Baars, are "the casual pat on the shoulder, the superficial compliment, the glib and hasty encouragement that is not attuned to the other person's feelings, as, for instance, when the mother tells her daughter on entering the dentist's office, 'Now, there is absolutely nothing to be afraid of, dear.' And we can add to this the premature or too quickly proffered advice that was not preceded by attentive listening."

Another form of false affirmation would be "permissiveness toward youth" which shows a parent's or supervisor's lack of care. There is a kind of "openmindedness," Dr. Baars insists, which betrays an indifference on the part of parents. They do not want to be bothered or to be involved with a child's well-being or development.

The Process of Affirmation

Affirmation is the reverse of denial, Dr. Baars believes, and it brings about growth. "For it is in being affirmed that a person's psyche is allowed to flower fully in its own unique way, to become open to its own goodness and that of others. Thus affirmation can be said to be truly life-giving, and as such is the source of another's psychic [psychological] birth."

He compares the affirming process to the effect water has on something immersed in it. The water respects the object and lets it be. "The water surrounds it perfectly and adjusts itself faithfully to the exact contours of the object without destroying it. It allows the object, if a living one, like fish, coral or plant, to grow and develop without hindrance by adjusting its own weight in relation to it. Moreover, it hides its defects from view."

Dr. Baars believes there is only one way of affirming others — and that is through an "emotionally felt love" that we reveal to others. He warns against any kind of *technique mentality*, whereby we think that certain external tricks or devices automatically bring about affirmation. He is wary of "pseudo-affirmers who say: 'All right. I'll say the right words, do the right things, but I don't care, or I just do this for a living.' It is his conviction that people who lead an affirming life at all times are the best affirmers."

At the bottom of affirmation must be a genuine love and "affectivity," according to Dr. Baars. And this is expressed through certain attitudes: If I want to affirm you, I need to be *aware* of your goodness, *be moved* by it and *reveal* my delight in it.

As Dr. Baars explains, I must first of all *"be aware of, attentive to, and present to* your unique goodness and worth." Secondly, I must *"be moved by, feel attracted to, and find delight in* your goodness and worth." Finally, I must *"reveal that I am being moved* by and attracted to you." And I reveal this attraction to you "by visible, sensible, physical changes — the tenderness and delight revealed in my eyes, my gaze, my touch, my tone of voice and choice of words. This causes you to feel and sense and see that you are worthwhile. You come to feel and know who and what you are."

Learning to be more aware of and responsive to another's goodness, asserts Dr. Baars, is a lifetime project and we must begin early to detect goodness in everything and in everyone. "You start off in childhood with things. A child should be given the opportunity to grow up and become aware of its environment and find out that the world is beautiful. The mud is beautiful, the toys and pet are beautiful, and, of course, human beings are beautiful."

Parents help by constantly leading an affirming life — affirming everything, all of creation and one another. The child's senses should become better developed and more refined all the time. Montessori schools are good at this, he believes, and our whole education system would do well to help children find a spontaneous joy in the goodness of creation.

"We must learn to be simply present to what is good and to be moved by it," says Dr. Baars, "but if I'm rushing around, I can't stand still and be present, for example, to the goodness and beauty of a tree or another person or whatever it may be. If I do take the time and let the goodness of things move me, then I affirm that creation. I become a *co-creator* with God of what He has created. That's another way of saying what an affirmer is: *a co-creator.*"

When asked to reflect on his own life in terms of affirming and non-affirming experiences, Dr. Baars revealed that "a most unaffirming experience in my life was having my freedom taken away by the Nazis and being imprisoned." Two years in Buchenwald, he says, "were a denial of my patriotism and my right to be a free human being." The reasons for his survival were his faith in God, his anger at the Nazis and a sense of self-worth given to him by "very affirming parents." He saw fellow prisoners "dying like flies from minor illnesses" because they had no faith or will to live or inner strength from affirmation.

"An even worse denial was a fairly recent betrayal by people whom I thought to be friends. I expect to be robbed of my liberty or life by enemies, but to have my professional work and ideas plagiarized and appropriated by 'friends' was certainly an extreme form of denial. Such an experience can unsettle you for a long time," he admits, "but it can never negate the inner strength my parents gave me — which is the basis for inner healing."

The most affirming experiences in his life, he says, are those which occur "when people let me be. For example, my wife lets me be. I let my wife be. We love one another. She lets me travel to lecture. She doesn't say, 'Why do you have to go again and leave me?' Feeling secure, she doesn't have to check up on me. This is what marriage should be: a letting be. Because I'm allowed to be, I like to share what I do and where I go."

Advice for the Unaffirmed

How can I become a more affirmed person? Although nothing can replace the gift of self we receive from an affirming other, Dr. Baars offers a number of suggestions we can follow in order to open the door to becoming a fuller human being.

1. "**Stop trying to affirm yourself,** that is, stop trying to *prove* to yourself and the whole world that you are worthwhile and good," advises Dr. Baars. There's a place for honest recognition of your own talents and achievements, but your self-worth doesn't depend on this.

So stop trying to impress others with your accomplishments; this illusory self-inflation only serves to put them down and keeps them from affirming you. Stop trying to make yourself seem important by amassing possessions, name-dropping, displaying degrees and honors, striving for power, fame, status or sexual conquests — or by other desperate efforts that only reveal your self-doubt. "Self-affirmation," Dr. Baars contends, "is always futile. Only another can affirm you."

Just relax and accept the good news that you are already valuable and worthwhile as created in the image of God, who always loves and affirms you.

2. "Just be yourself. This means," explains Dr. Baars, "to be *honest* with your feelings and opinions." If you can't be honest with your feelings at least in the presence of those who say they love you, warns Dr. Baars, you will torture yourself with the thought: "'I wonder if they would still love me if they knew of my anger, or how I really felt?' If you want to be loved for yourself and not for what you pretend to be, it follows that you must be yourself." If people are not going to allow you to be who you really are and express your true feelings, and if they refuse to give you the gift of yourself, do they really love you?

3. Avoid the "nice guy" syndrome. "If you have trained yourself for years to behave in the way you think others expect a *nice* person to behave, ask yourself the following question: 'What have I really accomplished by always being so nice, and never revealing my real feelings and thoughts?' "You may end up with no real enemies," Dr. Baars admits, but you also end up having "no real, close, intimate and reliable friends." The truth is, according to Dr. Baars: "Sooner or later every unaffirmed, other-pleasing individual discovers the tragedy of the whole masquerade of being so *nice* that he is still where he started — feeling unloved."

4. Accept your own emotions. "Reassure yourself inwardly, over and over, that it is good to feel whatever emotions you feel. It is especially necessary to stop repressing those emotions which you and so many others mistakenly consider 'negative' or 'bad' emotions, like hate or anger. There are no negative or bad emotions! All emotions are good!" Dr. Baars insists that emotions are outside the realm of moral judgment. Actions, based on these emotions, are of course a different matter. But there is no need to repress or be ashamed of the fact that you feel an emotion like desire or anger.

Dr. Baars demonstrated this by recalling how his own feelings of anger toward the Nazis helped him to survive against all odds at Buchenwald. He is convinced that anger was "a positive factor — a life-giving factor because my anger aroused me both psychically and physically to fight — to defend myself, to frustrate their desire to see me dead."

He said his anger was not directed to destroying them — in fact as a Christian he loved them with his will — but "to resist the threat of falling into despair and to stay alive no matter what. It gave me energy! It lent strength to my faith."

Therefore, we must become comfortable and friendly with all our emotions. If you want to be moved with love and joy in the face of what is good, "then you must feel comfortable also with the emotion of hate for what is not good or lovable and with the emotion of anger when you are treated shabbily, unjustly, or are slighted or manipulated."

5. Don't be ashamed to experience your feelings, even though you may have to restrain your actions. Dr. Baars insists that reason or love may require us to restrain our actions at times for the good of another, but this doesn't mean we should repress or feel ashamed of our genuine feelings. The repressing of a feeling and the restraining of an action are two entirely different things. "We should never repress our feelings," states Dr. Baars. But at the same time we accept, for example, our emotions of anger or desire towards another, we may have to exercise restraint in *expressing* these emotions for the good of the person involved.

"You never repress feelings of love," explains Dr. Baars, "but you might restrain certain manifestations of love because they are not good for the other person or they would be in conflict with the moral order."

6. Don't let the fear of hurting other people's feelings paralyze you. This fearful attitude, according to Dr. Baars, is widespread and "almost fashionable" today. "It stems from the mistaken belief that it is the highest virtue to go to any length to be considerate of the feelings of other people. Actually, it is merely a pseudo-Christian virtue not practiced by Christ in His life on earth. He always said and did what he knew was right even if it would hurt someone's feelings."

Dr. Baars finds that many people describe themselves as being *hurt* when it would be much healthier to say, "I'm irritated or angry." He advises that we begin identifying our *hurt* as *anger* and then speak frankly about it. He explains: "As long as you speak of yourself as being *hurt*, you'll have an image of yourself as being struck down, helpless, paralyzed, waiting for someone to come to your rescue. Your use of the word *anger*, on the other hand, will create a subconscious image of readiness to fight and defend yourself and therefore will cause you to feel courageous."

7. So learn to live a little more dangerously — "that is
—dangerously for you! — by doing and saying what you think,
know or believe is right, by not caring that you may be mistaken
at times. You'll learn from your mistakes."

He suggests that in quiet moments we use the "power of
positive imagining." For example, "Imagine yourself acting
and speaking assertively. Imagine people congratulating you
on speaking your mind or for acting assertively."

8. Be assertive. Dare to disagree or give an honest compliment. Be honest with your feelings in words and actions.
Express your feelings of anger or annoyance. Let people know
who you really are and how you feel. "You'll discover more and
more how you can do this effectively in the context of Christian ideals of love, patience and forgiveness, and if occasionally
things get out of hand, you can always apologize."

If you do not do this, you fall into "the non-assertive
person's vicious circle of feeling unloved." It works like this:
You feel inferior, inadequate and unloved, and therefore afraid
to let people know who you really are; you fall into the nice-guy
syndrome of seeking security by pleasing everyone, but they are
really not loving you for who you are. So you're back to where
you started — feeling inferior and unloved.

You can break this circle by being more assertive and not
putting so much energy into worrying about whether everybody
likes you.

Unaffirmed people, Dr. Baars observes, "hope to find
security by having everybody like them, but there may be a
lot more security in having x number of people like you and y
number hate you. It's better security to know who your enemies
are. Then you don't have to spend all that energy trying to please
everybody. Trying to please everyone for fear you will not be

loved is futile. It never assures you of getting what you want anyway: to be loved for yourself."

9. **Stop thinking that you are no good** and worth nothing because your parents or others in your early life failed to make you feel loved. "If you have not been loved by others," says Dr. Baars, "you come to the conclusion, whether consciously or subconsciously, that you must not be lovable and if you're not lovable, you must be bad. If I were good they would have loved me, so I must be bad. If I'm bad, then naturally I hate myself."

Dr. Baars reminds us that if our parents and others have failed to love us and affirm us as children, it is not because *we are bad or worthless* but very likely "because they themselves were never loved and affirmed or because they were emotionally repressed, rigid and fearful of their emotions; or they were too busy to love you adequately." He feels we must understand that those who should have loved us better were themselves unfortunate victims of a lack of affirmation. Therefore, our conclusion that "I am bad" is false and unhealthy.

10. **Be gentle with yourself.** Dr. Baars believes we must be compassionate, kind and forgiving with ourselves. Because we often suffer from self-contempt, he likes to quote the following words of Dr. Carl Jung on the importance of self-acceptance:

"Is there ever a doubt in my mind that it is virtuous for me to give alms to the beggar, to forgive him who offends me, yes, even to love my enemy in the name of Christ? No, not once does such a doubt cross my mind, certain as I am that what I have done unto the least of my brethren, I have done unto Christ.

"But what if I should discover that the least of all brethren, the poorest of all beggars, the most insolvent of all offenders, yes, even the very enemy himself — that these live within me, that I

myself stand in need of the alms of my own kindness, that I am
to myself the enemy who is to be loved — what then?"

What then? Well, both Dr. Carl Jung and Dr. Conrad Baars
believe we should stop condemning and raging against ourselves. We must learn to love and accept and forgive ourselves
and "receive the least among the lowly in ourselves with open
arms."

*Jack Wintz, O.F.M., is a Franciscan priest, ordained in 1963. He holds
an M.A. in English literature from Xavier University in Cincinnati.
He is the senior editor of* St. Anthony Messenger *and edits* Catholic
Update.

The Affirming Power of Love

We live in an age of confusion, both in religion and in morals. In the wake of the sexual revolution, falsely called liberation, we find compulsory sex, promiscuity, venereal disease, pregnancy outside of marriage, abortion and very little happiness. Though there can be much joy in sex, the happiness people were created for seems to be decreasing. We see more and more depression among young people, more suicides and escape in drugs.

As people who want to conserve what was good in the past, and to work toward improving that which needs improving in the present, we must dare to look at whatever in our religion or in our society has contributed to the present crisis. Let me briefly mention some of these.

There have been educators who taught our religion in ways that have led to unnecessary suffering among members of our faith, as well as among our Protestant brothers. Basically it has been an attitude of fear and suspicion towards human nature, especially our so-called lower nature. This fear and suspicion increasingly led to a repression of part of our nature. The situation was made worse by Calvin, who taught what the Catholic Church never taught: that human nature is corrupt as a result of original sin.

This repression led to the well known sexual neurosis of

the Victorian Age, to much scrupulosity and to an emotional illness which we regard as the opposite of scrupulosity or fear-based repression. We call it an energy-based repressive disorder, whereby people use emotional energy to repress part of their nature, to destroy the integrity or wholeness that God intended. The result is a total inability to successfully integrate the emotional life within the personality. Moreover, in our society we now observe a still different kind of emotional illness affecting our young people, as well as adults. We call it the syndrome of the unaffirmed person.

This illness in its most severe and crippling form is called Emotional Deprivation Disorder. Its victims suffer emotionally because they have been deprived of the fulfillment of their most fundamental need — to be recognized, to be known and loved for who they are. Our society is increasingly affected by this condition, resulting as it does in increasing psychological, spiritual and emotional weakness and debility, which makes us vulnerable to new and promising ideas that come along, even when contrary to long-held moral teachings.

We have been led to believe by certain "experts," not only among theologians but also among members of my own profession, that morality and moral standards lie at the root of sexual disorders. This is not true. Freud's faulty interpretation of the neuroses eventually caused the pendulum to swing to the other side. At present people are in terror of suffering neurotic repression. They hold the belief fostered by many members of my own profession, that all our emotions and feelings should be gratified. That, too, is unhealthy. In my very brief presentation today, we shall see how to correct this.

How can we deal with our emotions in such a way that we as adults can lead a healthy life? How can we lead our children to accept what we as parents, teachers, and counselors have to offer in the matter of leading good moral lives? We need a positive philosophy of human nature and of human sexuality. I intend to deal only with the first part, a positive philosophy of human nature. I shall present some of the basic principles of the authentically human way of life, the dynamic way of living as human beings, the life that Jesus Himself led when He was on Earth.

In order for me to live the affirming life, it is necessary that I be present with the full attention of my whole being to all of creation — not just with my thinking, or discursive mind, but also with the attention of my senses, my intuitive or contemplative mind, my spiritual sense, and my emotions.

As parents, counselors and teachers, we must be present in that particular way to our young people. We must become masters in seeing who they are, in seeing their goodness, in recognizing their unique differences. For that to occur, we have to not only observe, we have to listen and be sensitive. The discursive mind has to be much less active than the intuitive mind. In our society, the overactivity of our active minds and the overactivity of the utilitarian (assertive) emotions are a tremendous obstacle to leading the authentic human life.

The overactivity of our discursive reason and utilitarian emotions also prevents us from being responsive to the other group of emotions that God has given us. We call those the humane emotions, the emotions of love and desire, joy and kindness, affection, compassion, and tenderness. These emotions work directly under the guidance of our intuitive mind. Ennobled by the intuitive mind and guided by reason and will, these humane emotions should be the main source of being present to all of God's creation.

How do we relate to others, if we ourselves have been fortunate enough to grow up in an environment where we were allowed to be ourselves, where our humane emotions could develop properly? What happens when we were not conditioned to be afraid of those emotions? People will be able to sense our delight in their goodness.

When I am moved by the goodness of what I see around me, I automatically feel that I must protect that goodness. I do not wish to do anything that will interfere with this goodness. That is the source of my developing this love-with-restraint. I do not restrain the love itself; I always let it be and grow. I do restrain myself in the manifestations of my love, however, when I know that those manifestations cannot be received by the other person, when he cannot respond to me, or when I know that those manifestations of my love would be contrary to the moral order. Only in this way of relating do we allow the other person to be who he or she is and allow the other to become what he or she is meant to be in God's plan, both in his own time and at his own pace. At that point the deepest and most unbreakable bonds of friendship are formed, of mutual affirming and loving.

The first need of a person, then, is to be allowed to be himself. The second need is to know the truth. My obligation within this affirming relationship is to help the other to know who and what he is, and what he should do. The other will listen to me only because I have opened him to his own goodness, to the goodness of all creation, and to the goodness of God. When the other is disposed to listen to me, then I can tell him how he must live. Then I may correct him or instruct him — at the right time and in the right way — about what he has done wrong.

It is a most sensitive process, a delicately balanced process between being and doing, but it is the only way to get the coop-eration of our children so that they can learn from us. If we try to teach them without their being open to us, they are likely to turn us off. Once they feel that they can trust us, they become eager to be like us. They can become what they are supposed to be, moral persons. They learn to relate to other persons.

Everyone receives his or her physical existence from a

mother and a father. Every person must also be born psycho-logically, however, and this only happens as a result of the affirming presence of significant others. For the one affirmed, it is their psychic or psychological birth; and for the affirming person, it is the opportunity to co-create with God. This is why I called my book *Born Only Once*,[1] because it is dedicated to the millions of people who have not yet received their second or psychological birth, who suffer fear and loneliness because they cannot relate to other persons on an adult level. Only by being strengthened psychologically by other affirming persons can one develop the virtues of fortitude and temperance. The wish to lead the temperate and chaste life must come from within; it cannot be imposed from without. With temperance and chas-tity comes the fortitude to defend what is good, not only from within oneself but in everything that one holds dear and in which one believes.

People who have never lived in the orbit of an affirming person are psychologically, spiritually and emotionally weak. This explains why some people with a religious orientation, priests, religious and laity, are unable to defend the truth of their faith firmly and successfully. They are held back by their need to be popular or to be loved, because they never were loved themselves. They cannot be temperate in their relationships with others because their emotional life has not been fully integrated into their personality. They also continue to experience psycho-sexual difficulties.

The virtue of temperance gives us joy only when we have been reared without being denied, when we have been allowed to be ourselves, and to be the persons God wants us to be. This

---

[1]   Conrad W. Baars, M.D., *Born Only Once: The Miracle of Affirmation*, 1975, 1989. Preface by Suzanne M. Baars, Quincy, IL: Franciscan Press, Quincy University, 2001.

is the way we must rear our young people — not only by words but by our way of life. We have to let them know and feel that it is much more beautiful and joyful to relate to other people in the love-with-restraint rather than by sexual relations outside marriage.

Often I find that young Christians, who find it difficult not to go to bed with each other, will listen to me when I tell them in detail how we are supposed to function in God's plan, how beautiful it is when, out of love for one another, they restrain themselves from those actions that are against the moral order. Many come back and say, "I wish I had known this. I am much happier now. We find delight in respecting each other, in showing esteem for each other. We still show our affection and love, but not by going to bed. It isn't so difficult any more." Perhaps it is difficult once in a while, but the willingness and ability to live this way comes from within as the result of having been affirmed. Only through this process of being affirmed can people mature, and become the revealers of the goodness of others — co-creators, affirmers and healers.

Jesus came to Earth as the First Affirmer. He revealed to people, especially those who lived in close relationship with Him, the goodness that was within them. He gave them a mandate to carry on this process, to open their hearts to other people's goodness, to be strong and loving, to be healers.

The question is often asked, "If we have not been affirmed ourselves, what chance is there for us to become affirmed in the way you have just described?" My answer is this: if you have not been affirmed, you have to be opened to your own goodness by another person. You cannot force someone to do this for you, however. You have to wait until God brings this person into your life, yet there is much that unaffirmed or partially affirmed persons can do for themselves until the affirming person comes along. They should stop doing the things that unaffirmed persons usually do. Those things tend to make them less open to the love of an affirmed person when he or she appears in their life. To always please other people, for example, in order to gain their love or friendship makes you less like your real self. Moreover, it never really works, because one wants to be loved for who one is. If you always hold back certain thoughts and feelings because you are afraid that they will displease others, you will be liked only for what you pretend to be. It takes much courage for people to learn to be themselves, but it is precisely then that they discover that people like them much better than before.

Most of the unaffirmed people that I counsel tell me that they have no enemies. They say that everybody likes them. Then I ask, "Why are you here?" They answer, "I'm so depressed, doctor." Their depression is partly due to holding in anger out of fear that being assertive would hurt people's feelings and make enemies. I explain in the course of treatment that they will gain security from having some enemies, or at least from knowing who their enemies and their real friends are. They even gain a certain amount of energy when they don't have to put themselves out any more to please the people who don't like them.

Persons who have not received from their parents the assurance that they are indeed good and lovable will try to prove to themselves and to the world that they are good and worthwhile. They may do that by sexual exploits, or by amassing riches in order to impress others with their cars, houses and boats, or they may even acquire a number of academic degrees to list after their name. Such self-affirming people may also strive for power. You may find them in politics. In wartime, they torture and kill their victims in prisons and concentration camps. Unaffirmed and self-affirming people are conspicuous in the entertainment world. The result is always the same for them too — futility and frustration. Having climbed the ladder of success, of fame, of fortune or power, always expecting to find what they need — namely, the feeling that they are good and worthwhile — their hopes are dashed.

Doing things cannot give anyone the feeling of being good and lovable. One receives this sense of self only through another person who is willing to give this gift through his or her unconditional loving presence.

What makes matters worse is that self-affirming people cannot affirm others; they deny them or use them and thus weaken them, or even destroy them. Self-affirmation is like a cancer — its cells feed on the surrounding healthy cells until they are destroyed in the process. Self-affirming persons are not opened to being affirmed by others because they will not take the risk of receiving a gift that not even their parents gave them. Preferring to get what they want by their own efforts, they close their hearts to those who really care for them.

All of this goes on within the church also, made up as it is of large numbers of unaffirmed people. This must be corrected if our church is to become psychologically and spiritually strong. Unaffirmed people in religious life build their spiritual lives on sand. They cannot integrate the spiritual life with the rest of their nature. The affirming life also holds great promise for them. I am optimistic about the future, for by working together, we can help the church become a truly joyful church. By being co-affirmers with Jesus, we shall be joyful Christians who love one another, provide the right guidance to our children and help them to do what they will want to do, that is, lead virtuous lives.

CHAPTER V

Morality and the Christian Anthropology of Thomas Aquinas

It seems a valid assumption that insofar as the exposure to the teachings of Thomas Aquinas on the nature of the human person is concerned, today's priests can be divided into two groups — the few who have been exposed and the many who have not. Since it is my contention that the textbooks of moral theology used in the seminaries in the recent past did not present his *authentic* teachings on anthropology, it follows that his doctrine is simply not — or very little — known.

This has been and is a sad state of affairs, first of all, for priests themselves. I have seen a large enough number of them in twenty years of clinical psychiatric practice to know how needlessly they suffer as a result of their exposure to a distorted anthropology. Secondly, it is unfortunate for the countless people influenced by priests in catechism classes, confessionals, missions, etc. Thirdly, for the next generation, insofar as today's newly ordained priests and seminarians lack knowledge of Aquinas' authentic teaching regarding the nature of the human act, the passions, our free will and the virtues.

It seems that in spite of certain improvements in today's seminary education there is still something lacking in the process of helping young men to become masculine priests, leaders, teachers and affirmers of humankind. They possess good will, as did the older generation of priests; they are much less repressed, unlike the older generations, and thus they are freer and more open in their attitude toward the good. Yet, they are not well prepared to oppose evil. This may be because they tend to identify evil more readily in terms of social and economic evil rather than metaphysical evil, but also, and more importantly, because their psychological foundation in the virtue of fortitude leaves much to be desired.

I mention these shortcomings in the personality development of younger generations of priests solely for the purpose of spotlighting a potential short-cut in the necessary growing process toward a truly masculine and celibate priesthood. Even though the modern human sciences are increasingly contributing their share in the construction of this maturing process, the latter is as yet insufficiently complete and we cannot afford to overlook already available perennial truths from our tradition. Moreover, justice demands that the author of this knowledge — Aquinas — be given his due! This, more so than purely utilitarian motives, should prompt a re-evaluation of the wisdom of having eliminated the teachings of Aquinas from the seminary curriculum. Such an assessment should be undertaken, of course, in the light of Thomas' *authentic* anthropology.

Not being a learned medieval scholar myself, I must be satisfied with merely reflecting the results of studies by certain European scholars who in the fifties became familiar with the work of my colleague, Anna A. Terruwe, M.D., of Nijmegen, Netherlands. Her clinical validation of certain psychopathological theories relied on the ideas of a Dutch Redemptorist, Fr. Willem Duynstee, who in 1935 offered a Thomistic interpretation of the mechanism of neurotic repression, as a corrective to the Freudian explanation of the cause of repression. Duynstee's insights intrigued several European scholars to re-examine and rediscover Saint Thomas Aquinas' authentic doctrine on human nature and the moral life. Fr. Duynstee sought to correct the voluntaristic and repressive approach to ascetical practice by formulating a theoretical foundation for a more *balanced* approach to ascetical practice, which was applied to psychotherapy in Terruwe's *"mortification therapy,"* as I shall briefly note at the end.

I present the contrast between Aquinas' authentic doctrine and the mistaken views which influenced western Christendom, in the hope that a return to Thomism offers a solid foundation for the ascetical discipline and for the human sciences where, if applied clinically, will do much to relieve the suffering of persons with neurotic disorders. If incorporated into pedagogy, this sound anthropology will prevent the development of neurotic disorders in the future, and help men and women attain the happiness which the will is incapable of not willing[1] and for which one strives naturally and by necessity.

Actus Humanus

There was a common tendency in textbooks on moral theology and in ascetical literature which was influenced by voluntarism and rationalism to define the *actus humanus* (the human moral act) as an act done with full knowledge and with full and free consent of the will — *qui ex voluntate deliberata procedit... quorum homo est dominus.*

This focus on reason and will as the sole principles of human conduct, marked and determined the approach in much moral and ascetical literature. The human emotions were con-

---

[1] *Summa Theo.,* Ia IIae, q. 10, a. 2 (*Summa Theologica: St. Thomas Aquinas,* translated by the Fathers of the English Dominican Province, Westminster, MD: Christian Classics, 1981).

sidered, in principle, *extrinsic* to the human act and thus extrinsic
to the moral act. They were simply not considered part of the
human act. They were thought to exercise their influence on
reason and will from outside, only in a threatening fashion,
diminishing one's freedom — *passiones minuunt liberum*. While
it is true that the passions can diminish the freedom of a moral
act, it was forgotten that it is also true that they can enhance
the moral quality of an act. In the voluntaristic and rationalistic
view, however, the emotions were mentioned in one breath with
violence and ignorance as chiefly enemies of the will — *hostes
voluntarii*.

From this perspective, since the Fall, all human desire was
considered as *concupiscentia* — in the pejorative sense, of course
— which called for constant vigilance in this interpretation of
the *pugna* — the battle between flesh and spirit.

What most of these textbooks did not bother to mention
was Aquinas' constant teaching that what is human, rational,
voluntary and free in the human person has a twofold aspect
— *per essentiam* and *per participationem*. The passions participate
in the moral life as sources of the moral perfection of an act.[2]
Thus Thomas introduced the emotional life as a principal part of
the moral life. In other words, Thomas Aquinas explicitly stated
that not only reason and will but also the *appetitus sensitivus* are
principles of the human act.

In direct contradiction to some mistaken ascetical fearful belief that the emotions are solely an extrinsic threat to the
moral life, Aquinas explicitly stated that the passions have an
innate need to listen to the voice of reason — *passio nata est
obedire rationi*[3] — this insofar as the emotions participate in the
activity of reason — *prout substat rationi*. Thus he considered the

---

[2]   *Summa Theo.*, Ia IIae, q. 24, a. 3.
[3]   *Summa Theo.*, I, q. 81, a. 3; Ia IIae, q. 74, a. 3.

human emotions as typically human positive principles, which contribute moral value to the human act.

Let me interrupt my summary of Thomistic doctrine to mention that Terruwe theorized that in the person with a repressive disorder the emotions do not participate in the activity of reason and will. Rather, the repressing emotion wedges itself between reason and will on the one hand, and the repressed emotions on the other. This is one way in which neurotically distorted emotions can interfere with freedom. Of course, the other way is by giving into emotions without providing them with the guidance of right reason.

Thomas Aquinas' strong condemnation of the stoic exile from the moral life of the emotions as diseased entities — *aegritudines et morbi animae* — stands in direct opposition to the later teachings of Immanuel Kant, who considered all feelings as pathological. Kant's claims influenced widely held beliefs such as, "When you do something good when you do not like it and you do it with great effort and intense self-control, then your act is truly moral" and, "What counts is that you will the good (*actus internus*) and do it (*actus externus*), no matter how you feel."

This view was propagated, in spite of Thomas Aquinas' explicit teaching that there is in man something more closely related to reason and will than the act which proceeds from the will, namely the emotions, the feelings. Having a feeling, a liking for the good, definitely adds something to the moral value of the will-act. It is not only important to strive after the good with will and deed — but also morally better.[4] The human person is thus totally involved in morality, and this includes the feelings and emotions.[5] Aquinas: "Accordingly, just as it

---

[4]   *Summa Theo.*, Ia IIae, q. 24, a. 3.
[5]   *Summa Theo.*, Ia IIae, q. 24, a. 1.

is better that man should both will the good and do it in his external act, so also does it belong to the perfection of moral good that man should be moved unto good, not only in respect to his will, but also in respect to his sense appetite."[6] Instead of judging the moral value or the character of a person solely by what he or she does or does not do, Thomas thus provided another *signum*, namely, the delight, the joy which one finds in the good one does.

Ratio — Passio

In regard to the relationship between *ratio* and *passio*, the mistaken approach itself created a tension because it appears to hold that the passions can both diminish freedom as an extrinsic influence, and yet at the same time do not exert so great a force that they take away responsibility on the part of the intrinsic principles of human action: reason and will. This created the moral dilemma that a person can be diminished in freedom by his or her passions, yet also be responsible for these passions. In consequence of this negative attitude toward the passions, which are regarded as non-human, even infra-human or animal, some saw moral governance of the passions solely in terms of mortification and self-denial. The passions were to be dealt with firmly and severely: to be treated as dangerous for human beings. The very terms — passion, lust, sensuality, concupiscence, desire — sounded a pejorative note. Students were made to think that there was an essential conflict between *ratio* and *passio*, implying, of course, that one of them had to be

---

6   *Summa Theo.*, Ia IIae, q. 24, a. 3 [Editor's note: the validity of this passage for moral teaching has been recently confirmed by its incorporation *verbatim* into the text of the *Catechism of the Catholic Church*. Cf. 1767, 1770].

eliminated. Did some of them wonder whether there could be a more peaceful solution? Did they ever wonder if the authentic doctrine of Thomas had been utilized on this point? If so, they would have been pleased to learn that he had stated that the passion tends to the sensory good (*bonum secundum sensum*), but as a human passion it tends also toward reason and its *bonum rationis*.[7] This is not a conflict, but rather an invitation of the sense striving to follow, to be guided by, the rational striving without eliminating the former in the process. This invitation to integral moral maturity Thomas Aquinas called the ordering or the regulation of the passion.[8] This attitude on the part of reason, he held, is the proper way to bring about integration and harmony between the emotional and intellectual lives. This function of reason, it could be said, represents the Thomistic way of "sublimation" — quite distinct from Freudian sublimation, which is an unconscious, if not neurotic, way of dealing with the libido.

The only other ways for human beings to deal with passions, said Thomas, are to let them do as they please, even against reason, or to entirely suppress them (*tollere, repellere, exstinguere*). Neither of these ways was considered morally right by Thomas Aquinas. Christians have always recognized that the former way leads to vice and sin. We now know that the latter way is also psychologically harmful because it inevitably leads to development of a repressive disorder. Consequently, there is no justification for any form of mortification or self-denial which has a repressive effect on the emotions. Healthy, mature *mortification* in persons with neurotic disorders does not consist in causing the *death* of their emotions, but rather in reducing the

---

[7] *Summa Theo.*, Ia IIae, q. 30.
[8] *Summa Theo.*, Ia, q. 77, a. 4.

hyperactivity of pathologically overdeveloped emotions which hold sway over the emotional life, so that they may restore the proper role of reason and will in guiding the emotional life.

Voluntas

In regard to the *voluntas*, voluntarism taught that "the will is supreme. It is the force which enables us to control ourselves, to lead us to victory in a struggle between the flesh and the spirit. To will is to control, to master. You can do everything if you will it."

Since the passions were suspect and considered dangerous, it was considered the safest preventive approach to train the will as early as possible in life — by a variety of exercises — to overcome and master the passions. Such a one-sided emphasis on reason and will represented, in respect to the emotional life, a negative attitude which was both fear-inspiring and defeatist. Fear of one's emotions, we now know, is at the root of fear-based repressive disorders, such as scrupulosity, phobias, obsessions and compulsions. In these pathological states, fear, not reason, determines the activity of the will. Fear makes the will a despotic, suppressive ruler. Thomas Aquinas was not responsible for the disastrous results of these mistaken teachings which influenced western Christendom.

Thomas Aquinas, let it be known, explicitly said that the will is not an absolute ruler, not a despot.[9] The will is not the sole principle of human conduct. The will must respect and listen to the secondary principles of conduct, namely, the *appetitus sensitivus*. The will must rule the emotions democratically. It must do them justice in their tendency to also strive for the

---

[9]   *Summa Theo.*, Ia, q. 81, a. 3; Ia IIae, q. 9, a. 2.

bonum rationis. The will not only moves, it is moved itself. The will is a "moved mover" — moved by reason which presents the good, but also by the sensitive appetite,[10] which has such a strong influence on the practical judgment in any given situation. He taught that the will should listen to the emotions in order to guide them.

It should be noted here that in the time of Thomas Aquinas there were powerful reactionary movements in the Church which feared the rationalism of some uses of philosophy by the university professors. There were also voluntaristic movements which were fearful of the danger of determinism — if one were to admit that the will was not only a mover, but also itself was moved. Yet, Aquinas dared to affirm Aristotle's attribution of a passive aspect to the will, that the will must first be moved affectively,[11] in the sense that we use the word, e.g., "a moving experience" or "moved to tears." If at all possible, the good must please the will *via* the sense appetite and at the same time appeal to it *via* reason. To will, in the broader Thomistic concept, is first of all affective, and secondly, and dependent on this affectivity, is the will the mover — active, effective.

One may illustrate the significance of this concept of the will as follows. If a certain activity does not please me at all, if it holds no interest whatsoever for me, I can only force myself to do it. However, in the anthropology of Aquinas, there is no place for such an absolutely tyrannical will: "You can do all if you only will it." This is not to genuinely will it; rather, this kind of "willing" constitutes another type of activity: compliance.

However, if there were something in this life that would interest me or please me totally — which is only possible when

---

[10] *Summa Theo.*, Ia IIae, q. 9, a. 2.
[11] *Summa Theo.*, Ia IIae, q. 9; Ia IIae, q. 24, a. 3.

face to face with the Beatific Vision — then the only thing I could do would be to will it both affectively and volitionally. This kind of "willing" constitutes surrender.

Virtues

In regard to the formation of virtue, the mistaken approach held that "if everything depends on the will, then I must train the will, I must steel it." This was seen as virtue: the unrelenting training of the will. Could this have been why this approach was so unpopular?

Just what is virtue? It is the habitual perfecting and ordering of the *principia actus humani*. Since these principles include reason, will and the sensitive appetite — and not the two spiritual faculties alone, then the cultivation of the emotions is important along with the cultivation of reason and will in the development of virtue.

This is precisely what Aquinas explicitly held, viz., that virtue is not only in the will and reason, but also in the emotions.[12] Cultivation of the emotional life in its entirety, not its extinction or repression, is a prerequisite for *conformitas*, harmony, integration, and cooperation between reason and emotions. The emotions, with their psychomotor reactions (the physiological changes which accompany every emotion), exist in order to be integrated by reason; to move a person under its guidance toward the happiness for which he or she is created.

Any other idea, such as the theory that the emotions must be diminished or disappear, would make the existence of the sensitive appetite superfluous. As Thomas Aquinas said explicitly, such an idea or theory would be inane, absurd. Emotions

---

[12] *Summa Theo.*, Ia IIae, q. 56, q. 59.

do not exist for the purpose of being extinguished or repressed or even simply to be curbed. The emotions are not dangerous wild horses, as Plato held. Rather, they are docile, like a child with its parent, who must be taken by the hand and guided in the right direction. Of the four cardinal virtues,[13] justice is purely volitional; it has a typical business-like character since it deals with our relations to other people. Justice requires that others must be given their due no matter how one feels about it.

Temperance and fortitude, on the other hand, are virtues of the emotions, that is, they are precisely the moral formation of the concupiscible and irascible appetites. St. Thomas Aquinas made this clear in his differentiation between continence and temperance. Continence is a minor virtue — *aliquid minus virtute* — since it is a violent, painful dealing with or holding back — *se tenere* — of the emotions. With continence, the emotions retain their intensity; they never become tranquil. The process must be repeated over and over. Continence approaches virtue, and is often mistaken as the virtue of temperance, which is misunderstood to consist in energetic striving. Rather, Thomas taught, virtue consists not in the difficult, but in the good. Yet, to the mistaken ascetical viewpoint which overvalues striving, such continence may seem superior to the facility with which the person possessing the full virtue of temperance directs his or her emotions.

Of course, continence is much better than doing as one pleases without regard for the objective moral order, but it is definitely inferior to temperance. Temperance develops within the emotional life itself. There is an ever-diminishing need for repeated interference by the will from without. In the growing harmony and integration that ensues in the total cultivating of

---

[13] The four cardinal virtues are prudence, justice, fortitude and temperance.

true virtue, emotions learn to follow reason ever more readily as they are meant to do. They develop a habitual disposition to listen to their "master's voice" readily and effortlessly. In the temperate person their *aptitudo naturalis ad virtutem* has been allowed to develop to its fullest extent.

The temperate person has true rational and free dominion over the passions. The continent person has control-with-effort, not much better than suppression. If this person desires to become mature and temperate, he or she must learn to dare and grow beyond this pseudo-control, in order to gain true control. Here is where a sound ascetical theory and practice is needed so that the errors of the mistaken approaches can be avoided.

It is precisely such an ascetical theory which Fr. Duynstee proposed when he suggested that not only the emotions of the concupiscible appetite need to be curbed, but also those of the irascible appetite. This balanced approach to mortification indicated that ascetical discipline was not about fear of the emotions, for that would be to foster an imbalanced emotional life in which one stimulated solely irascible passions — such as courage and fear — as a means to suppress the feared pleasure appetite emotions of love and desire. Rather, as human nature is wounded since the Fall by disordered emotions of both the pleasure appetite (concupiscible passions) and assertive drive (irascible passions), it is both of these which need to be integrated under the guidance of reason and will. Asceticism endeavors to bring order into both sets of passions; hence there needs to be a mortification not only of the pleasure emotions, but also of the assertive passions of courage, fear, anger, etc. In light of Duynstee's theory, Dr. Terruwe developed mortification therapy to redress the imbalance between pleasure and assertive emotions which occurs in repressive neuroses. This balanced approach to the right ordering and mortification of all human emotions is based on the authentic doctrine on human nature as taught by St. Thomas Aquinas.

Conclusion

Why have the positive, humanistic, enriching thoughts of St. Thomas Aquinas about the nature of human beings been lost? Why were the textbooks of moral theology and ascetical practice so non-Thomistic? Additionally, in the closely related matter of authority and obedience, why has the voluntaristic, Suarezian *agere contra* doctrine of acting against the passions prevailed over Aquinas' intellectualistic doctrine?

It is not up to me to answer these questions. As a clinician, I can only point out that for generations people have been most adversely affected by the distortions and omissions of important facets of Aquinas' authentic anthropology. I can only note that the voluntaristic *agere contra* approach has dominated centuries of ecclesiastical attitudes and clerical *training*.

I am also happy and fortunate, however, to be in a position to point the way toward the proper cure and prevention of these repressive disorders and related emotional disturbances. Our Aristotelian-Thomistic understanding of the nature of the human person, our particular interpretation of the mechanism of neurotic repression, our integration of the Thomistic *concupis-cibilis-irascibilis* (pleasure — assertive) division of the human person's emotional life with observations in modern clinical psychiatry, and our many years of successful clinical application of this body of insights, hopefully will become a foundation for priestly formation. For this we can be grateful to the authentic teachings of St. Thomas Aquinas seven hundred years ago!

CHAPTER VI

Philosophy as Intellectual Affirmation
of the Seminarian

In the August 31, 1980 issue of the *National Catholic Register,* I had the privilege of expressing my professional opinion, as a Catholic psychiatrist, on the negative non-academic aspects of many American seminaries. For many years, I have suspected their academic programs as possible causative or contributory factors in our alarming vocation crisis. Yet for obvious reasons, I have never considered myself qualified to write on this topic. New information has become available, however, that enables me and other non-theologians to make an intelligent judgment on a seminary's academic program. I hope that, by sharing it here, concerned Catholics will be moved to shift their search for causes of the crisis from the "outside world" to events within the seminary walls.

It is true that for many generations a considerable number of priests have suffered from emotional disorders, spiritual afflictions, and a high incidence of addictions. It is true that to a large extent these were caused by incorrectly putting into practice the theoretically correct philosophical anthropology taught in the seminaries. It is true that there was a need to correct this serious defect in our seminary programs. It was wrong, however, to conclude that these sufferings could be cured and prevented by abandoning that very same philosophical anthropology and replacing it with the psychologies of the secular humanists with their considerable ill-effects on the lives and thinking of seminarians.

What about the abandonment of the source of philosophical anthropology, the teachings of St. Thomas Aquinas? Why do Catholics in general hear so little about this as a possible cause of the vocation crisis? Most Catholics I meet seem to be impressed by those who claim that the main reasons for the postwar vocation crisis are: the deteriorating family life with parents no longer fostering vocations among their children; the selfishness of the Me-generation; the overestimation of the need for sexual gratification and the alleged abnormalcy of celibacy, and so on. Often these claims are uttered in one breath with allegations of greatly improved, theologically updated, newly emerging seminary programs. A recent quote in a diocesan paper might be considered typical of such assertions:

> ...one of the most serious problems facing the Catholic Church in the U.S. and throughout the world is the phenomenon of the almost empty and dying seminary. There are good faculties, with fine programs — but there are no students. Very few Catholic seminaries or theological schools in the whole world aren't facing severe problems of shortage of students to support excellent and expensive programs of training.

It is also easy to be thrown off the track when "presidents" of seminaries write such *non sequiturs* as:

> Our attendance has been up slightly the last three years; this increase does indicate that bishops and

vocation directors are basically satisfied with the
program that XYZ seminary has to offer.... I find it
(the numbers of vocations) a great mystery.

These examples can be multiplied many times and undoubtedly have led most Catholics to direct their search for a
solution to the vocation crisis away from the changed programs
of theology and philosophy.

In the unlikely chance that it is not sincere ignorance on
the part of clergy and religious about the shortcomings of new
academic and psychosociological seminary programs, but rather
embarrassment about having to judge the various changes effected by fellow theologians that has led to this impasse in resolving "the great mystery of the vocation crisis," I decided to
seek out informed laity. I began by looking for lay members of
the Boards which all seminaries are supposed to have according
to *The Theological Formation of Future Priests* by the Sacred Congregation for Catholic Education, USCC, 1976:

Members of the Seminary Board will represent the
clergy, religious, and laity who share a concern for
priestly formation... and will include representatives
from the broader academic community and from the
various professions that can contribute to a more effective program, e.g., law, medicine, and finance.

Doubts lingered

When my admittedly limited search proved futile, I was
hopeful, almost certain, to receive answers to my questions by
contacting an officer of the world's largest organization of laymen dedicated to the promotion of priestly vocations. Surely, I

had never seen an article on that subject in its monthly magazine, but then I could have easily missed that during the many years I have been an active Serran. In response to my inquiry, Serra International's Executive Director ended his letter to me:

> ...he believes the seminarians in the United States are doing an excellent job in general. The administration is in good hands and is fully aware of the responsibility to help candidates in striving for spiritual development. One of the Bishops' major concerns is the quality of their seminaries. Apparently, most are quite satisfied with the job being done these days.

It seemed from this letter that thousands of educated professional and business men and women all over the world, none more dedicated than they in supporting the Church in every possible way, were all in agreement with the clergy: the seminary education in general is above reproach.

I was left with my doubts, fed from time to time by the reading of strange things going on in some seminaries. A good example was a sex seminar, held at St. John's Seminary at Plymouth, Michigan, for 22 first-year theology students, which presented "several films depicting male and female masturbatory, homosexual and unmarried heterosexual activity... depicted in an explicit, detailed and sympathetic fashion." This weekend-long workshop was conducted by a psychiatrist — an adjunct professor at St. John's — allegedly for the purpose of "'desensitization' and 'resensitization' of the participants' sexual emotions." Although I certainly cannot condone, either morally or professionally, such an approach of assisting young men to become mature and resolve existing sexual moral problems, I decided to write this seminar off as an aberration in what the bishops consider to be a satisfactory educational program.

Poland has a Vocation Glut

At that point, I was ready to forego my inquiry, when I reread Serra's letter more carefully. I then discovered that the favorable opinion of the prevailing status in American seminaries, conveyed by the Executive of Serra, did not represent the result of a well-conducted study by Serra's own lay members, but rather was that of a priest, Father Daniel Pakenham, for several years the former Executive Director of the National Conference of Catholic Bishops' Priestly Formation Committee! I had come full circle in my search for reasons (other than mainly psychological reasons) for the decline in numbers of candidates to the ordained priesthood. In addition to receiving still another subjective opinion of a member of the clergy, I reached a rather startling conclusion about Catholic laity who for decades have insisted that they want to be treated as adults by the Church. It seems that for many of them "Father says..." is still as much an obstacle to objective observation and judgment, as "Sister says..." used to be a tranquilizer for the parents of children attending Catholic grade school.

Having arrived at this impasse, I could think of only one question left to ask. Is there any place in the world where there is no vocation crisis on a large enough scale to validate conclusions about what a seminary should be like? where any Catholic can find objectively verifiable criteria by which to judge the quality of his or her own local seminary? where the laity can intelligently assist the Church in creating an overflow of candidates to the priesthood, eager to follow in the footsteps of fishers of men they can safely and constructively admire and emulate in all the dimensions of their being?

The answer to this question presented itself when I received from a colleague a book by Rev. Francis Lescoe, Ph.D., S.T.L. This book taught me that the ubiquitous claim to the effect that the vocation crisis is worldwide is simply not true. There is at least one country in this world where there is a vocation *glut*, not a crisis, where, according to Lescoe:

> The Polish Catholic Church is, by far, the most vigorous of all the Churches in European and North American countries today. The Churches of Poland are overflowing with worshippers — some parishes schedule 19 Masses each Saturday/Sunday. The seminaries are filled to capacity, the women's religious orders, which have discarded neither their habits, nor their prayer and community life in favor of apartment living, have waiting lists of applicants. St. Joseph's Order in Krakow, for example, has over 200 young women awaiting admission. Poland, today, is actually ordaining more priests than it needs, thereby enabling it to 'export' priests for service in such 'foreign' missionary dioceses as Newark, New Jersey, which recently accepted 6 priests from Krakow.

Suddenly Father Francis Lescoe, much to my surprise, had made it possible for all of the laity to determine, fairly and objectively, whether our seminaries have an academic program worthy of the name, by the publication of his *Philosophy Serving Contemporary Needs of the Church: The Experience of Poland.*[1] What does Lescoe have to say specifically about the seminary education of Polish candidates to the priesthood?

> There are 24 diocesan major seminaries (and 25 seminaries maintained by Religious Orders), teaching both philosophy and theology....

---

[1]   Francis Lescoe, Ph.D., S.T.L., *Philosophy Serving Contemporary Needs of the Church: The Experience of Poland*, New Britain, CT: Mariel Publications, 1980.

Of the 78 bishops in Poland all but three have EARNED doctorates.... A large number of these teach courses in their specialty in their own seminaries.... They are ACTIVE administrators of their own seminaries... and know all their students "first hand"... and *personally* know the strengths and weaknesses of the young men they ordain to the priesthood.... The late Archbishop H.J. O'Brien of Hartford used to complain, "I am now ordaining men for my diocese who are total strangers to me. I must take the word of others that these men are the kind of priests I need in my diocese."

... a seminarian must earn 38 credits in Philosophy... Logic, Epistemology, Philosophy of Man and Nature, Metaphysics, Philosophy of God and General Ethics form the systematic courses. The seminarian will also take 10 *additional* credits in Philosophy during his Third and Fourth year of Theology. These additional courses will be in Special Ethics, i.e., Social Ethics, Ethics of Marriage and Family and Medical Ethics.

In addition... the Polish seminarian takes Experimental Psychology, two years of Latin... one year of Greek and one year of Hebrew and two years of a modern language.

The American seminarian, on the other hand, is grossly undereducated. He currently takes (in most cases) only *18 credits* in Philosophy.... All too often these 18 credits are obtained not in Catholic, but in state and secular colleges and universities, where esoteric and exotic courses in contentless Oriental philosophies, which are alien to Christian thought, are substituted for foundational courses in the Philosophy of Man, of God, Metaphysics and Ethics.

On the subject of the American seminary Lescoe writes (p. 17):

> At the workshops on *Priestly Formation...* we could detect an almost universal agreement on the following points:
> 1. Seminary theological education is in disarray.
> 2. The failure in theology is due to a dismantling of the seminary philosophical curriculum.
>
> Conclusion: We must begin with a re-organization of the philosophical component of the seminarian's education, if we wish to improve his theological training.

On p. 19 Lescoe continues:

> The American deviant theologians have set back Christian Philosophy in the United States by 25 years.... It is only PHILOSOPHY — and not sociology, psychology, or some empirical science that can give to theology its sorely needed foundation and direction. If we do this, we shall restore the quality of our seminary education and ultimately, the quality of American Catholicism.

"Ultimately," Father Lescoe writes. "How long a time does he believe this will take?" He adds:

> Because of the dramatic decrease in seminary enrollments, many of the philosophy textbooks are now out of print. And because of the small market potential, there is little likelihood that authors will undertake to write new ones. Since the Lublin books have proved

to be so successful in the seminaries of Poland, we are in the process of undertaking the translation of these texts and of adapting them for use in our American seminaries.

That is good news indeed!

It seems that together with our already updated — theoretically as well as clinically — philosophical anthropology of Thomas Aquinas, future seminarians, if given the chance, can soon have available the very best in intellectual, emotional and spiritual strengthening. Once ordained, those future priests, authentically affirmed and free from crippling neurotic repressions, will be superbly equipped to serve the Church and the People of God in the troubled times ahead. No American Catholic can afford to be blind to the fact that the political future and safety of our democracy are not guaranteed any more than they are in Poland, where a leading Marxist publicly complained, according to Lescoe, "Marxism in Poland encounters a threatening opponent in Thomism as it is represented by the University of Lublin and preached from the pulpits in the Churches."

What will be done *now* in the matter of restructuring our American seminary programs will decide, I believe, whether Marxists in America in the years ahead will say the same of our clergy, our seminary directors, our liberation theologians, who, to quote Lescoe, "must strive to overcome a peculiarly American mental block, namely that St. Thomas is irrelevant and that Thomism is dead."

If we want to survive the ongoing and mounting battle between atheistic and Christian-Judeo societies and governments, all of us had better pray fervently that our American seminarians will be given as superb an education as those in Poland!

CHAPTER VII

Mature and Affirming Bishops

If we have people in positions of authority who are truly mature, then the subjects will flock to the authority. The authority is an author, *auctor*, one who creates, a co-creator who helps the subject to become mature. The task of the person in authority is to authorize the subjects who become more and more mature, so they in turn can become persons in authority. How do we get mature people in authority? For this we must have some psychological knowledge of what constitutes maturity and authority. Seminary education should be directed at getting mature priests, and the best of them will become persons in authority.

What influences those who now choose which men become bishops? Do faulty human considerations influence them? Do they seek in their auxiliary [i.e., bishop] a yes-man, a lackey? Are they sometimes afraid of a man who asserts himself? Do they want the nonassertive individual who never talks up and whom they feel won't cause any trouble for them? Do they want a man to whom they can say, "Jump!" and he will reply, "How high?" This is no basis for recommending him to be a leader! Do they want a priest who has pleased the bishop by his talent at raising money or administration? Or, nowadays we hear that a priest is to be chosen because he is 'pastoral' — but does that mean popular with lots of people? In either case these priests are actually people-pleasers, most often unaffirmed individuals desirous of being approved by their superiors or the multitude, for this is their way of obtaining the attention they crave. The priests who should be named bishops, however, are those who have been affirmed and are affirming, who are capable of self-restraining love without repressing, and are mature in their love without wanting anything in return.

Instead of wishing for honors — to be made a bishop, for instance — the mature and affirmed priest who is confident of his worth can leave such a matter up to God. He says, "Lord, do with me what you want." If the Lord wants him to be a bishop, He will bring it about. There is no need for the priest to imagine how it could be accomplished and to scheme how to achieve the ambition through political plotting. If he is unhappy in his current responsibilities, what makes him think that he would ever be satisfied? God wants him to be happy; indeed, God wills his happiness even more than he can will it himself! The mature priest simply does his present duties to the best of his ability, living the best possible life and ministry here and now.

Priests who have not been affirmed see in the status of bishop an enviable position which they imagine would gain them instant and constant flattery and attention. Actually, being a bishop brings many headaches and trials! The unaffirmed person, however, if he is energetic enough, will try to manipulate by whatever means he can to obtain honors and rank. Lacking in emotional development, because he is unaffirmed himself, (or because he has an underdeveloped emotional dimension due to repression), however, if he becomes a bishop or person in authority, he will only be able to give willed attention to his subjects. He shows a willed interest in them, and then walks away just as abruptly, because he has done his duty. He has learned all the right behavior, mastered all the nuances of appearing compassionate, the method of putting on a warm act

— but one without any heart in it. Not all people can distinguish the truly affirming person from the self-affirming person who can so cleverly appear to be concerned for them. One moment he smiles, and the next moment he is cold and businesslike. We all fall for this superficial act of interest in us occasionally. If we are with the individual for some time, however, we start to feel that they are only interested in themselves, and that they only go through the motions of pleasing us to get our cooperation, because they can use us in some way sooner or later. Their interest doesn't come from the heart.

If we have as bishops truly mature and affirming men, they will be able to empty themselves in a warm and loving service to their flock. People will feel that such bishops care for them personally. When they are in need they will go to their bishop, and he will say, "I have time for you." He will be someone who cared, who never got impatient, who did understand them even though they may not have been very kind to him or rejected him in return. He was not in too much of a hurry; he had time to be truly present to them. He will be a bishop who lets people be. He does not force himself on them. He gives them time to mature — and he lets them know in gentle ways "I care for you" and "I would like to be more for you." He is able to receive in love from them, too, appreciating and soliciting the best they have to give. Such a bishop is open to his subjects when they disagree with him, when they find his actions or directives unreasonable, when they feel they cannot go along with him and seek an alternative to be considered.

There exists a special need in the Church for fully emotionally mature and wise bishops who in self-restraining love can affirm the large number of priests and faithful who need them. A bishop must be familiar with the special needs of non-affirmed persons, and realize, for instance, that non-affirmed individuals when frustrated in their search for affirmation will attempt to affirm themselves through the acquisition of material goods, sexual exploits, power, fame or notoriety. The bishop must not be surprised, either, when these subjects respond to the inevitable failure of their attempts at self-affirmation with angry words and hostile acts, or even with claims that they do not value certain traditions or ties with their Church; whereas, in fact, they would love nothing more than to feel secure in those very same ties and traditions.

It will be no easy matter for a bishop to endure and have compassionate understanding for such behavior — in fact, he will often suffer deeply — unless he can affirm these subjects in self-restraining love, ever mindful that "God's word of love never returns to him without having borne fruit." This does not mean, of course, that the bishop should not set norms or provide direction, or that he should not help to correct a person's faults and defects. Not to do so would amount to pedagogical neglect, the non-affirmation of a person's need for guidance, self-control and independence, precisely as the non-affirmation of a person's need for emotional maturity constitutes emotional neglect.

In the process of Jesus' formation of the first priests, the apostles, Jesus did not hesitate to correct them. We see this in the startling manner of affirming Peter in his need to begin to understand the supernatural significance of Jesus' mission on Earth and of the task that Peter himself was to begin shortly as vicar of Christ on earth. Peter had already lived with Jesus for three years and had grown in strength in Jesus' affirming love. He was open to whatever the Lord wanted to teach him. Thus, when he remonstrated with Jesus that He should be spared the sufferings and death that Jesus had alluded to, Jesus affirmed Peter with the words, "Get out of my sight, you Satan! You are trying to make me trip and fall. You are not judging by God's standards but by man's."

When Jesus was ready to return to His Father, He left

behind men who were to continue His work of opening others to the infinite goodness and love of God. In response to Peter's revelation of Jesus' unique goodness as the Messiah, the Son of the living God, a revelation made possible through the indwelling of the Holy Spirit, Jesus said to him, "Peter, I declare that you are 'Rock', and on you I will build my church; to you I will entrust the keys of the kingdom of heaven." Jesus did not tell him to be a rock; that would have been denial, the opposite of affirmation. He lovingly revealed to Peter what Peter himself did not yet know about himself, that he possessed rock-like qualities strong enough to support an entire Church. Then Jesus added, "And now, Peter, now that you have been converted, (i.e., turned around toward me, living in and with me) now strengthen your brothers."[1] Now affirm your fellow priests who are to come after you, and your fellow men and women with the same keys with which you have been opened to the kingdom of my love and strength. It was Jesus' official mandate to all priests to be affirmers of all people, and of Jesus Himself in the daily sacrifice of the Mass and in the Sacraments.

When we recognize the need for bishops and priests to affirm their flock, we cannot fail to be impressed by our primary obligation, namely to heal the broken body of Christ. Here I do not refer so much to the longstanding scandal of our separated brothers and sisters in Christ, but to the rupture of most recent origin that is weakening the Catholic Church from within: the division between traditionalists, conservatives, progressives and radicals. From what I have presented here it is obvious that the least affirmed among them — those who live in fear of others who are different and therefore cannot defend their beliefs except on a purely intellectual level — cannot be expected to take the first steps in this process of healing.

---

[1] See Luke 22:32.

The challenge of initiating this healing is reserved for the most affirmed, for those who find delight in being present to others who are different and are able to reveal the goodness they perceive in such a way that the others are opened to whatever truths they may possess. Their task will be considerably lightened by studying anew the life of the First Affirmer. They will find courage and inspiration in discovering the varied ways in which Jesus revealed to the people their unique goodness and worth, and told them how to live according to His statutes and ordinances in ways perfectly adapted to their level of understanding.

For me, one of the most beautiful and instructive examples of the principle that intellectual affirmation (sharing the truth) must always be proceeded by emotional affirmation is Paul's instantaneous conversion on the road to Damascus. Instead of telling him that he should be ashamed of persecuting the Christians, Jesus shows His compassion for Paul's tireless and sincere efforts by saying, "It must be hard for you to kick against the goad!"[2] Jesus then reveals His faith in him by stating that He wants him, Paul, to work for Him. In one sudden moment, the former enemy had become the friend, and he abandoned his mistaken convictions in order to become the revealer of the real truth.

As bishops and priests sent out to heal the present polarization in the Catholic Church that is the result of mutual denial, of too many "you musts" and "you shall nots," and too few "you mays," it is important to remember that the affirming life cannot be lived in isolation. In order to be wholly creative and strength-giving it must be lived in a community of at least two persons. It will be solely in the complementarity of affirming relationships that bishops and priests will possess the power to

---

[2] See Acts 26:14

bring fulfillment to Jesus' prayer, "that all may be one as you, Father, are in me, and I in you." So it was with the apostles when Jesus sent them out in pairs into the towns without a walking staff, without sandals, without traveling bags. Their authentic affirming presence to one another, shared with and in Jesus, nothing more, provided them with the power to work miracles and heal the afflicted.

CHAPTER VIII

Psychological Aspects of Obedience

At a time when literature abounds with psychological descriptions of every possible human relationship and activity, I have found it difficult to locate studies which treat of the person who commands and the subject who obeys. Psychological texts treat only of the negative aspect of obedience, for example, the disobedience manifested at various stages in a child's development. In general, however, there is little or no recognition of obedience as such.

What is the reason for this silence about obedience? Could it be that we still judge our cultural and social development by the goals obtained in Europe through the French Revolution and in this country though the war for independence from Great Britain? In other words, "liberté, égalité, and fraternité" in Europe and independence in the United States are values that have been repeatedly threatened throughout the centuries, and people have had to fight desperately in order to safeguard or win those values. At a time that modern psychology had made its greatest strides, these same values have been seriously threatened in more ways than one. Therefore, it is not surprising that the psychological studies of human relationships have been devoted more to liberty than to interdependence, more to equality than to the relative inequality among people, and more to fraternity than to the ordinal relationships which exist in the family, the community, and the state.

Nevertheless, however important the emphasis of modern psychology and sociology on these values, one must be careful not to neglect other aspects of human relationships, and obedience is one of them. In fact, obedience is so fundamental that its abandonment would entail the destruction of all order in any society. Arnold Toynbee, the renowned historian, stated in 1950: "Obedience is indisputably one of the cardinal principles of medieval Western Christian society. It was indisputably thrown over when our secular, modern, Western society broke out of its religious chrysalis, and indisputably this modern society is now in grave difficulty. Is the repudiation of the principle of obedience one of the causes of our present plight? Was an abuse of the principle of obedience one of the causes of medieval Western Christendom's breakdown? No principle could well be more controversial, yet few controversies take us nearer to the heart of the riddle of our Western history."

The word obedience is derived from the Latin words "ob" and "audire" and it means to listen to or to hear. The Dutch word, "gehoorzaamheid," and the German word, "gehorsam," retain this same meaning. Through obedience, therefore, the subject hears and follows the voice of authority. As St. Thomas states: "Obedience is a special virtue, and its specific object is a tacit or expressed command."[1]

---

[1] *Summa Theo.*, IIa IIae, q. 104, a.2 (*Summa Theologica: St. Thomas Aquinas,* translated by the Fathers of the English Dominican Province, Westminster, MD: Christian Classics, 1981).

Complexity of Obedience

The act of obedience is a very complicated act requiring a number of integrated attitudes on the part of the adult human being. They are not easily distinguished in the adult, however, because they exist and operate simultaneously. If a person is to obey, there are certain conditions which he or she must fulfill. I shall mention later the conditions required on the part of the person in authority.

Requisites on the Part of the Subject

1. *Openness and Receptivity*

First, the subject must be open or receptive to the person in authority. The subject must not only be able to see or hear the other person and understand the meaning of the command, but must also be emotionally receptive to the command. This occurs when the command is seen as something good for the subject. If this is not the case, if the command does not appeal to the subject as a good, then the subject must at least be open and receptive to the person in authority. When does this happen? When the authority represents a good to the subject. The subject therefore needs to have developed a capacity to be moved by the values constituted in his or her relationship to the person in authority.

There are children in whom this openness, this receptivity or capacity to be moved, is seriously impaired very early in life. Such children easily become egocentric; their social development is seriously disturbed, with the result that no other person can enter into their world unless that person's presence furthers their selfish desires or needs of the moment. As children, and later as adults, they will find it impossible to relinquish anything which fascinates them at the moment. They cannot give up the present good or pleasure for the sake of something else.

2. *Feeling of Security*

A person will not usually be open and receptive to another unless he or she feels safe and secure with the other, and this is the second condition for obedience. To open oneself to another person always involves some risk, for one relinquishes something of one's own peace and composure. No one will take this risk unless he or she has full confidence in the one who gives the command and unless it is seen that something will be received in return, even if it is simply an assurance of safety and protection in the presence of the other person.

A child who has lacked the loving care of a mother will frequently turn out to be disobedient both as a child and as an adult, unless some greater fear makes the child submissive and servile. Such a child interprets every command as a violation of its own wellbeing by someone he or she considers hostile. Disobedience is therefore a manifestation of the inability to surrender to the authority who cannot be seen and felt as kind and loving. This is the result of the child's disturbed or unnatural relationship with the first human being encountered in its life. In such cases disobedience is often used unconsciously as an instrument of vengeance by the child who is otherwise weak and defenseless.

3. *Recognition of One's Limitations*

The third condition for obedience is a recognition and acceptance of the fact that one has certain limitations and is subordinate to others. If individuals do not recognize their limitations, there is no need to submit to others. For that reason, excessively selfish, egocentric people lack a sensitivity for the universal good because their intellect does not adequately penetrate their emotional life. They measure everything in terms of themselves; hence, they fail to realize their own limitations. Disobedience will therefore be a predominant characteristic in individuals with personality disorders and in normal persons during periods of increased egocentricity. If we consider the stages of development from childhood to adulthood, we shall find that the first manifestation of disobedience usually occurs between the ages of two and four, when children become aware of themselves, the influence of their actions on the world around them, their ability to will, and the power they can exert over others by their will. Often they will in order to test their power, which may lead to violent crises. The second period of disobedience occurs at the age of six or seven, when children enter upon the strange new world of the school. Their uncertainty in relationships with other people and things leads to a sense of impotency from which they try to protect themselves by refusing to obey. The third period of disobedience is early puberty, at about age thirteen or fourteen, but I think that this disobedience stems not so much from children themselves as from the attitude of authorities. Preadolescents are still in need of protection and help and should therefore naturally seek aid and not oppose it. I think that the rebellious behavior of preadolescents is normally caused by the faulty exercise of authority by parents, teachers, and others. Adolescents in their early teens resent unreasonable commands or an authoritarian attitude. They want authority and will accept it, but not as children who often obey out of fear of the consequences; they want it because they are beginning to understand its real meaning. What they need more than anything else is the opportunity to observe that the adults around them also do what is asked of them. They need practical demonstration that the purpose of authority and commands is not to keep people small and subservient but to allow them to mature.

4. Realization of One's Dependence

The fourth condition for obedience is the ability to recognize one's dependence. There can be no obedience without the realization of one's relative position in the existing order of things. Those who have a feeling of inferiority — and there are many — are very vulnerable in regard to this feeling of dependence; they often repress it and try to compensate for it by a feeling of superiority. They cannot tolerate any behavior that places them on the same level, let alone a lower level, in relation to other people. Though they give the appearance of being above all commands and conformity, deep inside they consider themselves worthless and out of touch with others. Consequently, they are often disobedient, and their disobedience must be handled by showing them the unreasonableness of their feelings of inferiority or inadequacy so that they may be led to a proper sense of self-respect. They have no feeling of worth for themselves and any attempt to force these individuals to toe the line will only strengthen their protective feeling of superiority. In this connection, I would say that the basis of true obedience is never found in complete self-negation but in an honest recognition of one's capabilities and a healthy sense of self-respect, which also includes the realization and awareness of one's relative position in the order of things.

5. Respect for Authority

The last condition for true obedience is respect for the person who gives the commands. Obviously, I am not referring primarily to the physical strength or sanctions which can usually evoke at least a servile obedience, but to the dignity of the position of the person in authority. The less one thinks of the person in authority, the less likely one is to obey that person. The subject should be able to feel — in the literal sense of the word — that through the person in authority he or she can come into contact with something higher from which one derives personal significance. It is precisely on this basis that any authority demands respect.

Unfortunately, not every person in authority conveys the significance of his or her position in a clear manner. Take, for example, the selfish, unloving conduct of many parents. While they should be the representatives of a higher world, and thus open the door for their children to a first image of God, often they close this very door. This is especially true when by their behavior and words they show that they themselves have no respect for any authority or law above themselves. The result is that their own children fail to develop any respect for them, and I believe that this is a predominant factor in our contemporary problems with obedience. Only through dignified and proper conduct is it possible for parents and others in authority to arouse the child's respect for that intermediary position of which St. Thomas speaks when he says that the superior stands between God and his subjects.[2]

Respect for one's superior includes showing him or her signs of courtesy and gratitude for the many opportunities the person in authority has given the subject — opportunities for education and growth in maturity. The subject affirms the person in authority by his loyalty. The subject denies the person in authority by putting the superior down behind his or her back. One affirms by an honest sharing of feelings and by asking forgiveness when one has failed the person in authority.

Respect for the person in authority develops in the maturing subject when he or she is able to understand the nature of authority and its role in society. We will say more about this topic in the latter part of this essay.

---

[2] *Summa Theo.*, IIa IIae, q. 104, a.5, obj. 2 and response.

Obedience and Compensation

If persons, in obeying others, relinquish something which at the moment is good for them, it follows that they must be compensated in some way, otherwise they will be deprived and frustrated. Aquinas quotes St. Gregory the Great on this point: "He who forbids his subjects any single good, must needs allow them many others, lest the souls of those who obey perish utterly from starvation through being deprived of every good." Saint Thomas adds: "Thus the loss of one good may be compensated by obedience and other goods."[3]

Adult persons are compensated for the loss of a good by the realization that they are obedient to what is truly higher, but for young persons — children or adolescents — this is extremely difficult, especially when the person in authority does not truly represent this higher good. It is wrong for parents and others to demand obedience to their commands simply on the basis of their position in authority or only to serve their own interests in some way. This kind of conduct fosters revolt and protest, because the obedience is frustrated and the subject is prevented from assuming his or her proper place in the order of things. Essentially the same thing happens when parents try to be pals with their children and conduct themselves as their equals. Their children do not develop a respect for a superior position and they obey for utilitarian or hedonistic reasons, but they never acquire true obedience. Moreover, they become uncertain and fearful, because, drifting as they do toward the pleasant or the useful, they cannot appreciate the transcendent, objective order which alone gives a definite standard for human action.

Obedience out of respect for the true worth of another per-

---

[3] *Summa Theo.*, IIa IIae, q. 104, a.3 ad 3.

son is likewise an important factor in the child's growth toward independence. The child should find in the father or mother a person with whom he or she can identify, a person whom the child not only obeys but loves. It is significant that the process of identification with the educator is based on the child's sense of personal inadequacy, on admiration for the excellence of the educator, on love, and on the belief that by surrendering to the other the child will in some way become like that person. Identification means a flowing together of obedience and love, and the obedience that proceeds from the desire to be like the admired and loved person is not an escape from responsibility but a participation in that responsibility, according to the capacity of the subject.

Abnormal Types of Obedience

There are certain abnormal types of obedience. Perhaps they are better classified as kinds of pseudo-obedience because they closely resemble true obedience but are the occasion of much of the criticism that is leveled against true obedience. In adults, pseudo-obedience may be the result of fear or a pathological need for security and safety. It may manifest itself as an exaggerated meekness, as is seen in those religious who show to every person they meet the same submissiveness they owe their religious superior.

1. Servility

This exaggerated meekness or servility, is often mistaken for the docility of obedience. Docility — derived from "docere," to teach — signifies that a person is easily taught to obey readily. This means that the person uses his or her intellect and is not merely a creature of pleasure and utilitarian appetites which can be trained — like an animal — to perform certain actions. Docility is exercised when the subject has an intelligent grasp of the meaning of a command given by a superior. Servility, on the other hand, is submission to authority that is motivated by fear — fear of asserting oneself, fear of the superior's reactions and fear of the effect on one's relation with the superior. Those who practice servile obedience will usually fail seriously when assigned to positions which require independent action and personal responsibility.

2. Identification with One's Superior

A related infantile form of obedience is based on identification with the person in authority. Although it is a normal process in children, it should be resolved in the course of growing up and it can be a dangerous mechanism when found in adults. For example, the young men and women who enter a religious novitiate are usually at the age in which they realize that they are different from others, in which they are beginning to develop opinions of their own, and in which they want to live according to their own initiative. It is just at this time, however, that they are emptied of everything they possess: parents, family and friends, personal possessions, former habits of life and their own independent initiative. If this emptying is done too rapidly and too radically, they may experience a feeling of impotence and may regress to an infantile attitude, especially that of identification in childish dependence on the superior or novice master or mistress. In that case, they can lose all individuality just as effectively as if they had been brainwashed.

3. *Submission Resulting from Repression*

Another form of pseudo-obedience is that which results from neurotic repression. In this case the obedience and submission spring not from fear but from emotional energy, and this is sometimes found in the most gifted persons. The repression in the subject is occasioned by a cold, unfeeling, rigid superior who will as often as not have an energy-based repressive disorder.[4] Feelings beget feelings, and lack of feelings begets lack of feelings; in other words, such a superior imposes his or her own neurotic disorder on his subjects. In such cases the obedience which follows from repression may lead to peculiar manifestations of disobedience in regard to other authorities. For example, the boy who is a model of good behavior at home because of an excessively strict father may be a troublemaker at school if the teacher is not equally severe. Again, religious who are perfectly obedient to a very demanding superior may show a callous disregard for law and authority when outside the jurisdiction of their proper superior. Their repressed feelings of self-assertion and their feelings of rebellion against their superior will manifest themselves in devious ways and in camouflaged forms unrecognized by the persons themselves.

The authority crisis in the Church may be a rebellion against authority's role in the frustration of the humane emotions and assertive drive[5] and in the repression of the emotions through premature and unbalanced prescribing of rules and commandments at a time that the still immature and growing individual cannot yet feel, or sense, their rational goodness. When the burden of repression or the intolerable frustration

---

[4] See *Psychic Wholeness and Healing: Using All the Powers of the Human Psyche* by Anna A. Terruwe, M.D. and Conrad W. Baars, M.D., Staten Island, NY: Alba House, 1981.

[5] Editors' Note: The humane or pleasure emotions are love, hate, desire, aversion, joy and sadness. The emotions of the assertive drive are: hope, despair, courage, fear and anger.

is opposed, the person in authority becomes the target of the revolt, for in some fashion the subject senses that he or she has been deprived rather than affirmed by the authority.

4. Abdication of Responsibility

Closely related to this form of pseudo-obedience is that of the individual who lacks sound judgment and initiative and insists that everything he or she must do needs to be spelled out clearly. The real purpose is to force the superior to be continually occupied with this person thus exercising a certain power over the superior. This is a special danger for women religious, because there seems to be something attractive to many women in the idea of giving up their will. By natural instinct the woman is inclined to submission and security, hence, to be taught in the novitiate that she must give up her will may mean for her that she no longer needs to make decisions or accept the consequences of her actions. Consequently, she cannot be blamed by God or another person for anything that goes wrong, as long as she was doing what she was told. Moreover, by giving up her own will, she is assured of salvation and is absolved from all personal responsibility.

To abdicate personal responsibility, however, is to condemn oneself to spiritual, moral, and psychological immaturity. Obedience founded on this type of surrender of one's will may lead to a perpetual childhood which, in turn, may be masked under the title of the "spiritual childhood" of St. Thérèse of Lisieux. A further danger is that the person will cease to think or judge at all, and quite logically, because if one is not to will, there is no need to think. Religious men and women who could and should have been artistically creative or apostolically original became sterile of mind and mediocre of spirit, and all because they had given up willing, and therefore, thinking.

5. *Obeying to Shame Others*

A form of submissiveness which is particularly irritating is that of persons who are a model of obedience and practice it in such an emphatic and obvious manner that they are a living reproach to everyone else. Such persons practice obedience in order to put others to shame. Additionally, there is the sadomasochistic form of obedience in which subjects delight in being restrained by persons in authority while the latter find equal delight in dominating their subjects. It is a mutual affair of torturing and being tortured. These subjects cherish their subordinate position by which they are a reproach to the ones who treat them slavishly; such superiors, in torturing their subjects, themselves experience the tortures they inflict on others. The more submissive the one, the more tyrannical the other. Such a sadomasochistic relationship sometimes develops between parent and child and may also be found in other relationships.

It should be evident that there is no true obedience in any of the types described. A truly virtuous person does not seek himself or herself, and true obedience is practiced only towards persons entitled to it, in matters where it is required and in the manner which is proper. All the forms of pseudo-obedience are basically camouflaged expressions of selfishness, but it does not follow that they are always practiced consciously or freely. True obedience, as I have said, is a complicated act, and it may be that the necessary equilibrium for obedience was never established in the subject because of mistakes in education, disturbed interpersonal relationships or faulty spiritual formation. If this is so, one must find ways and means of correcting these defects so that the subject may yet progress to equilibrium, maturity, and true obedience.

We usually assume that other persons are normal and mature, and persons in authority should surely act on this supposition, rather than suspecting some form of psychopathology. This does not change the fact, however, that in the face of repeated acts of disobedience on the part of an otherwise well-intentioned subject, those in authority should seriously consider the possibility of some developmental disturbance.

Purpose of Obedience

Before an individual can give an adequate human response to authority through obedience, he or she should understand why there is and must be authority. In attempting to determine how authority should best operate in order to foster obedience it is essential to keep in mind that the purpose of obedience is not obedience itself, but the fulfillment of the person who obeys. Furthermore, authority will not necessarily be weakened by a critical evaluation of its role; rather, it should be strengthened.

To begin with the excess of authority, I think it is evident to all that authoritarian discipline has become meaningless, not only in religious and ecclesiastical life but also in the military profession and in business corporations. Moreover, the blind obedience which is the expected response to authoritarian discipline has also proved inadequate. Whether blind obedience was ever adequate is a question I shall leave unanswered, but nowadays few persons would deny that authority, which relies heavily on explicit instructions to be obeyed to the letter, without reference to the goal sought or on threats and sanctions, merely tends to produce mechanical compliance without any true development of the individual or any sense of personal responsibility on his or her part. However, is it not true that blind obedience has often been extolled as the perfection of the virtue of obedience?

One of the defenses for blind obedience in religious life is the notion that the vow of obedience requires that an individual give up his or her own will. What this may lead to in a subject has already been discussed above, but such a notion also has an effect upon the superior. If the subject can avoid exercising personal judgment in the name of obedience, so can the superior.

If all the directives of a religious superior are considered the will of God or an inspiration of the Holy Spirit, the superior can, under this pretext, avoid prudent consideration before giving a command. If the superior happens to be impulsive, petty, or abusive, it is easy to see what will follow. Actually, what the Holy Spirit wants is the proper use of one's faculties and powers. He wills that our actions be fully human acts, and it is therefore important that both subject and superior exercise mind and will prudently, consciously and justly.

So-Called Fraternal Authority

In attempting to avoid the excess of authority and concomitant blind obedience, some today advocate substituting a type of "fraternal authority" for paternal authority. There is great danger, I believe, that this so-called fraternal authority will deteriorate into the "fraternité" idea which tends to destroy the role of true obedience. "Fraternal authority" seeks to give as much discretion and independence as possible to the subject by specifying the objective rather than the means. Accordingly, a religious superior is expected to say: "Don't bother me with every little detail; make your own decisions" rather than: "Keep the rule and the rule will keep you." Subjects, in turn, are no longer to ask permission for such trivialities as writing a letter, making a telephone call, obtaining a toothbrush, and the like.

Such an approach to authority, as I have said, could possibly deteriorate into the "fraternité" approach and the abdication of authority. Rather than being brothers or sisters to their subjects, I believe that superiors have to be strong and secure in themselves and should have recourse to an authority higher than themselves, namely, the Holy Spirit. They should not allow their subjects to excuse themselves for failure by saying that they were simply following orders, but they should give them the freedom and duty to make decisions. To do this, of course, superiors need subjects who are responsible, self-respecting and mature, and superiors themselves have to be knowledgeable. They must know as much as possible about the goal that is being sought, and to this end they should allow their subjects every opportunity to supply information, personal ideas, and opinions.

This means that there must be adequate communication between superiors and subjects. In a seminary, for example, the rector must not refuse to have staff meetings with the faculty. Then, when the person in authority has made a decision after consultation, he must see to it that it is properly communicated to the subordinates and understood by them. This is necessary if the cooperation of all is to be obtained. Furthermore, the superior should seek the willing consent of his subjects and not the compliance of blind obedience, which is psychologically impossible. Insistence on blind obedience leads to resentment, if not rebellion, because it is a complete denial that the subject is a rational, self-determining being.

Requisites on the Part of Authority

1. Benevolent and Affirming Love

First of all, persons in authority must possess a benevolent and affirming love for their subjects. Benevolence is an essential element of friendship, whether it be between equals or between superiors and subjects. Benevolent superiors desire what is good for their subjects, as subjects, and to that end they will treat them as persons, respect their individual temperaments, further their development, and help them to fulfill their potentialities. To do this, superiors must be fully aware of their responsibility for their subjects.

This matter of benevolent love is one that is often completely misunderstood by those involved. One reason for this is that we frequently tend to make too great a division in the act of loving between benevolent (generous) love and concupiscible (self-centered) love. In any concrete situation it is not so much a question of whether the one or the other kind of love is present, but rather, which of the two types of love will predominate. If the benevolent love is to be sensed, it needs to be made manifest through the involvement of the humane emotions. There has been a tendency, however, especially in the spiritual and religious life, to insist almost exclusively on love as an act of the will and to ignore or even reject the affective, sensory love. "Pure love of the will," however, is a psychological impossibility, for volitional love always involves emotional love to some extent; indeed, volitional love without emotional love would be an imperfection.

I am convinced that one of the reasons why many well-intentioned persons find no happiness in the priesthood and religious life is that it has become an uninterrupted repression of emotional love.

Benevolent superiors will not use their subjects as a means of attaining their own welfare, nor sacrifice them for a utilitarian good of the community, even if it be in the works of the apostolate. Rather they will be a "servus servorum," seeking like a good father or mother to have the good of the subjects at heart.

They will allow their subjects to obey commands in their own particular way, just as they will govern in their own particular way. In giving orders they will exercise patience and tact, because they realize that it is a risk for subjects to obey, since they must relinquish one thing for the sake of something else.

2. Respect for One's Subjects

A second condition is that a superior should have respect for his or her subjects. Mutual love implies mutual respect. The subject is not merely a useful tool in the hands of the superior but a person with his or her own life and goal, and these may never be sacrificed to the arbitrary will of a superior. The content of every command and the manner in which it is given must always be, directly or indirectly, in accordance with the rational nature of the subject. This means that a superior is never justified in giving unreasonable commands, for to do so shows a lack of respect for the human person's rational nature, nor should the authority interfere with or suppress the natural strivings and drives of the subject in the emotional, intellectual and spiritual life by inspiring fear, demanding elimination of all feelings, or by refusing to explain directives and demanding blind obedience. The authority should instead be sensitive to the feelings and emotional dimension of his or her subjects. The authority should listen to their opinions and suggestions, carefully reflect upon them, and take them into consideration. St. Benedict gave directions for this kind of consultation and invitation for a consensus among the subjects in his rule of order for the abbot of the monastery. The authority should also leave room for initiative and judgment on the part of the subjects.

3. *Avoidance of Foolish, Excessive Commands*

It goes without saying that a superior should not give foolish or petty commands. Such commands lessen respect for authority and insult the dignity of subjects; they create resistance to authority or foster servile submission which, in turn, forms a distorted judgment in subjects and destroys their ability to make independent decisions. At best, they make the superior appear ridiculous in the eyes of his or her subjects.

The person in authority should also avoid an excessive number of commands or precepts that tempt to regulate the tiniest details of daily life. These drive subjects to desperation, rebellion, or cause them to become slavishly dependent on the superior. Such a superior is a meddler who distrusts the initiative, rationality, or good faith of his or her subjects. St. Thomas says in this regard: "If a superior makes a heap of precepts and lays them upon his subjects, so that they will be unable to fulfill them, they are excused from sin. Wherefore superiors should refrain from making a multitude of precepts."[6]

Then, of course, commands or prohibitions should be presented in a reasonable manner, so that subjects may obey from a free choice that derives from personal deliberation. Related to this is the need for the authority to be sincere, not only as regards the content of a command but the manner of issuing it. When a superior gives an order and believes that no further motivation or explanation can be given, he or she should say so, rather than giving some fictitious reason and thus risking the chance of appearing dishonest and small in the eyes of subjects who detect that the phony reason is a mask for the real purpose of the order. It is vital that the superior be mature and set a good example of obedience.

Superiors must be above personality conflicts and must

---

6   *Summa Theo.*, IIa IIae, q. 105, a.1 ad 3.

not humiliate subjects that they consider to be a threat to their own position. A seminary professor, for example, must not rashly accuse a brilliant and sensitive student of being proud, or lacking docility. Neither should a superior stretch obedience to include the conscience or interior life of the subject. I believe this is a special danger with superiors of religious women. Although canon law forbids it, it is not unheard of that superiors or novice mistresses have demanded an account of a subject's imperfections in writing or have refused a legitimate request to seek confession or spiritual help from a priest.

When subjects are young and immature it is often the person of the superior that determines the degree of respect and obedience in the relationship, but with older and adult subjects the authority must see to it that he divorces himself from this personal respect. If this is neglected, a child will grow to maturity without respect for what is objectively good, but only for the person in authority. Those with a weaker nature will then become servile, law-abiding persons who lack initiative and responsibility, while the stronger ones will sooner or later rebel against all authority. I am firmly convinced that modern juvenile delinquency stems to a great extent from this basic error in education.

At the opposite extreme is another fault, that of eliminating all personal authority from our education. Here the educators — teachers or parents — lower themselves to the level of the children. They let children judge for themselves, or they try to reason too much with them. They want to save children from strict obedience in the false belief that it will warp their personalities. The consequences of an education lacking in obedience and authority, however, are no less harmful than those resulting from authoritarian discipline. The principle effects are a breakdown of self-control and self-discipline and a lack of respect for anything beyond the children's own feelings and biological drives. Connected with this problem is the false notion that one should always reason with children. It is true that gradually, as their level of understanding develops, children need reasoning at a time of discipline. The younger the child, however, and the more undeveloped the intelligence, the more the parent should rely upon emotional and sensory communication, which is the way in which a smaller child gets the message.

4. *Prudence*

Lastly, persons in authority should exercise prudence in giving commands. They must consider the personalities of their subjects. Thus, the obedience demanded of a forceful, domineering individual must be different from that required of a person who is docile and subservient. The overly sensitive person must be handled differently from the cold person. The same type of authority should not be exercised over adolescents as over children. Most important of all, superiors must recognize that here, as in other areas, they must respect the law of gradual development. All growth takes time and it should never be forced. Any attempt to do so will be a kind of violence which invites rebellion, and even if the rebellion is repressed, it will manifest itself sooner or later in an indirect and disguised fashion.

We will discuss under the section on philosophical roots the necessity of the person in authority having a sound philosophy of law, authority and obedience. The philosophical aspect underlies many of the psychological aspects which we have been presenting.

Development of Obedience

It will be profitable to discuss briefly certain developmental acts of obedience. Like all the acquired virtues, obedience is an operative habit engendered in a person by repeated acts. Such a habit may be defined as "a quality, difficult to remove, which disposes the subject to function with facility for promptness, and delight. It gives the subject facility for operation because every habit is an increase of energy in relation to its corresponding action; it gives promptness because it constitutes, so to speak, a second nature in virtue of which the subject quickly gives himself to action; and it causes delight in the operation because it produces an act which is prompt, facile, and connatural."[7]

This psychological description of an operative habit may give some the impression that all that is required for true virtue is the endless repetition of certain actions from an early age. If that were true, however, we would have no problem with fallen-away Catholics who in their years at parochial schools were regimented to go to confession, Mass and Communion at frequent intervals. If we admit that we cannot force people to be virtuous, it is strange that we have not put this knowledge into practice but have almost forced our children into religious practices which not only do not lead to the desired results of producing virtuous adults but are even obstacles to the formation of responsible, personally committed Christians. I would venture to say that many Catholic school graduates who become indifferent in the practice of their religion or even fall away from it altogether are people who were pushed into attendance at daily Mass and weekly confession in grade and high school.

The question is: Why this tragic consequence of so much

---

[7] *The Theology of Christian Perfection* by Antonio Royo, O.P., and Jordan Aumann, O.P. (Dubuque: The Priory Press, 1962, reprinted by Our Sunday Visitor, 1982), p. 55.

zeal on the part of educators? Certainly, in these practices, aimed at making a saint out of every person whether he or she wants it or not, there is a lack of consideration for the psychological need of each person to be allowed sufficient time and opportunity to develop a desire for the good to which these acts are directed. In other words, to enjoy a good to the fullest, to be happy in its possession, it is not sufficient that the person merely possess the good. It is also necessary that the person has had time to develop a desire for the good psychologically. One way to kill or stifle the desire is to give the person the good prematurely. This is the basic principle which explains why some children are spoiled, and it applies, I am sure, to the spiritual realm as well, where one spoils children for religion and the infinite good by giving it to them prematurely.

Maturity, the Goal of Obedience

The use of approval and reward or disapproval and punishment as a means of promoting obedience in a subject has significance only if one realizes that obedience as such is not the goal of education. The only goal to be considered is the person's spiritual, intellectual and emotional maturity.

How do we define spiritual maturity? A person may be called spiritually mature when he or she has become independent and capable of self-surrender. Independence in this sense means rational control of natural drives and emotions, not repression; it requires objectivity, initiative, foresight, and wisdom. By surrender I mean that one is capable of giving oneself to other things and other people without seeking self alone and without losing oneself. Spiritual maturity and obedience are not always synonymous, however. Those familiar with boarding schools and seminaries surely recognize the danger of thinking all is well merely because the students adhere to the rules in a strict and orderly fashion.

Pedagogical Value of Reward

If approval or reward (which is a materialized form of approval) is to have pedagogical value, it must be directed to the goal of maturity. The pedagogical reward — which is essentially something different from a reward in the usual sense — aims at bringing subjects, whether children, adolescents or adults to that which is good for them by means of something that gives them joy. This is in accord with the deepest stirrings of the soul, for in normal people the performance of good acts brings inner joy and calm. In the pedagogical reward, educators accentuate their approval, which becomes the instrument of their love in its function of fulfilling their subjects, of making them good and whole.

In striving toward the good and the avoidance of evil, subjects are helped much more effectively by means of approval than through punishment. The reward loses value, however, when it is not made clear that it constitutes an approval of what is good; in other words, when it loses its symbolic value. When this is the case, educators achieve the opposite of what they strive for: the subject's moral growth is retarded, for the good is done simply because of the prospect of a reward, not because it should be.

The subject runs the danger of regarding the material reward as the natural consequence of the good deed and risks becoming an egotist. It is for this reason that one must frown upon excessive praise, gifts, and the promise of favors or rewards. As far as the natural environments mentioned are concerned, one must look at the system of rewards for good behavior as a problematic one.

Much more efficacious are those signs of approval which indicate, first, that the educator is content and, secondly, that the act itself is good. This is done by a smile of approval, a pat on the back, a word of praise, even a reward, *provided the reward is unexpected and essentially one that would not expect to be repeated.* Those signs of approval also give the subject the courage to make an effort when the going gets difficult, because experience teaches us that the individual cannot do without this sympathetic participation of the educator in the subject's advance toward maturity. The older the subject gets, of course, the more the reward loses its value. Like punishment, it must recede more and more into the background to make room for awareness of, and interest in, the task at hand, a sense of duty, and love of virtue.

All this explains why the reward must not be determined solely by external conformity, but by an honest intention and a willing effort. Youngsters who are talented and successful always run the risk of being praised for things which they have done without effort, and sometimes even with selfish intention. This does not mean that these individuals have no need of approval, but only that the educator should try to stimulate their good intentions, for example, by encouraging them to help others, to refrain from pushing themselves into the spotlight, and to praise the achievements of their competitors.

What I have discussed so far is analogous to the Catholic doctrine on the human person's eternal reward.[8] The Church teaches that eternal happiness is the reward for the good we

---

[8] Editors' Note: "We can therefore hope in the glory of heaven promised by God to those who love him and do his will. In every circumstance, each one of us should hope, with the grace of God, to persevere 'to the end' and to obtain the joy of heaven, as God's eternal reward for the good works accomplished with the grace of Christ." (*Catechism of the Catholic Church*, Washington, DC: United States Catholic Conference, 1994), no. 1821.

do, but this does not mean that virtuous deeds should be done simply for the sake of an eternal reward. To do so would make us forget the gratuitous character of God's gifts, including the promise of eternal salvation, and could easily lead to pride. Eternal happiness is a reward in the sense we have discussed reward here; it is the consequence of good deeds done for God and not for any reward independent of Him.

What is the correct manner of applying a reward? Since a reward should express approval, and approval in turn presupposes that a good action has already been done or is being done, it follows that gifts and favors should never be promised in advance. As soon as one separates reward from approval, one has robbed it of its pedagogical value.

Pedagogical Value of Punishment

Just as approval has as its aim to enable subjects to reach their goal by means of joy, so disapproval, and more specifically punishment, tries to do this by way of suffering. What, exactly is the pedagogic element of punishment? Undoubtedly it aims at keeping subjects from the wrong path and at steering them toward the good, but what is the relationship between the suffering and the desired improvement? I must emphasize here that I am not speaking of the child's early training period in which the educator appeals to the pleasure appetite of the child in order to make him or her do something which is objectively good or avoid what is objectively evil. During this training period, one cannot speak of reward or punishment in the proper sense of the word. Rewards merely constitute the training aimed at habit formation and serve a preparatory function, namely, to train the very young child to do certain things in a particular sequence and context because it elicits a feeling of pleasure.

Is the purpose of punishment to teach the older child to avoid suffering? If so, it would be wrong, for then one leads the child to believe that obedience is for the prevention of punishment. One forces the child to believe in the right of the stronger, and that is precisely what one wants to avoid. Punishment must be the explicit manifestation of disapproval on the part of a person who has the right and the duty to show disapproval and, therefore, someone who would neglect that duty if he or she were not to show disapproval. Punishment as an educational means is valuable only when it appeals to the conscience of the subject. Therefore, it must be evident to the subject that the punishment is not the result of anger, irritation, hurt feelings, or pride, but stems solely from love, and is given with sincere regret, in order to arouse sorrow and improvement. One may say that punishment must be such that honest and sincere repentance is possible.

In order for punishment to promote growth to maturity, it must be in keeping with human dignity. Beatings, as formerly practiced in English schools, are out. They are a means of training, not education. For the same reason one must avoid every punishment which is humiliating, of too long duration, or having little actual relation to the wrong done. When demanding obedience, one must allow punishment to remain absolutely in the background. At times it may be even better not to punish, especially when it is already clear to the subject that his or her wrong act is deserving of punishment. The reason for omitting punishment in such a case is to accentuate even more strongly the proper educational values.

It must gradually dawn on each subject that obedience is an appeal to his or her free will, which does what should be done from an ever-growing realization of God's love. Educators, therefore, must be deeply convinced that the will can never be coerced. One may be able to force a certain action by fear or threats, but this does not move the will itself.

In the past few decades much opposition has been raised against the use of punishment, as we all know. Some stems from an exaggerated faith in human nature, which is thought to need no restriction of any kind; some stems from too great a respect for the child. The majority of opposition is aimed, and correctly so, at the many faults of modern education itself, at all the questionable things which are being said and done because of mistaken ideas about the purpose of pedagogical punishment and the reasons for disobedience and delinquent behavior.

Progress in the psychology of education has made it clear how much insubordination and other misbehavior of children is caused by a totally inadequate educational milieu and an equally inadequate educational activity. Whenever educators become aware of an increase in disobedience on the part of their subjects or realize that they must step up their use of punishment, they should seriously examine their own attitudes as educators. Educational activity that is inconsistent, indifferent toward, and neglectful of young people as individual personalities never fails to bring out bad behavior and disobedience, as do a conforming and constricting milieu, unreasonable demands, and the lack of true love.

Philosophical Roots

When a psychiatrist observes in the realm of the psychologically abnormal the many consequences of the repression of the natural drive of self-assertion, self-realization, and self-

---

[9]   In these sections we rely upon Fr. Willem Duynstee's insights, in particular those expressed in "The Law and Legal Obligation of the Law" and "The Essence of Retribution," available only in the Dutch original.

fulfillment, he or she becomes aware of the importance of considering authority and obedience from the philosophical point of view.[9] The psychiatrist sees the need to inquire into the nature of our obligation to obey a law, whether it be a positive law or the natural law. In other words, the psychiatrist wants to know why, in the final analysis, one must obey. A correct answer to this question is extremely important, because, as we shall see later, a wrong answer can have far reaching ill effects both in the area of emotional health and in the spiritual life, whether for an individual or for a community, such as a seminary, a convent, a house of religious formation, a family, or even the Church herself.

Ever since the Middle Ages, two divergent views have existed on the nature of the obligation which every law, positive or natural, imposes on its subjects. These two positions — the intellectualistic and the voluntaristic — stem from different philosophies and therefore lead to two different mentalities or attitudes. The proponents of both views agree that every law is the product of the combined activity of the intellect and will of the legislator, and is directed to the intellect and will of the subject. They differ, however, as to which element is primary. Is the law essentially and primarily the work of the intellect or is it primarily an act of the will of the lawmaker? Or, from the point of view of the subject, does the obligation to obey derive from the fact that the law is a rational directive, or from the fact that it is imposed by the will of authority? Although in this essay we will not consider a higher synthesis of these two views, such a possibility is becoming available to us through the renewed anthropology of the *affective* and *effective* sides of the human person. The former dichotomy of intellect/will is resolved, not by eliminating the distinction between them, but by obtaining a more refined understanding of the nature and function of both. For the purposes of this essay, however, we will limit our consideration to the former categories in which these two faculties are polarized — a phenomenon due not so much to the original thinkers on this subject but to many of their less gifted disciples who hardened the lines of difference and took principles to an extreme limit. A correct appreciation of both the intellect and will as affective (to be moved) and as effective (to move) offers us a new perspective which has yet to be developed and applied to topics like obedience.

St. Thomas Aquinas

St. Thomas Aquinas viewed the law as an ordination of reason (*ordinatio rationis*) and the obligation to obey it as stemming from the human person's natural inclination toward the good, namely, that which corresponds to the person's rational nature. When an object appeals to someone as necessary for the attainment of a rational good, there arises within the person an obligation to strive after that object. In other words, a moral obligation is engendered.

It is the task of the person in authority to point out what these objects are. Once they are made known to the subject, a moral obligation arises to pursue them. Authority, it is true, must exercise its will to make reason issue an actual directive to the rational good. It must often exercise its will to compel obedience for the common good, but this does not change the fact that the reason why the proposed law or rule should be obeyed lies in the circumstance that the law is rational, in accordance with reason.

Duns Scotus

At variance with this view of St. Thomas is the voluntaristic doctrine, which maintains that one's obligation to obey the law is determined by the will of the authority. According to this position the rationality of the law, although required to be present, is not considered to be the determining element of one's duty to obey. In other words, one does not obey the law because it is reasonable, but because it is imposed by the authorities. It is not a question of the superior's intellect appealing to that of the subject, but of the superior's will imposing a duty on those who are subject to him or her.

The Franciscan, Duns Scotus, an adherent of this voluntaristic doctrine, was the first to oppose St. Thomas' teaching on this point. His view was based on his answer to the profound theological question of his time: Which is primary in God, His intellect or His will? For Scotus, God's will was the primary determining factor of His activity. "If you ask why the divine will is directed more to one than to the other of two opposing things, I reply that the only reason why the will wills this, is that the will is will." In this view no appeal is made to the intellect of the subject to whom the superior's will is made manifest. All the subject has to do is to conform his or her will to that of God, and the subject is free to do this without any appeal to reason, for in the subject also the will is primary.

As a good son of St. Francis, Duns Scotus could say this because he always connected the manifestation of God's will with God's love; however, his voluntaristic view made it possible for Ockham to draw the extreme conclusion that as a measure of good or evil, God's will could have no limitation or restriction whatever. To hate God, if God were to will this, would be a good and meritorious act, according to Ockham.

The teachings of Duns Scotus and Ockham continued to

make themselves felt in England. One of their followers, Hobbes, held that the will of the State and not that of God was the determining factor of morality. "Every human act is by nature indifferent. What makes the act good or bad is determined by the rules and laws of the lawful kings."

On the European continent the teaching of St. Thomas prevailed, namely, that God's wisdom precedes His will and that all creation is governed by the expression of that wisdom. The plan of divine wisdom is the eternal law, in which man and woman participate by virtue of the natural law. This intellectualistic doctrine was enlarged by the outstanding scholastics of the sixteenth century, Cajetan, Medina, and Soto.

Francisco Suarez

Yet, there were exceptions. The most important one was the foremost theologian of the Society of Jesus, Francisco Suarez. The doctrine of Suarez on this point, and not that of St. Thomas, is the one that has exerted the greatest influence in the Church during the past several centuries.

In one of his works, Suarez asks whether the law is an act of the intellect or of the will. After presenting different opinions, he supports the voluntaristic view that law is an act of the will of a person in authority by which he wills the subject to be bound. Suarez applied this conclusion first to positive law, and later also to the natural law, even though he did not want to deny that what the natural law requires or forbids is intrinsically good or evil. In order to solve this apparent contradiction, he arrived at the following compromise: "Although there is a kind of moral value independent of God's commandments, the natural law derives its character of law and legal obligation, in the fullest sense of the word, only through the will of the divine authority."

This, of course, is quite different from the conclusion drawn by St. Thomas and his followers that every obligation stems from the human person's natural orientation toward the good of reason, from the necessity to strive for and attain this good.

Predominance of Voluntarism

The influence of voluntarism on theological thought was strong in Calvin and Luther. Luther maintained that God's will is the source of all law. Calvin, originally a lawyer, expressed this by saying that God is king or sovereign prince; He is above all laws because He is law for Himself and for everybody else. Rousseau, Hobbes, and Leibnitz promoted voluntarism in jurisprudence. In philosophy it was Immanuel Kant who solidified the influence of voluntaristic thinking. Kant had concluded that nature in itself could not be known; hence, God as author of a moral law, or a moral law written in nature, could not be discerned. He therefore had no choice but to appeal to a categorical imperative of practical reason which urges, "Thou shalt." Since Kant's time it has generally been held that only positive law is law and that the will of the legislator is its determining factor, while the law's reasonableness is at most, a necessary quality. In other words, the supremacy of the will has been established.

Solution

Law directs humans to their goal, but only through an appeal to their reason, for human beings are rational, free, self-determining beings. Given the natural inclination toward their own well-being, whether or not they will strive for a specific goal is something that they have to decide for themselves. Not even physical force can deprive them of this freedom. For them to strive freely for a concrete good, however, it is basically necessary that they know what that good is. Since respect for their dignity demands that they be left free to choose, it follows that authority cannot go beyond providing them with what they should know, unless the common good or the good of another person is genuinely threatened by their chosen course of action.

One might object that such direction can no longer be considered law or commandment; that rather, one should speak in this case, as in earlier times, of the *"lex indicativa,"* because the subject depends on authority solely for the indication of what is good. This objection would be valid, except for one important point: the obligation to obey the law stems in the first place from man's necessity to attain his goal, his good. What the law indicates as a necessary means to this goal is the human person's rational good, and one is morally obliged to obey that law by reason of his natural drive toward fulfillment. The obligation, therefore, does not derive from the formal making and imposition of the law, which are actually necessary to make the obligation known, but from man's natural orientation toward his goal.

Problem with the Voluntaristic View

In favoring the voluntaristic concept, one runs into difficulty. In response to the question why the willing of the law obliges to obedience, one can give two replies: First, what authority wills must be done because it is reasonable. This answer is, of course, entirely correct, but because the determining motivation here is reasonableness, one is back to the intellect-ualistic doctrine. Secondly, one can reply that the obligation stems from the law, not because it is reasonable, but simply because one is subject to authority, that is, to the will of another. This, however, tends to deny the truth that human beings are free and responsible in determining their own actions and goals. It shifts the determination and responsibility for one's actions to another person.

From a philosophical point of view, therefore, it would seem to the author that St. Thomas' doctrine is the more ac-ceptable. His teaching seems important, not only philosophi-cally, but also from a practical viewpoint. Each opinion leads to a different mentality, a different way of thinking in regard to law and authority. This is true not only for the law of the state but also for the law of God, and it is not very difficult to see how the attitude of civil or of religious authority is influenced and determined by either view.

From the intellectualistic viewpoint, the task of superiors or authorities consists in pointing out to their subjects what constitutes the rational good. It is the task of the law to show subjects how to go about attaining this good, which is found in the common good. This means that authorities are concerned with the common good of the community and the particular good of its members. It is the task of superiors to serve the com-munity and its members, and if superiors lose sight of this fact, their work loses its value and the laws their binding force.

If the voluntaristic viewpoint prevails, the will of the authority is the determining factor, the compelling force. The authority is the master. Of course, the authority must be good and reasonable, but before everything else, he or she is the mas-ter, and the community and its members are the authority's servants. If the authority's law is unreasonable, it is a poor law, but his or her will must still be obeyed.

Resulting Attitudes

Obviously, this way of thinking can have dangerous practical results. First, persons in authority may tend to consider it their prerogative to determine whether a rule is reasonable or not; and secondly, they may be inclined to identify reasonableness with their own will. We see, then, that this attitude can lead to abuse of authority, as we have witnessed in extreme German militarism and in the tyranny of the Roman Empire. "Ours is not to reason why; ours is but to do and die." It leads to the use of authority for "obedience training" in the performance of external acts and disregards the individual's need to grow in personal responsibility by means of obedience. In genuine education, obedience is aimed at the formation of conscience; in mere training it is aimed at the performance of certain acts. In this connection it might be well to consider the popular use of such expressions as "training for the priesthood," "training for the religious life," "psychiatric residence training," "highly trained experts," and the like.

A similar difference in mentality is found in subjects. Citizens who think and feel from an intellectualistic rather than from a voluntaristic viewpoint recognize authority and law as their rational good and tend to conform to them as such. They freely adhere to the law in the full realization of their own personal worth. "To serve is to reign" truly applies to them. The attitude of voluntaristically oriented citizens, however, is based on the principle of human dependence. They obey because they must, not because the command is reasonable. This, of course, leads to the servility of slaves rather than to the cooperation of free persons. It is indisputable that this is contrary to a human being's free nature and, as such, cannot be accepted inwardly.

Attitudes Toward God's Law

How about our relationship to God? Here the proper mentality is of even greater importance. For persons whose view of law is intellectualistic, God's commands are gracious helps. In creating human beings, God suited their nature to the perfect happiness which He had prepared for them. What is more, God allows human beings to be themselves; He respects the freedom which He has given them as the most precious gift of their nature. If persons do not will what is good for them, God will never force it upon them. Yet, on His part, God will do everything possible to help human beings to realize their happiness. This He does in part by giving them His law; this is the purpose of God's law.

For the persons whose view of the law is voluntaristic, on the other hand, God is the Lord, on whom they are utterly dependent and whose will they must do because they are subject to the superior will of the Lord. Here the motivating force is not the rational good but God's power and will. God's infinite and supreme power as well as our dependency on God are fully recognized in the intellectualistic doctrine; humans recognize their dependence as true, and realize that to live according to this truth is their highest good. In contrast, in voluntaristically-oriented persons, such recognition plays no role. It is God's law as such which obliges them to obey. Actually, this goes against their very nature and for that reason they are, in the final analysis, unable to accept it — even from God. Certainly persons can force themselves to acceptance, but acceptance can never be achieved in the innermost depths of their soul. For this reason such persons live under a continual strain, or pressure.

How persons will react to this pressure, this oppression, will depend on their personality. They may, first of all, resist the pressure and throw it off, but in doing so they will also reject

God. In this case, the doctrine of dependence on God as such proves itself untenable in actual living. Again, persons may do violence to nature and force themselves to obey, regardless of their feelings, by a determined act of will power. If they do, they will become hard and unbending (persons with energy-based repressive disorders), recognizing only God's coercion and not His love. Thirdly, they may endure this pressure in fear (scrupulous persons), if not anxiety. In this event, the joy and freedom of the children of God will be foreign to them.

These brief notions have been presented in the hope that the Thomistic doctrine on obedience and legal obligation will play some part in restoring to a state of calm persons with obsessive-compulsive repressive disorders whose condition is directly or indirectly related to the dangers which have been outlined above.

Summation and Conclusion

In understanding and promoting obedience as a virtue, we must put greater emphasis on the role of authority than it usually receives, and relatively less on that of subjects. We must look beyond the function of obedience and see it as a stepping stone on the road to full maturity, where persons stand without fear before God, ready to make a decision of either surrendering themselves to Him or rejecting Him. We must come to realize that when subjects fail in obedience, it is far more likely that this is, or has been, the fault of present or past authorities. We recognize, too, that when an authority fails in obtaining obedience from his or her subjects, the most important single cause is the lack of true love for them.

The acquired virtue of obedience, like the supernatural habit, must, as it were, be infused into subjects by the love of their educators. We must, I believe, have greater faith in the goodness of human nature, in the sense that human nature, imperfect as it is because of original sin, still spontaneously strives for the good. When persons are forced to be obedient, however, they will eventually rebel or lose their humanity in pseudo-obedience and servility.

We must arrive at a deeper understanding of the meaning and importance of the free will and the ways in which its liberty may be impaired, and realizing the free will's importance, we must encourage our children and subjects to use this freedom in willing. We must hold out the rational good in the clearest possible manner, in an atmosphere of unselfish love. Then, because we have allowed subjects not only to understand but also to feel and to sense the goodness of virtue and the badness of vice, we can firmly expect them to choose the good while permitting them to remain free to reject it.

We must remember that this was precisely what God did with Adam. Endowing Adam with a perfect human nature, God then held out an even greater good and let Adam decide freely whether he wanted to accept it. God never forced Adam to accept His greatest gift... that of eternal life. So precious is the gift of free will that God considers it a greater evil to force His highest gift on Adam rather than to allow Adam to incur the evil which he freely willed.

In obedience, therefore, human beings never give up their will. Rather, they continually direct it in freedom toward the good held out by persons in authority. Authorities have the important task of drawing subjects to this good by the love they bear for them — a love which goes out to subjects in such a way that the latter not only recognize it intellectually but feel it sensibly.

CHAPTER IX

A Priest for All Seasons: Masculine and Celibate

More than ever — or perhaps just as much as in past periods of crisis — the Church of today needs masculine and celibate priests; not merely priests who are "not married," but *caelebs* in the true sense of the word; not merely strong priests who can do a good day's work, but mature, masculine priests ready to do battle against evil for the sake of the good, ready to be hurt, but also, if need be, ready *to* hurt!

These words sound strange in times that many see in optional celibacy the promise of stemming the tide of defections from the priesthood, of drawing new blood to the depleted ranks. They sound strange in times in which so many wish for love and fulfillment, and equate charity with not hurting other people's feelings. They sound strange in times that too many priests, in seeking to promote peace and justice, seem to do so more with a view to exterior, rather than inner peace, and seem meek in the defense of absolute truths.

Are these words strange, however, if in our concern with maturity and identity we grasp the true meaning of celibacy, if in our cognizance of the metaphysical fact of the existence of evil we grasp the true meaning of masculinity?

Caelebs — Not Married?

In a discussion of celibacy, certain fundamental difficulties are encountered. Almost always the word "celibacy" is understood as "not married." Most dictionaries like the Thomas Aquinas dictionary of Deferrari define *caelebs* solely as "not married." The implication is that the married state is the natural, the celibate state of life the deviant one. The popular views concerning sexuality which prevail in our culture do little or nothing to counteract this prejudicial opinion.

This contrasting image between celibate and married life does not benefit from the realization that in our Western culture the practical concept and experience of married life is not necessarily a healthy one. It is not an exaggeration to say that a majority of marriages must be defined as states of obsessive-compulsive preoccupation with genital sex. Such a married state is by definition characterized by a lack of or diminished degree of freedom in sexual matters because of an obsession with sexual thoughts, images, and desires, and such a strong compulsion to gratify these desires that it all too readily spills over into premarital and extramarital activities.

Similarity Between the Celibate and Married States

If a knowledgeable person is to make a comparison between the celibate state and the marital obsessive-compulsive state of preoccupation with genital sex, he or she is struck not so much by their generally assumed difference, but rather by their similarity! The celibate life is characterized all too often by a similar preoccupation with genital sex, although this may go unnoticed at first glance. The only difference is that the celibate's obsessive-compulsive expenditure of energy is directed at repressing the sex drive, unlike that of the married person who finds outlets for it. At least this was largely true before Vatican II, as since that time an increasing number of priests and religious have tried, understandably so, to throw off this repressive yoke. That in doing so some of them have found themselves caught in an obsessive-compulsive striving after sexual fulfillment as part of their personality fulfillment was to be expected. In such a reaction the pendulum always swings too far in the other direction. This striving has been expressed either directly or indirectly, for example, in defections from the priesthood and religious life in order to marry, in the demand for optional celibacy, in shallow catechetical teachings (if existing Church laws or directives by the Magisterium are seen as interfering with personal concepts of love and sexual needs) or in proclaiming as a moral norm only what is attainable by the psychologically person and thereby implying that the latter is incapable of growing as yet toward the ideal of perfection.[1]

If in the past married life has been seen as the natural state and the celibate as the preferred one, even though at the same time the latter has been seen as the union of the abnormal with the supernatural, the view which emphasizes their similarity rather than their differences holds greater promise of a deeper understanding of both life styles. As priests and married people have been reared and *trained*[2] in like manner and exposed to the same cultural and religious values and beliefs, it is to be expected that in both the obsession with and tenuous repression of genital sexuality will continue from puberty to well beyond the taking of vows.

---

[1]   See Chapter I, "How to Treat and Prevent the Crisis in the Priesthood."

[2]   Editors' Note: as opposed to *educated*. See also *Feeling and Healing Your Emotions* by Conrad W. Baars, M.D., Rev. ed., Suzanne M. Baars and Bonnie N. Shayne, eds., Bridge-Logos: Gainesville, FL, 2003.

In either lifestyle, this obsession may lead sooner or later to compulsive masturbation, extramarital activities, homosexual or heterosexual affairs, or furtive viewing of pornographic movies and magazines. Both styles of life will manifest the side-effects of this continued repression in tension, anxiety, restless striving or psychosomatic disturbances. If alcohol is used to alleviate these symptoms, addiction may be a consequence in many. Both ways of life will manifest the repercussions of continued sexual repression in a diminished capacity to love and be loved, in a certain atrophy of the emotional life in general, and in various degrees of aridity in the spiritual life.

Inasmuch as the incidence in our Western culture of immaturity or emotional illness in priests and lay people seems to exceed the number of those possessing an integrated sexuality and mature capacity to love unselfishly, there is ample reason to study the psychological factors responsible for this state of affairs.

Degree of Maturity at Time of Vows

In view of what I have said about the similarity between the married and celibate state, it is obviously futile to expect a "horizontal" comparison of these life styles to provide a meaningful value judgment of either. Generalized claims that the celibate life is better than the married life, or vice versa, are meaningless. The issue is always what each person brings to and makes of his or her chosen state of life. Each state of life must be evaluated on its own and in a "vertical" comparison with the individual's personality development prior to a vocational commitment. It may be said that the degree and quality of personality development which exist at the time the person commits to the marital or celibate way of life prognosticate its "normalcy" or "abnormalcy." If prior to this commitment — marital or religious — there exists a sufficient inner order and integration (and of course a properly directed will), the person who marries has a much greater than average chance to become happy and find fulfillment with his or her beloved. Of course, to some extent this will also depend on one's chosen partner, but the chances are that one's choice will be a good one. A mature person is not in a hurry and will not focus on such accidental matters as beauty, wealth, popularity, and the like. He or she will be able to recognize and evaluate the shortcomings in the other, and unlike the immature person will not marry in order "not to burn," (1 Corinthians 7:9) or to escape parental domination or avoid other obligations.

The person who is already mature at the time he or she decides on a religious vocation is virtually assured of finding fulfillment in the love of many. Yet even so it would be possible for the personality of that person to be adversely affected if exposed for several years to an attitude of repression toward the emotional life, or an abuse of authority on the part of immature or neurotic staff members in the major seminary. It has been only too true in the past that some seminaries trained men to be boys!

If prior to one's commitment there does not exist a sufficient degree of maturity, either style of life will present obstacles to happiness and fulfillment. Both will accentuate existing shortcomings of personality and character and more readily precipitate emotional illness and conflicts with spouse or authority figures. Neither style of life can be counted on to be therapeutic for incomplete personality development, whereas both do contribute significantly to further growth in wisdom and happiness if at the time of vows the person was already well on the way to maturity. The latter is true if only because the Grace of the sacraments is vastly more effective in a well-ordered personality.

To Be Mature is to Be *Caelebs*

How does one gauge the degree of maturity of a person on the threshold of making a vocational commitment? It would be impossible to describe here all the positive signs of physical, emotional, intellectual, moral, and spiritual maturity, or the various signs of emotional immaturity, neuroses, psychoses or personality disorders. Suffice it to say that a mature person should evidence a sufficient degree of assimilation of the lower orders of his or her nature by the higher. In a mature person, one can see a rich, balanced emotional life which responds readily to direction by intellect and will without being suppressed in the process, a spiritual life which is ennobled by the fullness of feelings and emotions, a joyful other-directed unselfishness, and an unshakable sense of self-worth and self-love. To a large extent, that person must be the realization of his or her unique natural disposition, possessed of a readiness and capability of going out freely toward the good and opposing the evil, and thus capable of possessing the happiness for which human beings are created.

That person must possess himself or herself lovingly and gratefully as man or woman, as being — in peace and harmony — what in the ultimate analysis each person is — singular and alone. In other words, the person mature enough to commit to either the married or religious state of life must already have become a free, self-possessed, unique masculine or feminine *celibate* — for that is precisely what *caelebs* means: singular and alone!

Having been affirmed in the goodness of his or her being by loving parents who respected and treasured their child's uniqueness and "otherness," the person who is *caelebs* has come to love himself or herself unselfishly — so much so that this love overflows toward others (whether one or many) toward God and toward the world. If such a person has been affirmed and at the same time protected from a grave distortion of human nature through repressive training, the truly celibate priest or married person is free to *be* his or her sexuality as man or woman — free to love others sexually without compulsion to be genitally active. To say it differently, the person is free "to be love" without having "to make love." In marriage, free to practice periodic continence in the joyful love of restraint. In religious life, free to abstain from genitality with joy and ease. This freedom to be one's sexuality far surpasses in excellence a freedom to act sexually as one pleases, or a freedom from "being bothered by one's sexuality!"

The Future of Modern Humanity

It must be admitted that these thoughts sound idealistic and that modern humanity is not yet disposed to incorporate them into its present lifestyle, yet it is necessary that we allow these ideals to give direction to our future way of living, when humanity finally becomes sated and disillusioned with sexual and sensual abandonment, frustrated by having repressed reason and will in an attempt to be an "enlightened liberal" and to escape from neurotic disorders and immaturity through a "new morality." We must prepare for the practical application of ideals founded on a sound psychology of the normal human person, on intellectually satisfying and morally correct interpretations of clinical psychiatric findings, and a newer and sounder philosophy of human sexuality, of masculinity and femininity, and of marriage and celibacy. We must have the courage of our convictions and abandon a way of thinking that idealizes genital behavior at the expense of true sexuality and which creates a false need for contraceptive techniques, legalized abortions, and euthanasia. We must not be afraid to adopt a new sexual philosophy, even though it would expose a staggering incidence of frigidity and impotence among modern men and women!

Misconceptions about Sexuality

How, one may ask, is it possible to define one's true sexuality as man or woman if we continue to subscribe to misconceptions about sexuality which reflect a mistaken philosophy of human nature? For example, it is commonly held that our sexual need virtually equals that for food and oxygen. Yet the truth of the matter is that our sex drive only *seems* much more insatiable and stronger than it actually is, chiefly as the result of it having been affected since early childhood by repressive influences. If it were only our glands and organs that determined the intensity of our sex drive, these repressive factors would be of no consequence. It is our mind and feelings which are responsible, however. If these sexual feelings and desires are allowed to benefit from a growing assimilation by and a natural tempering or moderating action by the intellect and will, then the sex drive will not develop the obsessive-compulsive character which makes itself felt so intensely and all consumingly as in the person with obsessive-compulsive repression or scrupulosity, for it is an unassailable fact that anything that has been repressed will keep pushing itself to the forefront of our mind — and with a vengeance. Human emotions have an innate need in their striving for their object to be guided by reason. If frustrated in this need by the repressing action of another emotion, a constant energy-consuming battle ensues between the opposing emotions. This battle becomes clinically manifest in an obsession with the repressed emotion and a compulsion to gratify it.[3]

Sexual Need vs. Sexual Appetite

There is a common failure to distinguish between sexual need and sexual appetite which contributes to the false belief that our sexual need virtually equals in intensity our need for oxygen and food. The French theologian Jean Guitton has made a succinct and pertinent observation in this regard. "Man's sexual need," he said, "is but slight as compared with his sexual desire, which knows no bound and makes itself felt at the slightest stimulation. We live in an aphrodisiac society which multiplies our sexual desires!"[4]

Another grave obstacle to our becoming our sexuality as man or woman is the present day so-called sexual and sensual revolution, rooted largely in the mistaken belief that in order to avoid a neurotic disorder and become fulfilled and mature, one must freely gratify the sexual drive and feelings. This belief that one must counteract fear of sex by a — not less neurotic or immature — relentless striving after sexual gratification can be held and defended only by those who do not understand the

---

[3] For the sake of completeness it must be mentioned that there is yet another reason for the sex drive's seemingly extraordinary intensity, namely an absent or greatly diminished regulatory action by the will as the result of either congenital factors as may exist in a personality disorder or of acquired factors as in pedagogical neglect or spoiling (See *Psychic Wholeness and Healing: Using All the Powers of the Human Psyche* by Anna A. Terruwe, M.D. and Conrad W. Baars, M.D., Alba House, Staten Island, NY, 1981).

[4] Jean Guitton, *Human Love*, Franciscan Herald Press, Chicago, IL, 1966.

fundamental difference between neurotic repression of emotions and their rational guidance. As a result of ignorance of psychological matters or fear of becoming neurotic or not growing to maturity, some will consider masturbation normal or recommend extramarital sexual relations and divorce on grounds that one's feelings of love must be expressed without restraint lest they be repressed; however, this way of thinking cannot be allowed to go uncorrected. Modern human sciences do provide us with psychological and psychopathological insights which support and confirm the natural law and moral laws.[5]

We offer a final observation on prevalent misconceptions about human sexuality. To the extent that "modern morality" bothers with the formality of marriage, it considers it a foregone conclusion that premarital sexual experimentation is necessary in order to determine sexual compatibility and thus prognosticate the chances for a lasting marriage. Yet, before marriage, the optimal test of true sexual compatibility in marriage lies in the measure of joy and happiness experienced in the persons' freely willed restraint from genitality — and from other goods for that matter — for the sake of the beloved.

Human Nature

If these and other distorted notions of human sexuality cannot satisfy us, how do we define our sexuality as man or woman in its all-encompassing sense? Of course, the answer to

---

[5]   Conrad W. Baars, M.D. and Anna A. Terruwe, M.D., *Loving and Curing the Neurotic*, Alba House, Staten Island, NY, 1972. [Editor's Note: *Loving and Curing the Neurotic* is out-of-print but has been republished as two volumes: *Psychic Wholeness and Healing* and *Healing the Unaffirmed: Recognizing Emotional Deprivation Disorder* by Conrad W. Baars, M.D. and Anna A. Terruwe, M.D. (Rev. ed., Suzanne M. Baars and Bonnie N. Shayne, eds., Bridge-Logos: Gainesville, FL, 2003).]

this question will depend on our view of human nature. Since Aristotle, the idea that the human person is fundamentally an animal is one that is deeply ingrained in Western civilization. Humans differ from other animals merely by being rational. In more recent times, Freud has defined the human person as a sublimating animal whose instinctual, animal energy is "made sublime" by being directed into behavior conforming to the ideals of society. Freud considered this sublimating process not a rational, but an unconscious one, and essential to mental health. If this process fails to resolve the tensions produced by the confrontation of the instinctive urges from within the person with the social pressures from without, the superego of the human person has no choice but to repress. It is this process, also unconsciously motivated, that Freud considered to lead to emotional and mental illness.

In my opinion, Freud's theories, as distinct from his brilliant clinical discoveries, leave much to be desired with respect to his explanation of the repressive mechanism and his philosophy of the normal human person. His idea that a person's mental health, or lack of it, depends largely on unconscious processes is no improvement on Aristotle's insight into the role conscious reason plays in making the animal human.

Is there a better philosophy of human nature than that offered by Aristotle and Freud? As a Christian psychiatrist convinced of the unsoundness of therapeutic concepts based on experimental animal models, schools of behaviorism which reflect the idea that the human person is an animal to be trained, or the philosophy that the human person comes into existence as the termination of a biological process, I am happy to say that indeed there is such a philosophy. One finds it not in the handbooks of the sciences, but rather where all the great ideas concerning humans have been found through the centuries, namely in the writings of dramatists, poets, novelists, and philosophers. It is in the work of two young philosophers, Mary and Robert Joyce, that we find a delightfully common sense approach to a newer understanding of human nature, yet more profound than one would dare to expect from such a young married couple. Not only are their ideas delightfully profound, they fit hand in glove with a psychology and psychopathology of the human person — described in *Psychic Wholeness and Healing*[6] — that found its origin in a grave disillusionment with twentieth century psychiatric thinking about human beings and their psychic [psychological] sufferings. Rather than attempting to summarize the Joyces' views of human nature and human sexuality as man and woman in a few sentences, I will use, with their permission, some direct quotes from their *New Dynamics in Sexual Love*.[7]

> "If man is basically an animal, then an animal is basically a vegetable, or a plant-substance with vegetative powers for growth and reproduction. But the fact that animals grow and reproduce in common with plants does not warrant the assertion that animals are basically vegetative things or that the energy for an animal's behavior is a plant energy. An animal's walking, running, crawling, seeing and other acts of sensing are not expressions of a plant energy but of a new energy. This new energy assimilates or draws into itself the energy of vegetative life.

> "Due to this phenomenon of assimilation, the very things that animals have in common with plants are basically different in animals than in plants. The an-

---

6 Terruwe and Baars.

7 *New Dynamics in Sexual Love: A Revolutionary Approach to Marriage and Celibacy* by Robert E. and Mary Rosera Joyce, St. John's University Press, Collegeville, MN, 1970. See also: *Let Us Be Born* by Robert E. and Mary Rosera Joyce, Franciscan Herald Press, Chicago, IL, 1970.

imal is basically a sentient creature and not basically a vegetative creature. In a similar way, man, though he has powers in common with animals, is not basically an animal. In man, still another new energy, a mind-energy, assimilates and transforms the energy of animal life.

"Evidence of such assimilation of the lower into the higher appears already in the newborn child. On the first day of life his difference from the newborn of animals is striking. The latter are able to walk and run almost immediately. In most cases the characteristic animal-power of locomotion is ready to go at birth. But the newborn of man barely moves for months. If he is held erect with his feet touching a surface, his legs may begin a stepping motion. But because the child is unable to walk, he must *mentally absorb* his environment as the place where his walking will begin one day. He must *discover* his legs and feet. After pulling his feet toward his head, after feeling and biting his toes, he discovers that these belong to him and that they can be made to serve his purpose. Only after the child's legs and feet, as well as his environment, have been assimilated into his mental life is he able to begin his stumbling progress toward human locomotion. The walking of a baby is a human act with a mental foundation. From the very first this creature is not an animal!"

Training vs. Education

In order to further clarify the difference between human beings and animals, the Joyces clearly distinguish between training and education.

"The well known experiences of the Montessori schools have shown us that in a prepared environment children develop an affection for the materials they work with and have their inmost energy set free to assimilate movement and sense experiences into their own inscrutable purposes. Their growing toward maturity and loving union with the environment is not forced from without, as Freud would have it with his social pressures and sublimation, but by a spontaneous movement from within. This movement will depend on the degree and quality of freedom the child is given *to be* and to *become* himself. When the child's mind is controlled and manipulated by adults, it is trained under social pressure. But mental training fails to release the inmost energy of the human mind. In fact, such a training forces the child to repress much of his true nature and to remain unconscious in his motivation. His sublimated behavior is willed behavior that does not benefit from his natural and spontaneous feelings. He is made to repress these feelings under the pressure of the superiority complex of adults and the ironic tyranny of loving parents. This tragedy of repression is the social sickness in man that Freud described well but did not interpret correctly, as his view of human nature is derived from sick, repressed man, not from man as he is when *educated* in freedom.

"Whether one approaches the subject from a philosophical or psychological point of view, the final conclusion is the same. Training is an inadequate method of developing man's emotional and mental life, precisely because the human creature is not an animal! Education is based on respecting children as human beings, on giving them the freedom within a prepared and safe environment with an adult to act as a guide rather than a trainer. Only in education, never in training, are children allowed to be and to become what they really are: uniquely themselves. Only when affirmed by mature parents and educators, i.e. loved for being what they are, even for their 'otherness,' and allowed to assimilate spontaneously in their own tempo their whole being into their mental and spiritual life, only then will children find their unique identity and fulfillment, never to be plagued by an identity crisis in later life!"

Nature of Human Sexuality

Whether or not one agrees with this particular view of human nature, the Joyces' equally profound way of thinking about the nature of human sexuality and the being of man and woman, of masculinity and femininity, deserves serious consideration too. The psychology of the priest's masculinity, as I shall describe shortly, finds its roots and confirmation in the Joyces' philosophy of the nature of human sexuality. Theirs is a much more profound philosophy than Freud's expanded concept of sexuality. Although he intended it to be more than mere genitality, Freud and his followers never advanced beyond the view that the psychological eros in its genital functions formed the center of the human person's sexual nature.

The Joyces, however, believe that contrary to ancient and even recent assumptions, genitality, as well as generation, is no longer to be considered the central value of our sexual nature. They believe the true center of the human person's sexual na-

ture to be something still more radical than these two sexual
functions, namely: the person's power for actively *being* his or
her sexuality without *necessarily* engaging his or her sexual
functions. This is one way of saying that the original and most
authentic meaning of genuine sexual freedom is the centering
of the sexuality of man and woman in their capacity for *being*
love without necessarily *making* love in a genital manner.

This is another way of saying that the masculine and
feminine aspects of human nature are not only or primarily
physical and oriented toward sexual communication. Rather,
they are also and primarily psychic and trans-psychic, i.e.,
oriented toward the being of all things. These masculine and
feminine aspects serve the purpose of sexual communion, the
revelation of what man and woman are, the being consciously
aware of the goodness of the other, the process by which they
give the other to himself or herself, and the process by which
they affirm each other.

"The meeting of persons as beings — so necessary in
the process of finding our identity and giving others
theirs — is hindered severely if we place our primary
value in the physical aspect of sexuality. To do so
also leads to a grave misconstruction of the nature
of sexual equality. Many women insist that the only
difference between man and woman is a difference
in anatomy, that sex is biological only. The only difference then left to man and woman — their physical
difference — must be played to the hilt thereafter and
exploited as a compensation for the lack of deeper
difference and complementarity. As a result, either
women have become, more than ever, the play-objects
of men, or both men and women have become slaves
of the one sexual interaction they allow their nature

to have. Women need to realize that the limitation of sexual difference to the human anatomy is not the way out of their ancient subservience to men, nor the way into the joyful freedom of friendship with man.

"It is very difficult for the human mind to sustain the notion of fundamental difference within fundamental equality. Though man and woman are equal, they are different in the very depths of their existence. Their more apparent anatomical differences are not mere accidentals or mere attachments to their common human nature; differences in the body are *revelations* of differences in the depths of their being. Since the human body is an expression of the human soul, an essential difference in any organ of the body is an expression of an essential difference in the whole being of the living person. If this is not true, the human body is not really united with the human soul. The idea that sex is biological only is a serious affront to the unity of the human person."

Hands and Intellect

"Though the hands are not the organs in which man and woman differ most, their hands are revelations of the difference within equality that constitutes their true relationship. The hand may be described by its complementary acts of *feeling* and *grasping*. These physical acts are revelations of the deeper power by which man knows the *existence* and the *natures* of things in the world. The human intellect, in its complementary acts of feeling and grasping, is very much like the human hand, and vice versa. In its intuitive act of perception, the intellect touches and feels the existence of things. In its act of abstracting, the intellect grasps the nature of things. Knowing *that* things exist and knowing *what* they are, are complementary acts of man's spiritual hand, his intuitive-rational intellect.

"Even though man and woman both have hands with powers for feeling and grasping, it is apparent that their sexual difference extends to their hands. Generally, man has greater size and greater muscular strength in his hand. He excels not only in the grasping power of his hand, but also in the grasping power of his intellect. This is why man was given dominion over the earth. Adam's mental hand was able to grasp the essence of each creature individually, and his mind was so grasping strong that whatever he apprehended each creature to be, that was precisely its nature (Genesis 2:19). But it was not good for Adam to be alone. It was not good for the master of the earth to be alone without another hand in his, keeping it flexible and open. Lest Adam forget that beings are good not only for their service to man, but primarily, and always, just because they exist, another hand was placed in his. Grasping without feeling degenerates into exploitation."

The hand placed in his was that of a woman. Gentle and sensitive, it is oriented toward touching and feeling the existence of things, toward protectively taking hold of things. Her hand expresses the intuitive act of perception of her intellect. As intuition is knowledge of what is actually present, this intuitive knowing is without doubt the perfect form of knowing.

Thinking, on the other hand, is knowledge of what is absent; the necessity for thinking is due to a failure of intuition. In our scientific age which expresses the power and the reason emphasized in man, it would be well for women to become aware of the crucial role they have to play if humankind is to be saved from itself. The special sensitivity and intuitive intellection emphasized in woman is the source of the wisdom needed to modify man's technical power before it degenerates into weakness. How man and woman are to experience sexual communion, their original and most fulfilling form of sexual relationship, one will learn from reading and rereading Mary and Robert Joyce's revolutionary approach to marriage and celibacy.

Man and Woman

Similar concepts, like these of the Joyces, concerning the fundamental differences between man and woman are expressed by yet another contemporary philosopher who unfortunately did not live long enough to further develop these ideas. German Jewess, student of Husserl, convert to Catholicism, Carmelite nun, refugee to the Netherlands, but eventually victimized by her fellow Germans in the gas chambers of Auschwitz, Edith Stein [Saint Teresa Benedicta of the Cross] wrote:

"To nurse and keep and shield and help grow — this is every woman's natural, motherly desire and skill, and to them are joined her desire and skill as companion. Her gift and happiness are in sharing in another person's life, and sharing means to her sharing in everything that concerns the person she loves, in

the great things and the small, in his joys and sor-
rows, in his works and his problems . . . And it is
her overflowing wealth of heart, her almost limitless
ability to devote herself, her patience, that help her
partake in man's life, a partaking which awakens his
strength and multiplies his achievements. She does it
with patience, for while man may be able to do more
she can endure more; while he has greater thrusting
power, she has more energy in store.... Because man
serves his cause more directly and woman more for
his sake, it is appropriate that she do so under his
guidance.... If their partnership is seen under the
image of a tree, man is the tuft, woman the root, the
whole hidden root bearing even the highest tuft and
the sunlit tuft bearing even the furthest root, the root
filling the top with its strength, the top governing the
root by its encompassing power."[8]

Observations in Psychiatric Practice

Insights like those of the Joyces and Edith Stein are
confirmed over and over again in daily clinical practice by
psychiatrists and psychotherapists who have kept a balance
in their profession and, not unduly impressed by speculative
psychoanalytic theories, animal experiments, sex laboratories,
and statistical acrobatics, are sensitive to and willing to learn
from their patients. Whether neurotic, psychotic, or liberated,
every woman's nature reveals to the sensitive observer, in spite
of repression, withdrawal, or denial, the feminine characteristics of motherliness, compassion, and endurance. She finds

---

[8] John Oesterreicher, *Walls are Crumbling*, Devin-Adair, NY, 1952.

fulfillment and becomes whole when others respond to her wisdom founded in her intuitive intellect and sensitivity, just as she withers away or reacts in rebellion when her uniqueness as woman is denied and she is merely used by the other sex. Every man's nature reveals, in spite of neurotic distortion, passive submissiveness, or other culturally determined aberrations, the typically masculine characteristics of being a thinker, builder, leader, competitor, protector, and fighter. Yet his natural bent toward working and subduing the earth would surely degenerate into exploitation and utilitarianism if it were not for his ability to feel the goodness of the being of things. Man's technical power and scientific accomplishments without an accompanying feminine sense of beauty and wisdom always degenerates into weakness.

It is a matter of course that each individual human being should possess both masculine and feminine characteristics in an appropriate ration. A woman will not be more equal to man if she has assumed the envied male traits at the expense of those peculiar to her own sex. A man will not be more masculine to the extent that he has eradicated or suppressed his feminine characteristics. On the contrary, the latter are most desirable since they bring tolerance and militate against excesses in typical masculine pursuits. This is particularly true for members of what should be one of the most masculine and mature vocations — the priesthood. Priests who are required to function at present as celibates — and of course also as *caelebs* in the sense described before — have a special need for an appropriate admixture of feminine traits within their own personality, because they must be father and brother to many. In this twofold role, he must be friend and gentle companion, as well as teacher, leader, protector, and fighter against the many evils that threaten those whom he wants to help find the One he represents. This is not to say, of course, that a priest who is truly *caelebs* should not be allowed to directly experience the beneficent influence of a mature woman's wisdom and her sense of the goodness of things. If it pleases God to put a mature woman on his path with whom he can experience the *amor amicitiae* in a proper, mature love of restraint, his work as a priest may be expected to bear even greater fruit.

Man — A Fighter

The idea of modern man (and a priest at that) being a fighter may seem ridiculous when those to whom the welfare of society has been entrusted seem to imagine that, as Josef Pieper says, the power of evil is not so gravely dangerous that one could not "negotiate" or "come to terms with it." It seems that personal charity, brotherly love, and fortitude need to play only a subordinate role in a welfare society whose liberalistic world view — characterized by a resolute worldliness, an earthy optimism, and a middle-class metaphysics anxiously bent on security — is blind to the existence of evil in the world of humans, as well as in the world of spirits (evil in the twofold form of guilt and punishment, i.e., the evil that we do, and the evil that we suffer).[9]

It cannot be denied that there exist in this world many evils, over and beyond the less personal and more "remote" social and culturally determined evils which, because they touch the moral core of the human being, require a good deal of personal courage, risk taking, dedication, conviction and determination. Yes, even a readiness to be hurt or even to die, and a readiness to hurt rather than merely relying on a government to provide protection from social evils from the cradle to the grave.

---

[9]   Josef Pieper, *Fortitude and Temperance*, Pantheon Books, NY, 1954.

In fact, it is precisely when that government abandons moral principles and refuses to recognize and protect such a fundamental right as the right to life of its citizens — whether already born or yet to be born — that individual men and women, but most of all priests and religious, are called upon to fight these evils. Men are called on to attack with their thrusting power and physical strength while women are called on to attack through endurance in their kinship with pain and their closeness to the goodness of being.

This is even more true, to quote Pieper again, when it is not only the government which is too fearful to shout an angry "no" to the evil which threatens the community from without, but even religious leaders who embrace an ethical life which has become falsified into an unheroic, unthreatening way of existence free from sorrow and harm, where the good is attained effortlessly as a plant-like unfolding and growth. When governed by morally weak or indifferent persons, when living in a timid Christianity, men and women, priests and religious — but precisely priests as the appointed leaders and teachers — each in their own masculine and feminine way are called upon to deal courageously with the evils which threaten them as individuals, as members of families, society or church. It is precisely then that each man and woman, each priest and religious, must assess his or her courage, or lack of it.

It is only by feigning blindness to the very real evils, for instance, of atheism, atheistic communism, heresy, amoral sex education classes, the anti-life forces of contraception-abortion-euthanasia, planned corruption of youth and society through sexual abandon, pornography, and drug traffic and by closing our eyes to the higher goods in dire need of preservation against these evils that persons can spare themselves the painful realization that they no longer possess the virtue of fortitude. They may delude themselves into believing that they fight a valiant battle when they clamor for greater love of humanity and participate in anti-war rallies, when they demand peace for the sake of coexistence rather than for the sake of truth and goodness, or when they labor for ever more government supported programs to help the poor rather than being personally involved in works of charity. They may not even realize that when evil does overcome them, they are the very opposite of the truly brave man who knows how to bear it with equanimity without his spirit being broken by grief, while preserving his serenity of mind and cheerfulness. But unlike the brave man, modern persons, when overcome by evil, lack the patience which excludes sadness and confusion of heart but not energetic and forceful activity.

Virtue of Fortitude

What could be the cause of this apparent lack of courage to oppose evil in modern society, of this apathy and apparent blindness in the face of threats to life and property? Undoubtedly there are many causes, probably often interrelated and rooted in a common psychological matrix. Whatever the answer, in regard to the latter, one thing is certain. Fortitude, more than any other virtue presupposes a healthy vitality, not only in the moral and above the moral order, but also in the pre-moral or psychological order. It is to the latter that I shall confine myself when discussing some of the reasons for the modern human person — layperson and priest alike — to live as a semi-invalid, a half-person so to speak, who wants the good, but is at a loss what to do with evil.

If humans are disposed to oppose evil in the moral and supernatural orders they still need a ready preparedness in the psychological order to carry out their good intentions. To the extent that a person's psychological underpinning of the virtue of fortitude has been crippled or insufficiently developed, he or she is powerless, or at best only partially effective in striking out against evil. Much of the energy needed to do battle is dissipated either in a senseless intrapsychic battle between the emotions themselves, as in persons with repressive disorders, or in the inevitably futile search for self-affirmation or self-fulfillment, as in persons with Emotional Deprivation Disorder.[10] Neither type of neurotic individual, nor for that matter the person who is immature because of non-neurotic reasons, is equipped to utilize the emotion of anger in its natural function of serving the virtue of fortitude. In fact, the person may not even be aware of this particular function of anger, as Christian ethics has excluded it as something alien and incongruous, while its assertive activity is repugnant to good behavior regulated by "bourgeois" standards.

On the other hand, a psychiatry which has construed its concept of the normal person from clinical observations of patients with neurotic disorders has done little to help the person in the street to understand the goodness and necessity of his or her emotion of anger. By failing to distinguish clearly between the emotion of anger itself and its subsequent expression, between neurotic repression of anger and its rational direction, and by the rather indiscriminate use of the word anger in association with terms like aggression, hostility, vengeance, immaturity, and the like, psychiatry, in fact, may well have contributed its share in keeping persons from using their emotion of anger to the best advantage of themselves and society!

---

[10] See *Healing the Unaffirmed*.

Courage, Hate, Anger

Those suspicious of anger may say that it suffices to experience the emotion of courage in the face of a threatening evil in order to have fortitude. Indeed, courage is of the essence in arousing people to action aimed at opposing the evil in order to protect themselves from harm. If it is merely self-preservation they are concerned with, however, they will be satisfied to terminate their courageous action once they know they are safe from the evil that threatened to harm them. It also requires the additional capacity to feel the emotion of hate for the evil itself in order to be moved to destroy it and to prevent it from spreading and harming others too.

In other words, the feeling of hate for the non-good is necessary to move persons to oppose it effectively even when it no longer constitutes a personal threat. That this should be done, of course, under the guiding action of the will informed and enlightened by reason does not change the fact that the emotion itself must be experienced if persons are to be aroused *in toto* and act in the most efficient way, spontaneously and yet not precipitously. When the "motor" of the emotion functions in cooperation with the "motor" of the free will, persons function as a whole. If trained to function solely or predominantly on the "motor" of their will, their actions are relatively sterile when it comes to moving other persons. For example, preaching the message of the gospels in a strictly intellectual manner leaves the faithful largely unmoved either toward the good or away from the non-good.

Although it is not necessary for a proper understanding of the emotion of anger to analyze it as a composite of two other emotions, hate and courage, it does make for a more profound insight into the purpose of this most important assertive emotion. It suffices to see anger as the ultimate emotion to arouse humans, both psychologically and physiologically, to a vigorous effort to throw off the evil that has overcome or threatens to overcome them, or to surmount the obstacle which separates them from a desired good. All that is necessary — and this is true for every emotion — is first that it is experienced and really felt within, and second that its expression is directed by reason in such a way that it is optimally effective in dealing with the evil or the obstacle. The more closely the emotional life and intellectual life have been permitted to become integrated during the growing years, the more intensely the good is loved and the non-good hated emotionally, the more experience that has been accumulated as to how anger can be expressed in infinitely varied ways, and the greater the knowledge of which form of expression of anger is most effective in a given situation, the easier it is for persons to deal with evil effectively and thus to experience greater joy.

Those who have been unfortunate, for whatever reason, not to attain this integration of the two orders and have been *trained* to rely only on the so-called "good" or "positive" emotions, if not solely on the will without benefit of any emotional arousal, are doomed to wear a pseudo-Christian mask of meekness, of not daring to hurt the feelings of others, of being afraid to offend them, and of rationalizing the evil way. Those people must be content to proclaim their verbal support of combating less personal, more remote social and cultural evils and profess blindness to the more personal ones. While they must suffer the inevitable consequences of repressing their feelings of anger — growing resentments, tension, insomnia and depression, to mention only a few — the evil around them is perforce allowed to go unchecked and spread and grow. As they are prevented from establishing and testing the depth of emotional rapport, the roads to better interpersonal relationships, real friendship and Christian charity are closed off.

Love is Not Enough

Love alone is not enough in a world in which the existence of evil as a metaphysical fact cannot be denied. One's capacity for finding deep joy in loving the good must be complemented by a capacity to hate intensely the non-good and to feel the sadness of being exposed to it. If it were to be left solely to the rational and volitional faculties of the individual or to the impersonal action of a government body to deal with evil, it could not but grow and spread like a cancer in apathy, the non-emotional *laissez-faire* of a people brainwashed to believe that only love is good, not hate and anger. There are, of course, those already experienced "political psychologists" who are exploiting this timidity of the modern human person to the full. The ultimate conquest of those believing that truth and goodness prevail of themselves, without demanding any personal commitment to defend them nor a readiness to die in battle against evil, will only be a matter of time.

In order to be convinced of the goodness of all human emotions it is necessary to realize that all divine commandments concerning love and hate refer solely to the volitional aspect of love and hate, not to their emotional or feeling part. Emotions or feelings cannot be commanded, although in time they may perhaps, in the best and most saintly of persons, follow the movement of the will. What is meant by this may be clarified by an attempt at paraphrasing the commandment to love one's enemy. *"In addition* to feeling the emotion of hate toward your enemy — and thus being prepared both psychologically and physiologically to defend yourself when attacked — you must also will him or her well." It is because your intellect tells you what your emotions or senses cannot tell you, viz. that your enemy is also your brother or sister in Christ and is also created for eternal happiness. To will that for your enemy, and to be ready to express it outwardly if at all possible — that is to love your enemy according to God's commandments. To feel hate toward your brother or sister and to freely assert to the desire that evil befall him or her, *that is a sin*. Sin lies in the will, not in the emotion.

A Time for Love, A Time for Hate

Some possible consequences of not distinguishing between emotional and volitional love, the two components of mature love, and of holding that only love, not hate, is appropriate in the scheme of living, are presented in the writings of Erich Fromm. In *The Art of Loving*[11] Fromm has many true and beautiful things to say about love. Yet by remaining silent on the subject of the necessary role of the emotion of hate, or by implying that to hate is not civilized or a sign of immaturity, Fromm has no choice but to advocate, however indirectly, pacifism, anti-capitalism, and socialism as the ideals of humanity. In this partial exposé of human nature, this progression of ideas would be a logical one. For, if it is true that only love is noble and that human beings must eliminate such unacceptable emotions as hate and anger, Fromm's disciples can only hope to survive by putting themselves at the mercy of their enemies. Only by proclaiming themselves pacifists, persons who are forbidden to hate can hide from themselves the fact that they are psychologically powerless to defend themselves. Likewise, if only "good" or "positive" emotions are acceptable to Fromm then he must, of necessity, advocate a political system in which all are so equal that there is simply no room for "bad" or "negative" feelings because another

---

[11] Erich Fromm, *The Art of Loving*, Harper and Row, NY, 1956.

person has more than he or she does. That this way of thinking is totally unrealistic is self-evident, at least to the Christian, for it certainly does not allow for the necessity to combat moral evil — but then there is no need for this in Fromm's philosophy, as for him there is no God and thus no sin.

Fromm's Philosophy Appeals to the Non-Affirmed!

Philosophies like those of Fromm do appeal to modern persons, especially non-affirmed persons, even though they are fatal. The latter's absent or inadequate sense of self-worth, feelings of loneliness, inferiority, and existential fears, as well as the futile search for identity in self-affirmation, has left his or her psychological structure weak and vulnerable. To be advised by a psychiatric expert that there is no need for hate and anger, that by loving one and all one will find peace, fulfillment and happiness, and that all evil can be reduced or eliminated through government action, has an immense appeal to the non-affirmed. These persons view hate and anger as absolute obstacles to their frustrated need for love and identity. To them anger excludes the possibility of being loved. Their own anger makes it impossible for others to love them. They welcome any excuse to refrain from being angry and they will berate themselves for their own occasional, seemingly unexplainable outbursts of anger, while they will excuse and overlook those of others.

Effect on Women

The ever increasing and deepening lack of affirmation in our day, which is even affecting millions of human beings who have not yet seen the light of day,[12] is one of the more important reasons for the increase of violence and hatred in the world, for the disappearance of the qualities of true maturity and masculinity, and, as a consequence of the latter, for the phenomena of Women's Liberation activists insisting on being equal with the very men they despise, and of some Catholic women demanding the right of admission to the ordained ministry of the Church. To the extent that these demands represent a woman's mature concern for the preservation of the goodness of beings, threatened nowadays by the failure of too many men to defend it with masculine fortitude, these women may well represent the last stronghold in the perennial battle against evil. Their predominant representation and successful activity in pro-life movements, for example, testify to their courage and determination to protect humankind from the evils which male-dominated policy-making bodies and governments promote directly or indirectly.

To the extent that a woman has become frustrated by man's vanishing masculinity and does not possess those personality characteristics necessary to be actively engaged in the defense of humankind, she is in even greater need of experiencing the strong, yet tender guiding and supporting hand of a masculine, mature man. This is true for both married and religious women. Both will benefit when the priests of the future are able and willing to assume their God-given role of being teachers and leaders in the Church and thus in the world. It will only be when priests once again have become truly masculine and celibate teachers and leaders that other men can follow their example and become warm, loving, strong, masculine and mature husbands, fathers, and brothers, in whom women can be fulfilled in their never-changing feminine need to relate to a man as the

---

[12] Conrad W. Baars, M.D., "The Psychiatrist — Friend or Foe of the Pregnant Woman?" in *Linacre Quarterly*, Nov., 1971.

roots of a tree to the tuft and its branches.

Insofar as the human sciences have contributed to modern man's un-manly role, it needs repeating that nobody, least of all the non-affirmed individual or person with Emotional Deprivation Disorder, benefits from a psychology which does not understand the nature of the human person in relation to the Creator and creation. It is true that modern secular psychological schools have contributed a variety of interesting facts and theories. However, if they prove to be in violation of an as yet unsurpassed psychological-philosophical view of the normal human person like that of St. Thomas Aquinas, their value is of little consequence.

Anthropology of St. Thomas Aquinas

Oft repeated observations that hate and anger are bad because they may lead to war and violence merely testify to the impact of modern schools of psychology on popular thinking. It is only when one fully grasps the magnificent anthropology of Aquinas that one understands why the truly gentle, kind and compassionate person, the *alter Christus*, is the very one whose capacity for the emotions of hate and anger is well-developed and integrated with, and therefore readily guided by, an unselfishly oriented will informed by reason. It is the meek, passive, submissive pseudo-Christians whose credo is their determination or fear never to hurt another person's feelings, who will manifest their repressed emotions of anger and hate in unpredictable outbursts, chronic irritability and resentments, faultfinding and depression. They are the victims of twentieth century psychologism, whose view of the normal person is biased, unbalanced and incomplete.

It should come as no surprise that the priesthood has been

seriously contaminated by these prevalent psychological forces and attitudes. The Church draws her priests from the community of laymen whose emotional health is greatly affected by the Church's own teachings on the formation of personhood and character, as well as by the secular city's attitudes toward mental health and illness. The Church's longstanding fear and suspicion of the emotional life has influenced all people. Her lack of awareness of the significance of the emotional life for the supernatural life and spirituality has prevented the structuring of a firm psychological basis for the priest's fundamental mission — to be the chosen affirmer of Christ and the faithful. This psychological underpinning, anchored in the soma during the years of personality development, is an absolute requisite for the priest to be able to love the good and to bring others to the universal good in love, as well as to hate what is not good and inspire them to fight evil, including the ultimate evil, Satan.

Aquinas vs. Suarez

It is one of the tragedies of our times that in this world which needs heroes and anti-heroes, the Church has been blamed for contributing to the repression of personhood by giving preeminence to the teachings of the Universal Doctor. Although there cannot be any question of blame in this matter, it is necessary to set matters straight if the priests of the future are to profit from the unparalleled fount of knowledge St. Thomas Aquinas has left us, and the seminaries are again to include his legacy in their curricula. What the anti-Thomists of our day do not seem to realize is that the philosophy of every-day living as taught by the Church for several centuries was pervaded and determined largely by the doctrine of the Jesuit theologian Francisco Suarez, rather than by the anthro-

pology of Aquinas. Insofar as the latter did play a role, it was
not his authentic thinking on the nature of the human person
that prevailed, but rather the distortions and omissions in the
work of his translators. From a psychological point of view, the
voluntaristic doctrine of Suarez, characterized so well by his
development of the noted *agere contra*, together with a non-
authentic anthropology of Aquinas contained in the popular
handbooks of moral theology for so long, must be considered
largely responsible for the current crisis in the priesthood.

This is no idle claim. On the contrary, it is well supported
and documented by the dissertations and research of several
outstanding Dutch and German scholars in the late 1950's.[13]
Therefore, it would seem that those who have driven Aquinas
out of the seminaries are in duty bound to familiarize themselves with the facts and hasten to reverse the current academic
trend to deprive candidates for the priesthood of what should be
one of the most important sources of maturity and priestly identity — the authentic anthropology of St. Thomas Aquinas.

The New Earth

If the new earth of which St. Peter speaks is to become a reality, it will be necessary for the Church to attract large numbers
of young men to the seminaries. Throughout the ages, young
men have been in need of challenges in their idealistic concern
with improving the world of human beings. The young men of
our day are no exception. Witness their interest and voluntary
participation in such projects as the Peace Corps, Vista, and

---

[13] Prof. J. van Boxtel, "Moraal en Gevoeisleven volgens Thomas van Aquino," in
Tycischrill voor Philosophie, June, 1959. C. van Boekel, MSC, *Katharsis*, 1957. Stepha-
nus Pfürtner, O.P., *Triebleben und Sittliche Vollendung - Eine Moralpsychologische
Untersuchung nach Thomas von Aquin*, Freiburg, 1958.

Teen-Corps. That in their altruistic desire to help others in need, they are drawn more to secular projects than to those providing for the spiritual and moral needs of others, stems, I would venture to say, at least in part from the virtually absent masculine and mature priest image with which they can identify, and the relative overemphasis on the need to combat social and cultural evils rather than moral ones as a possible overreaction to hell-and-brimstone teachings of the past.

There is no doubt in my mind that young men will once again respond in large numbers to the call of the priesthood when the following conditions have been met.

1. Children must be prevented from becoming spiritually spoiled by not being given too many spiritual goods too early or too soon. This was done in the past, for instance by insisting on their daily attendance at Mass during grade-school years.[14] Children's innate desire to grow toward a greater knowledge and love of God must be given time to develop gradually in childhood. This requires a firm belief in the fundamental goodness of human nature on the part of the Church, parents, and educators.

2. A doctrinally sound presentation of the Catholic faith and morals by means of a pedagogically correct catechetical program is a must in the elementary grades.

3. A high school religion program centered around the application of basic moral principles to the problems of the modern, secular world should be taught by mature, well-informed priests, sisters, or lay persons who welcome discussion and quotations from students and are able to provide direction and answers consistent with the teachings of the Magisterium.

---

[14] Conrad W. Baars, M.D., "The Psychology of Childhood Confessions," in *St. Anthony's Messenger*, 1965.

4. Young people should have ample opportunity in all stages of personality growth to develop their individual, unique selves in an affirming, non-repressive atmosphere in the home, school, and Church.

5. All young people should be constantly exposed to masculine and celibate priests in the sense described in this paper. There can be no virtue (from the Latin *virtus* = manliness) without virility (from the Latin *vir* = man).

6. On the college level, students should be stimulated intellectually in a most profound way by a well-rounded liberal arts program covering the humanities and the tradition of Western civilization. In the seminary, they should be exposed to a theology of the Gospels and a systematic theology based on a philosophy of reasoning, with ample opportunity for their practical application in well-organized and supervised pastoral programs.

7. During the seminary years, college students should be challenged to mature further through diverse friendships, competitive activities and sports, community living, and courses in becoming leaders in service and shepherds of the faithful. They should have ample opportunity to develop mature obedience in response to mature authority on the part of superiors fully aware of their awesome task of being an author, i.e. an *auctor* or creator of others.

The only difficulty in meeting these requirements may be the matter of time. They have to be effected by the people of God who, whether as priests, religious, or laity, have been psychologically affected in various degrees by the Church's past fearful and suspicious attitude toward human nature. In this time of crisis, it will be necessary for those least affected and handicapped to assume leadership, and in doing so take care not to neglect or harm those more seriously affected.

I foresee that a large number of priests and religious who now suffer the psychological, somatic, and spiritual consequences of non-affirmation and chronic repression will effectively be helped in a special therapeutic and educational center operating on sound anthropological, psychological, psychiatric, philosophical, and theological principles. Once restored to health in this center, these priests and religious, too, will become available to do their share in restoring the Church to her rightful position of being a Church of love, a Church whose mature, human love affirms all people, stimulates their love and joy, and invites mature obedience to the laws of God.

Once the conditions set forth above have been met, I cannot see how young men, whole, *caelebs*, virtuous, masculine, and well-educated could fail to respond to the call of the beautiful and masculine vocation of the priesthood. I cannot see how they could not be eager to assume the priest's task of bringing all people the love of God by being an *alter Christus,* by teaching the divine truths without fear of hurting people's feelings or being unpopular, by exposing and opposing heresies, by upholding the law of Christ, by their willingness to risk betrayal, imprisonment, torture, and death in bringing Christ to the captive nations, by being leaders in the unrelenting battle against moral evil. I cannot see how mature young men could not long to affirm the living Christ in His continued, infinite love of all people by responding to His love in the name of many — could not long to affirm others by aiding them to become free persons, free to love God without fear or irrational striving for perfection — could not long to affirm people by aiding them to obey the more difficult teachings of the Magisterium, instead of instructing them to ignore those teachings in misplaced sentimentality and ignorance of the fact that by doing so they deny them — the very opposite of affirmation.

What I have written in these pages I have written in love

and gratitude as a tribute to all priests — to those already masculine and celibate because they have effectively built on the wholesome personality structure they received as a gift from mature and loving parents and educators and to those who never had the opportunity to become *caelebs,* due to no fault of their own, because they have tried so heroically to achieve what was impossible, no matter how much they had to suffer. My admiration for them is endless, my compassion heartfelt, when I reflect on the irony that they became neurotic as a consequence of what were held to be solid Christian beliefs and teachings. Of course, by this I do not infer any criticism or accusation of the Church, as there simply cannot be a question of culpability in the Church's failure to help the faithful to mature without repressing their emotional lives prior to our recent discoveries about affirmation — the essence of human love — and the nature of the neuroses.

It is a deep source of joy and gratitude that I may offer the Church insights which hold out the promise of a new priesthood, a community of mature priests capable of inspiring humanity to reach out for the good, of leading the faithful in the battle against the evil that separates them from the universal good, and of making this a new earth.

I am humbly grateful to God for enabling me to affirm the Church in her sincere desire to serve all of humanity by teaching each man, when called, to become A Priest for All Seasons — Masculine and Celibate.

CHAPTER X

The Homosexual's Search for Happiness

Introduction

Psychiatrists writing on the subject of homosexuality have several strikes against them from the start. For one, opinions on homosexuality expressed by psychiatrists are neither invited nor considered welcome unless they carry the unequivocal seal of approval of persons in the Gay Liberation Movement. Second, passions run high in reaction against past suppression and condemnation of homosexually-oriented individuals, regardless of their sexual behavior. The present turn-about in attitude on the part of society and Christian churches is long overdue, but in the absence of a calm, objective atmosphere, the danger of the pendulum swinging too far in the opposite direction is considerable.

If the psychiatrist is Catholic, his or her professional opinion on "homosexuality" is likely to be suspect by some if that judgment concerning the psychological soundness of homosexual acts parallels or supports the Magisterium's stand on morality. Although these two subjects, "homosexuality" ["homosexual orientation" or "same-sex attraction"] and "homosexual acts" are two distinct entities, they are not so in the minds of many people, which may lead them to accuse the Catholic psychiatrist of letting the Catholic religion's moral judgment of a person's acts cloud his or her evaluation and conclusions about the psychological state of that person.

In this presentation, I intend to proceed along psychophilosophical lines, letting the opinions of the Magisterium and persons in the Gay Liberation Movement stand on their own merits. Nevertheless, it must be realized that my professional conclusions about the psychological soundness of homosexual acts cannot be expected to be in conflict with moral judgments of human acts if both moral theology and psychology have as their starting point an intellectually responsible philosophy of the nature of the human person. In nearly thirty years of clinical psychiatric experience, the school of psychology which I have discovered fulfills this criterion most adequately is that which blends *authentic* Christian anthropology with the best of modern clinical psychiatric observations and contemporary philosophic thought. This psycho-philosophical framework has, in my experience, proven a most valid tool for gauging the validity of certain disciplinarian-ecclesiastical teachings, proscriptions or attitudes regarding such topics as obedience, authority, pedagogy and family planning, to mention only a few.

Another factor that can be expected to have a bearing on my conclusions is, of course, my personal attitude toward homosexual persons. It is probably best illustrated by the fact that I seldom remember my homosexual patients — and I have seen hundreds in these past thirty years — as homosexual. I recall most of them as unique individuals with distinct personalities whom it was a privilege to meet in my journey through life. In fact, it is not seldom that I realize that I had forgotten that they were or still are homosexually oriented until a casual remark in a letter or phone call again brings this to mind. One reason for this, a minor one to be sure, may be the fact that a certain number of them sought my professional help primarily for a depression, alcoholism, a spiritual crisis, or for any or all of the symptoms of the condition I shall describe shortly, while the symptom of their homosexuality was only brought up as a secondary factor in therapy. The other reason is the fact that once they had been helped in accepting their homosexual orientation without feelings of guilt, self-condemnation, self-pity, or an angry need to become a "gay militant," the subject was referred to, for reasons to be explained later, with decreasing frequency during the therapeutic process.

Homosexuality as a Diagnostic Category

For others again, my aforementioned reference to "modern clinical psychiatric observations" will be somewhat suspect, I am afraid, since the credibility of such observations, at least as the subject under discussion here, seems to have been undermined to some extent by the 1973 controversy on homosexuality. I am referring to the then widely contested statement by the American Psychiatric Association that "homosexuality by itself does not necessarily constitute a psychiatric disorder," a statement which led to the decision to replace the diagnosis of homosexuality in the American Psychiatric Association's *Diagnostic and Statistical Manual of Mental Disorders*[1] (DSM) by "sexual orientation disturbance."[2]

As a member of the American Psychiatric Association, I

---

[1] DSM: The official manual of approved diagnostic terms of mental disorders, with definitions, for use by psychiatrists and psychotherapists in office practice, mental hospitals, clinics, mental health centers and in consultation to courts and industrial health services. American Psychiatric Association: *Diagnostic and Statistical Manual of Mental Disorders*, Fourth Edition, Text Revision. Washington, DC, American Psychiatric Association, 2000.

[2] Editors' Note: The DSM II (1968) was used at the time this article was written. This diagnosis is no longer found in more recent editions of the DSM. "Sexual Disorder Not Otherwise Specified" can be diagnosed for persons with "persistent and marked distress about sexual orientation" (DSM-IV-TR, 2000, p. 582).

voted against its proposed change in diagnostic category, even though I agree with the Association's assertion that "homosexuality by itself does not constitute a psychiatric disorder." In fact, I would go even further and exclude homosexuality from the DSM altogether. After all, the American Psychiatric Association holds that "in order for a condition to be included in the *Diagnostic and Statistical Manual of Mental Disorders* it must regularly cause distress or it must regularly interfere with social effectiveness." Even if I were to agree with the Gay Liberation Movement's claim that active or inactive homosexual persons would not be distressed by their particular orientation nor hampered in their social effectiveness if it were not for centuries of outright condemnation and persecution, this would not be my main reason for eliminating homosexuality from the DSM.[3] Neither would I allow this claim to move me to conclude that homosexuality is normal and that homosexual practices are just as normal as those of heterosexuals.

The reason for wanting to exclude homosexuality as a diagnostic term from the DSM is that I do not consider homosexuality a "mental condition." Although we are not accustomed to think of heterosexuality as a mental state or condition, we do so of homosexuality. To consider homosexuality a "mental condition" — whether normal or abnormal — would make sense only if we hold the same for heterosexuality. Never has it been claimed that the heterosexual orientation or preference is synonymous with, or proof of, a healthy mental or psychological condition. A heterosexual orientation can be present in well-integrated, mature individuals, just as it can be in immature, selfish persons or persons with neurotic, psychotic or personality disorders. Therefore, if we make no claims for the

---

[3]   From what follows in this article it will be evident that I would include homosexuality as a *symptom* of an underlying emotional disorder.

heterosexual orientation being a healthy or unhealthy mental condition, why should we do so for the homosexual orientation or preference? There is no reason for this. In fact, I intend to show that the entire longstanding dispute about the normality or abnormality of homosexuality as a mental or psychological condition, diametrically opposed to heterosexuality, can benefit decidedly from a different perspective.

A Different Perspective

This perspective is one of looking at the homosexual orientation or same-sex attraction strictly as a *manifestation* or a *symptom*, rather than as a *condition* or *state*. We may find a homosexual or heterosexual orientation in a person with a "normal" makeup just as we may find a homosexual or heterosexual orientation in a person with an "abnormal" mental or psychological condition as currently defined by the DSM. Using this manual as the sole criterion for determining what a normal or abnormal condition is, the homosexual orientation as a symptom can exist in such universally recognized abnormal mental or emotional conditions as a neurotic disorder, a psychotic disorder or a personality disorder, as well as in what psychiatry considers a "normal" person, i.e. a person whose mental condition is not listed in this manual. There exists, however, a certain emotional condition characterized by a constellation of various typical symptoms of emotional illness or dis-ease which psychiatry has not yet officially recognized in adults as a separate clinical entity, and is therefore not listed in the DSM. It is possible for this condition to masquerade as that of an "average or normal person" and therefore go unrecognized.

Emotional Deprivation Disorder

Emotional Deprivation Disorder is the condition called the syndrome of non-affirmation which occurs in a person who has been deprived in early life of most or all fundamental affirmation[4] by a significant other. Even a cursory look at this condition will show that it constitutes just as much a sharply-defined syndrome as the classical Freudian neuroses, whether hysterical, obsessive-compulsive, phobic or depressive. These neuroses have been universally recognized as the consequence of the repression of unacceptable emotions since childhood.

If the "average or normal person" can be said to be reasonably mature, integrated, unselfish, and able to relate to self, other people and God in a mutually satisfying manner and to cope reasonably successfully with the vicissitudes of life, then the unaffirmed individual, especially the *totally* unaffirmed person or person with *Emotional Deprivation Disorder,* who lacks these qualities deserves, no, *needs,* to be recognized and listed in the DSM. Emotional Deprivation Disorder is a distinct clinical entity to be distinguished from the classical Freudian repressive neuroses by a particular constellation of neurotic symptoms, described in detail in the book *Healing the Unaffirmed.*[5] These symptoms are not the result of an intrapsychic process of repression of emotions which began in childhood, but rather of an environmental deprivation or frustration in early life of the fundamental psychological need to be loved for one's unique self.

---

[4] The term *affirmation* was introduced into the psychiatric literature by Dr. Anna Terruwe and me in the early sixties, and has a specific, well-defined psychological meaning.

[5] By Conrad W. Baars, M.D. and Anna Terruwe, M.D., *Healing the Unaffirmed: Recognizing Emotional Deprivation Disorder,* Rev. ed., Suzanne M. Baars and Bonnie N. Shayne, eds., Alba House, Staten Island, NY, 2002.

Recognition of Emotional Deprivation Disorder, which represents merely the most extreme form of the non-affirmation syndrome, can show us that from this perspective there is a striking similarity between the promiscuous homosexual individual and the promiscuous heterosexual person, between the gay or lesbian and the "straight" person whose preferred sexual activities have been considered in the gay or lesbian person as psychologically abnormal and immoral, and in the "straight" person as simply immoral, but not psychologically abnormal.

The observation that both the unaffirmed homosexual and the unaffirmed heterosexual individual have much in common to explain their sexual behavior would be too easily ignored if we were to focus solely on their differences as to preferred object choice and genital mode of relating and obtaining sexual gratification. Their personalities are better understood if seen as fundamentally similar but accompanied by different behavioral phenomena, ranging from a compulsion to be promiscuous to a voluntary abstaining from homosexual or heterosexual promiscuous activities for reasons of conscience, fear of detection, or whatever. In other words, in this particular perspective we must distinguish between the totally or adequately affirmed individual who is always heterosexually oriented on the one hand, and the partially or totally unaffirmed individual who can be either heterosexually or homosexually oriented on the other. The reason for claiming that all fully affirmed individuals are heterosexually oriented is that any of the factors which in very early life cause the innate predisposition to a heterosexual orientation to change to a homosexual one are at the same time detractors from or obstacles to full affirmation. This will become clear in the following description of the unaffirmed person and how the unaffirmed state moves the person to behave sexually.

Affirmed Persons

Individuals who have been adequately affirmed during their developmental years by unselfishly loving, affectionate, mature parents and/or other significant persons can be said to have received the gift of themselves. They feel worthwhile, significant and lovable. They possess themselves as man or woman. They know who they are. They are certain of their identity. They love themselves unselfishly. They are open to all that is good and find joy in the same. They are able to affirm all of creation, and as affirmers of all beings are capable of making others happy and joyful, too. They are largely other-directed. They find joy in being and doing for others. They find joy in their loving relationship with their Creator. They can share and give of themselves, be a true friend to others, and feel at ease with persons of both sexes. They are capable of finding happiness in marriage or the freely chosen celibate state of life. They are free from psycho-pathological factors which hamper one's free will and are therefore fully responsible — morally and legally — for their actions.

Unaffirmed Persons

Unaffirmed individuals, on the contrary, can be said to have been *born only once*; their second or *psychological birth* never took place[6] (or, since it is a protracted process, was never completed). They were not made to know and feel their own goodness, worth and identity. They have been thrown back

---

[6]   Conrad W. Baars, M.D., *Born Only Once: The Miracle of Affirmation*, 1975, 1989. Preface by Suzanne M. Baars, Quincy, IL: Franciscan Press, Quincy University, 2001.

upon themselves by denial on the part of significant others in their life. They are like prisoners — locked in, lonely, and self-centered — waiting for someone to come and open the door of their prison, waiting to be opened to their own goodness and that of others. No measure of success in business, profession or otherwise can adequately compensate for their feelings of inferiority, inadequacy, uncertainty and insecurity. Both the married life and the celibate life accentuate the fundamental loneliness of these persons and their inability to relate to others as equals. Their spiritual life suffers as time goes on, and their basically joyless way of life changes more and more to a state of depression until death seems the only way out.

Most importantly, unaffirmed persons have only one concern and need: to become affirmed, to be loved for *who they are* and not for *what they do.* They are literally driven to find someone who truly, unequivocally loves them. This is in marked contrast to affirmed individuals who look for someone with whom they can share their love, who can give love as well as receive, who can wait and are not hurried, driven, or compelled to find someone who will love them. If affirmation by a significant other is not forthcoming, many unaffirmed persons will use their talents, intelligence and energy to try to convince themselves and the world in a variety of ways that they *are* worthwhile, important, and significant, even though they don't feel that they are. The most common ways of doing this are by the acquisition, display and use of material goods, wealth, power, fame, honor, status symbols, or sex. As I have described in *Born Only Once,*[7] Adolf Hitler sought to affirm himself by power, Marilyn Monroe by fame. Both failed tragically.

---

[7] Ibid., 61-73.

Self-Affirmation

For the purpose of this paper, it suffices to confine myself to discussing those attempts at self-affirmation which aim directly at the attainment of what people did not receive gratuitously from others: *affirmation* — namely, unselfish, life-giving love. There are two ways by which unaffirmed people will try to obtain this love. First, by always being "nice" and pleasing others, by never getting angry, and by never hurting other people's feelings — in short by nonassertive behavior. Second, in sexual contacts using the mistaken notion that sex equals love. The more total the frustration of the fundamental need for affirmation, the greater the drive and the more desperate the desire to bind another to oneself. Some young women demonstrate this by getting pregnant before marriage through the careless use of contraceptives. The greater the drive to find love, the more indiscriminate one's willingness to hop from one bed to another, to look for love in group sex, and to engage in sexual acts which, compared to other sexual and sensual, other-directed and other-respecting, intimacies, are least likely to lead to a lasting, satisfying and mutually affirming relationship. By and large these sexual acts (I am referring here to "oral sex") represent a measure of the depth of a person's fundamental deprivation, since they indicate either the intensity of the need to please others (by what many have told me they consider self-debasing sexual acts) or the fear of being rejected or considered "unmanly" in the "gay" world.

It is to be expected that the compelling drive of self-affirmation affords neither the homosexually nor the heterosexually unaffirmed individual an opportunity to find what he or she so desperately searches for: love — authentic, unconditional love, and being loved for his unique self. There are two reasons for the fact that self-affirmation, by whatever means, is always futile. First, authentic affirmation can be given only by another already affirmed individual. Second, affirmation is a gift, not something that can be bought, demanded or obtained at the price of self-debasement.

The unaffirmed person is unlikely to meet an affirmed person in the places where homosexual and heterosexual promiscuity flourishes. If the unaffirmed person were to meet such a person, the affirmed person would exclude genital sexual activities, even if he or she were to desire them. The affirmed person knows or senses that genital involvement would not be good for the unaffirmed individual because as soon as genital sex becomes part of the relationship, the unaffirmed individual cannot help but wonder sooner or later, "Does he (or she) love me for my unique self, or merely or largely for my body?"

Sexual pleasures sought for selfish reasons or in compulsive striving for affirmation have no affirming component, as is true for those experienced by two truly mature persons, i.e., persons in whom the sexual feelings, as well as all other emotions, are readily responsive to the person's will to seek the happiness of the other person first. Moreover, even though there is much pleasure in sexual acts as such, there is little joy unless the acts are the ultimate consequence of a mutually affirming relationship. Where there is no joy, there can never be enough pleasure — hence the compulsion to be promiscuously active. The joy of being loved for one's total self, of being found worthwhile and significant for who and what one is, can only be given by an already affirmed other who finds his or her greatest happiness in that of the other person. Since it cannot be found in promiscuous sexual contacts, the ensuing frustration drives the unaffirmed individual to new sex partners, to other beds, or parks, or bars, or baths, only to be frustrated again and again in a vicious circle.

Elimination of Sexual Frustrations

This frustration can be eliminated only if these contacts are strictly limited to non-genital touching, caressing, stroking, etc., without, and this is most difficult yet absolutely necessary, proceeding to genital gratifications. Only then can they possibly have some affirming value. That would depend on whether these actions proceed from authentic feelings of love for the other, or are engaged in for selfish pleasures. This, of course, is a far cry from homosexual and heterosexual contacts in which the genital organs are made the primary if not sole object choice in the search for "love," and substitutes for the unique, personal qualities that are to be found only in the total physical and spiritual person, not for example, in the size of the penis as an object of uniqueness (a common preoccupation among homosexual men). The foregoing observations have been confirmed by Dr. Anna Terruwe and me in a combined total of 50 years of helping unaffirmed persons and those with Emotional Deprivation Disorder of either sexual preference through affirmation therapy.

Before describing some aspects of this therapy, I want to remark briefly on the not always clear genesis of the homosexual orientation. Whether this orientation is constitutionally determined — hormonal, genetic, or otherwise — or the result of early life environmental influences, or both, is, in the context of the particular perspective presented in this paper, of less importance than the always present and commonly reported association between the individual's homosexual orientation and a disturbance of his or her sense of worth and identity. In my opinion, this disturbance has both a causal and effectual relationship with the homosexual orientation and, when treated successfully, has a decidedly beneficial effect on the person's capacity for happiness even without a change in sexual orientation.

Therapy of Unaffirmed Homosexual or Heterosexual Persons

What happens in the treatment of homosexually or heterosexually oriented unaffirmed individuals, whether lay or religious, who possess diminished moral responsibility in several areas because of the gap between their undeveloped or underdeveloped emotional life and their intellectual and volitional life?

As they begin to receive emotional and intellectual affirmation from the therapist, their sense of self-worth and identity gradually grows and their compulsive need to look for love indiscriminately and at all cost diminishes at the same rate. When they develop a sense of their own goodness, they become more open to what is good around them. To the extent that they lose their fear of others, they are able to love and affirm them. The more they affirm others, the more they are affirmed in return, and the more they are able to love themselves and God. They increasingly realize the difference between being loved for who and what they are and for what they do to please others. It also becomes easier to say "no" to sexual activities, which before seemed to offer the only promise of fulfilling their frustrated need for affirmation. Their compulsion to be sexually promiscuous diminishes, and in time disappears altogether. Their sexual drive and desires become increasingly accessible to guidance by reason and will. In the end, they are free and responsible individuals whose actions, sexual or otherwise, have become truly human acts subject to moral judgment. This is true even when the homosexual orientation has remained unchanged during therapy.

In the therapy of homosexual and heterosexual unaffirmed persons, the vicious circle of feeling unloved → seeking/buying love → being frustrated → and feeling more unloved is broken, and their growing sense of self worth, goodness and significance causes them to lose interest in their previously active promiscuous life. Where moral considerations alone never had this effect on them (except perhaps temporarily and at the cost of intense emotional suppression through fear or guilt), the psychological resolution of the restless drive to find affirmation in sexual intimacies always succeeded.

When unaffirmed individuals become affirmed, they are at last free to follow any course of action they choose. They no longer feel compelled to act out sexually. Heterosexually oriented persons are able to find happiness in marriage or the celibate life of religious or laypersons. For homosexually oriented individuals, the situation depends on whether or not they have retained their homosexual orientation in the course of affirmation therapy. Not infrequently, this orientation disappears by itself if there has been no overt homosexual involvement prior to therapy. If it persists, it can be dealt with additional psychotherapy if indicated or desired. In a certain limited sense it does not make too much difference for celibate religious persons, whether they are homosexually or heterosexually oriented, for in either case they must deal with their sexual feelings in the same manner: they must guide them rationally toward total abstinence. In each case, the client's attitude and feeling toward his or her homosexual orientation will determine the need for further therapy. The desire for change in orientation is often more pronounced in lay persons, even when the compulsion to act out sexually has disappeared. The desire for marriage and children is one of the factors that plays a role.

In those persons who have been quite sexually active in the gay or lesbian world, the ultimate change in orientation is not easily effected, if at all. Therapy is usually time-consuming, since deeply ingrained habit patterns are not easily erased. Which type of therapy is most effective is difficult to say. The widely divergent results of psychoanalytic treatment of homosexuals are rather confusing. The more orthodox and impersonal analysis has little affirming value and therefore does not resolve the restless striving for finding affirmation in sex. Pure intellectual understanding of the reasons for the homosexual orientation does not diminish this striving. I would expect that the analysts who report successes in their treatment of homosexual patients are largely warm and affirming individuals themselves and thus provide the emotional and intellectual affirmation their clients require primarily.[8]

Generally speaking, the type of therapy which produces the best results is that in which the process of affirmation by the therapist blends and overlaps with the gradual resolving of conflicts and tensions that resulted from those early life experiences which obstructed the establishment of gender identification. The various causes for this obstruction are well known. To mention some: a pathological family constellation, parental role reversal, hate or fear of the parent of the opposite sex, repeated sexual involvement by an unaffirmed child with one and the same older individual of the same sex, which constituted a satisfying and pleasurable substitute for not feeling loved by a parent of the same sex, boys being attracted by the increasing number of non-assertive men who do not constitute a threat to their weakly developed self-image, while being repelled by the increasing number of non-feminine feminists who are a threat to them, and young women being turned off by passive, submissive men who frustrate their innate need for a truly masculine partner.[9]

---

[8] See "Ferment in Psychoanalysis and Psychoanalytic Psychotherapy" by H.H. Strupp, Ph.D. in *Success and Failure in Psychoanalysis and Psychotherapy*, Edited by B. B. Wolman, Macmillan Co., 1972.

[9] For a description of masculinity see Chapter IX, "A Priest for All Seasons: Masculine and Celibate."

Therapeutic and Pastoral Guidelines

These can be readily combined as far as affirmation therapy for unaffirmed individuals is concerned. Only very depressed or anxious unaffirmed persons, persons with Emotional Deprivation Disorder, and persons with "marked and persistent distress" due to their homosexual orientation[10] should be referred to the psychotherapist. Affirming unaffirmed persons is something that concerns everyone — all people — priests and religious, laypersons, pastoral counselors, physicians and surgeons, and ministers of healing. In this matter each and every one can be said to be a healer — a creator of the human person's psychological being. Their role as affirming healers is essential in the resolution of the sexual compulsion and the maturing process of promiscuous homosexual and heterosexual persons.

The following guidelines can be expected to be effective only if they are followed by healers whose authentic affirmation provides the framework within which the pathological aspect of their client's behavior and attitude can be examined and redirected. These guidelines will be ineffective and futile in the hands of pseudo-mature, pseudo-affirming healers.

1. Since sexual involvement is one of the several ineffective methods used by unaffirmed individuals to secure authentic love, the immediate cessation of genital activity is to be strongly recommended at the start of therapy. However, not all clients will be able to abide by this recommendation. If it is impossible for certain clients to immediately discontinue their promiscuous activities, they should be advised — and this pertains particularly to homosexual clients — to at least

---

[10] See footnote 2.

abstain from those acts which shift their focus of awareness from the other person to the other person's sex organs. Instead, these persons should concentrate on discovering the uniqueness of the other as a person and determine what the other has to offer as a loving, helpful friend.

2. Clients are to focus on the expression of affection through tactile, non-genital contact and learn to distinguish between those expressions that are other-directed, gentle, warm and caring, and those that are self-seeking, grasping, hurried and aimed at genital sexual gratification. The latter are to be rejected and avoided. These persons should be encouraged to find pleasure and satisfaction in unselfish, other-directed affection, and not to spoil its effect by proceeding to genital sexual gratification.

3. Clients who cannot yet abstain from genital involvement should be advised to dare to say "no" to offers or requests for "oral sex," not only for the aforementioned reasons, but also because they present opportunities for learning to be assertive, a quality which is lacking in most unaffirmed individuals. Most homosexual men consider "oral sex" the "masculine" thing to do, and scoff at the "feminine" search for affection by the minority of members of the "gay" world. However, this scoffing attitude represents a repression of their basic need to find authentic love. Homosexual clients should understand this and dare to admit their basic need for affection. Only then will they dare to become different from "masculine" homosexual persons and succeed in their search for happiness.

4. Clients are also to be assisted in becoming assertive on other levels of relating. They must dare to run the risk of not being loved by some individuals when they are truly themselves, rather than try to buy love through giving gifts, repressing

their anger, never hurting other persons' feelings, never disagreeing, etc. They will discover that their assertiveness is a most effective antidote for the dependency and exploitation of which they were victims and which they had invited and encouraged by their fear of incurring the displeasure of others.

5. Clients are to be encouraged to make friends with members of both sexes, but not solely on the terms of other persons like unaffirmed individuals do. Their own terms should play an equal role in every relationship in the growing expectation that they will be respected. After all, clients are seeking to be loved for who and what they truly are, not for what they pretend to be or in spite of what they hide for fear of not being loved. Likewise, their sense of self-worth and self-respect will be enhanced by behavior which is in accord with their values. It takes courage to set forth their values and beliefs, to defend them, and to live by them in the face of criticism and attack. Through the authentic affirmation of the mature healer, this courage will gradually replace the chronic fear of not being loved and thus become a source of behavior leading to greater self-respect and self-worth.

6. Healers who are unable to practice self-restraint in their love for their clients must realize that they will harm their clients. In fact, the condition of unaffirmed persons, especially persons with Emotional Deprivation Disorder, will be adversely affected by the healer who takes advantage of his or her clients' need for love and uses them for personal pleasure. Such self-seeking behavior more than cancels out the affirming effect the relationship may have in other respects.

7. The most beneficial relationships for homosexual and heterosexual clients are those with individuals of either sex

who are themselves largely affirmed and can find joy in a relationship which does not include genital sexual activity. Such persons, whether professionals or friends, are the most important source for helping clients to find themselves and to become free, self-determining persons.

8. Confessors and spiritual directors who have an aversion to sexually promiscuous homosexual and heterosexual persons and can only moralize, or at best, go through the motions of counseling without truly affirming their clients, do best to refer them to a confessor or director without this handicap.

9. Clients must always first be shown the psychological reasons for the necessity to abstain from promiscuous sexual activities. The moral or religious reasons follow from these. It must be understood by clients that it is primarily for psycholo-gical reasons that such sexual activity arrests and prevents growth to full maturity.

10. When a client's homosexual orientation diminishes and heterosexual desires make themselves felt, the healer should not make the mistake of encouraging the person to have sexual intercourse. Such a course of action, rather than proving or solidifying the changing sexual orientation, impedes and retards the therapeutic progress. The client must be advised to allow plenty of time to let the attraction to and desire for a person of the other sex grow from within. This advice is based on the psychological principle that all human faculties need time to develop their fullest potential by gradual and timely exposure to their proper objects. (This, by the way, is the reason that premature sexual experiences in young people block, rather than promote, their personality development!)

Gay and Lesbian Groups

It makes little sense for homosexuals to group together on the basis of a single symptom, unless they all desire to support one another to become affirmed individuals. Alcoholics unite in Alcoholics Anonymous to support one another, not to demand their right to drink. The same is true for individuals with diabetes, multiple sclerosis, etc. The *dis*-ease of homosexually oriented persons does not find its source so much in the sexual orientation, but rather in the person's emotional underdevelopment as the result of lack of affirmation. Group formation by gay or lesbian persons would benefit, I believe, from participation by heterosexually oriented, unaffirmed as well as affirmed, individuals sympathetic to the plight of their less fortunate unaffirmed fellow human beings. Together they can do much, since in the matter of affirmation we all need one another. The already affirmed person needs the response of the non-affirmed person almost as much as the latter needs the affirmation of the former. Therefore, unaffirmed homosexual individuals contribute significantly to their own welfare and that of others — affirmed and unaffirmed — by discontinuing their efforts at self-affirmation in sexual encounters. These encounters as well as all other means of self-affirmation are insurmountable obstacles to being affirmed.[11]

Conclusion

In conclusion, I hope that the perspective explained in this article will help to alter the focus from a person's sexual

---

[11] Rollo May's unfortunate and unacceptable use of the term self-affirmation in his book, *Power and Innocence* (New York: Norton, 1972), is refuted in my book *Born Only Once*.

orientation and/or activities (whether homosexual or hetero-sexual) to the underlying syndrome resulting from emotional deprivation. Since this syndrome is widespread in our largely non-affirming society, it affects the majority of men and women. Although it is a well-crystallized clinical syndrome, it may at times be mistaken for a Freudian repressive neurosis — especially when these types of neurotic disorders are associated in one and the same individual — or even a so-called "normal" or "average" human condition. Fortunately, this syndrome responds well to affirmation therapy described summarily in this article. Besides the promise of alleviation and cure of the sufferings of the unaffirmed state and the reversal of the homosexual orientation, it may be hoped that the perspective presented in this article will assist a rapprochement between homosexual persons and the psychiatric and healing professions. It is hoped that it will exert some influence, albeit slight at first, on the over-reaction of militant gay and lesbian groups, which bring little, if any, authentic happiness to their members. Their happiness can only come through authentic affirmation, as herein explained.

CHAPTER XI

The Alcoholic Priest

Of the multi-faceted subject of the alcoholic priest, I only want to discuss the personality of the alcoholic priest here — or rather, his personalities, for just as there is no one personality of a priest, nor of an alcoholic, so there is not just one personality of an alcoholic priest.

What all alcoholic priests have in common is the disease of alcoholism. This disease arises out of complex genetic factors which, when exposed to alcohol for a sufficient length of time, produce permanent abnormal body reactions responsible for the varied and progressive symptoms of the clinical disease. The earlier in life the exposure to alcohol and the greater the amounts consumed, the sooner the disease with its compulsion to drink becomes manifest. Once developed, the disease can only be arrested by total and permanent abstinence, and the elimination or correction of whatever psychological, social, economic, or spiritual factors that led to the excessive use of alcohol.

Probably the single most important reason for the use of alcohol is its relaxing effect, its ability to quickly and effectively reduce or eliminate tension (more so than anxiety), and thus produce a sense of well-being, of feeling free and more oneself. The occasional, moderate drinker welcomes this effect in addition to the other pleasures alcohol provides, as much as the problem drinker, unable to cope with his tensions in more realistic ways, craves it. Either one, if genetically predisposed, will become an alcoholic sooner or later.

Tension results from the action of two opposing forces. A stretched rubber band is under tension. A stiffly extended arm is tense because the extensor muscles exert a greater force than the flexor muscles. One is tense when one fears and desires a surgical operation at the same time. If members of a family oppose each other, there is tension in the home. Of all possible symptoms occurring in mental and emotional disorders, tension is the most universal. It is also experienced frequently by healthy, mature people, but because they are well equipped to deal with the source of the tension, it is only felt temporarily and transiently.

To understand the personality of the alcoholic priest, it serves little purpose to study the causes of tensions which are part of the daily life of every priest. Most of them are usually resolved within a reasonable span of time, unless the priest has been *trained* to repress his emotions or is handicapped as the result of deep-seated psychological conflicts. In that case many of the daily tensions become chronic and, added to those stemming from the repressive process and the conflicts themselves, invite drinking.

Neither would there exist a particular need to write this article if our knowledge of psychological conflicts did not extend beyond the commonly recognized mental and emotional disorders. Since the discovery of the syndrome of Emotional Deprivation Disorder and its sub-clinical states of the non-affirmed individual, however, our understanding of the alcoholic and the individual with a neurotic disorder has been enhanced considerably. It also explains the remark of so many observers that a goodly number of alcoholics, once they have been detoxified, "look so little like typical psychiatric patients."

Since space prevents me from giving a detailed description of the syndrome of the Emotional Deprivation Disorder and the non-affirmed person, I refer the reader to *Healing the Unaffirmed*,[1] written jointly with my colleague from The Netherlands, Dr. Anna Terruwe. I shall quote here some passages which deal with the presence of this syndrome in alcoholics.

> The actual prevention of Emotional Deprivation Disorder is not necessarily simpler than that of the repressive disorders for, though it is relatively easy to understand the fundamental principle, its application in everyday life is far more difficult. Witness the great and ever-growing number of unaffirmed people in our society who suffer from full-blown Emotional Deprivation Disorder, or lead unhappy, lonely, insecure lives, not knowing why they suffer from recurring depressions, irritability, chronic alcoholism, chronic fatigue, or vague physical complaints which respond to medical treatment only temporarily, if at all (p. 181).

Insofar as we can judge, the increase in the number of unaffirmed people is frightening. One would be hard put to count them all, but it would be no surprise if they represented a fourth of the population of the Western world. Among them we would have to include a large percentage of alcoholics. There have been many unaffirmed people with Emotional Deprivation Disorder among our alcoholic patients, and we have been struck repeatedly by the reports of authors,

---

[1]   Conrad W. Baars, M.D. and Anna A. Terruwe, M.D., *Healing the Unaffirmed: Recognizing Emotional Deprivation Disorder*, Rev. ed. Suzanne M. Baars and Bonnie N. Shayne, eds., Staten Island, NY: Alba House, 2002.

who, in attempting to describe an "alcoholic personality," almost always mention the main symptoms of the syndrome of Emotional Deprivation Disorder. To quote, for example, from a recent psychiatric study which describes a characteristic lifestyle, rather than specific personality traits of the alcoholic: "A deeply felt sense of inadequacy is invariably present... the earliest memories center on damage or abandonment, and the reaction of helplessness... a distinctive *hypersensitivity* is present, especially noticeable in personal relationships and in attitudes about talent, creativity, and success. Achievement is frequently discounted and is not experienced as success or as the fulfillment of genuine ambition... compensates for his deepening sense of inadequacy by ascribing to himself special qualities or talents, and by setting grandiose goals to prove that he is worth more than others think...."

From a widely circulated book by a recovered alcoholic and respected member of Alcoholics Anonymous we quote: "He has been too dependent throughout his life on some person... feels insecure, incompetent and childlike... essentially a lonely class of people... anxious, fearful and tense in the real world... can't stand reality... is guilt-laden and rigid... takes the joy out of everything he does... the central desire of his whole nature is that of being caressed by his mother... the source of his craving for attention is often a lack of self-confidence... failure to accept and love himself...."

The relatively few remaining personality features in this particular chapter, not quoted here, are typical of alcoholics with repressive disorders and alcoholics with psychopathic personality disorders. This corresponds to our clinical impression that the largest percentage of alcoholics is made up of unaffirmed people without a superimposed repressive disorder; the next smaller group consists of individuals with a repressive disorder; and by far the smallest group is comprised of psychopathic personalities who, of course, have little or no need to seek relief from alcohol since they suffer very little tension or anxiety.

Being familiar with the various types of disorders enables one to make sense out of a rather bewildering array of personality characteristics attributed to the alcoholic. Moreover, insights based upon this classification complement the A.A. approach to the disease of alcoholism, pointing out the need not to treat all alcoholics according to the same principles, except, of course, those pertaining to alcoholics as human beings with a common addiction. Beyond the A.A. approach which represents a combination of *will training* and a certain degree of mutual support, alcoholics require specific psychotherapeutic treatment if they are to enjoy lasting sobriety. Interestingly, the distrust, if not complete rejection, by many A.A. members of psychoanalytic therapy for alcoholics finds its justification in our understanding of the different types of neurotic disorders. If our opinion is correct that psychoanalysis is indicated only in people with a hysterical neurosis, who constitute a very small percentage of persons with repressive disorders, and, of course, an even smaller percentage of all people with neurotic disorders, it follows that only a very small number of alcoholics could be expected to benefit from this type of psychiatric treatment.

The unaffirmed alcoholic with Emotional Deprivation Disorder needs, in addition to active membership in A.A., one kind of psychotherapy; the alcoholic with a repressive disorder another. Some alcoholics require a combination of both A.A. membership and psychotherapy while the non-emotionally disturbed alcoholic requires only the straight A.A. involvement directed at total abstinence. The psychopathic alcoholic, of course, will rarely benefit from any form of treatment for a prolonged period of time (pp. 195-197).

The problem of non-affirmation and Emotional Deprivation Disorder is also a very real one among priests and, for that matter, among religious. The most severe states begin to develop in early life because of a lack of affirmation by the mother. Somewhat less severe are those occurring in priests whose fathers failed to affirm them during puberty and adolescence. Not infrequently their condition seems to improve during the seminary years if they are fortunate to live among professors and older priests capable of affirming them. The most critical period, however, follows ordination, as the non-affirmed priest is no longer the center of concerned educators and in his new assignment is usually dependent for his needed affirmation on a far smaller number of people — his pastor, superior, and bishop. Unless their capacity to affirm is particularly great, the non-affirmed priest will seek it outside this circle, find relief for his growing tensions in alcohol, or compensate for them by attempts at self-affirmation.

Judging by my observations in private psychiatric practice, I believe that the lack of affirmation on the part of pastors, superiors, and bishops, for whatever reason, as well as failure to recognize existing emotional illness in candidates for the priesthood, have contributed significantly to the crisis in the priesthood during the past several years. Priests with intrapsychic emotional illness, such as scrupulosity and other types of obsessive-compulsive repression, usually realize that there is no special advantage in leaving the priesthood as far as their illness is concerned. Their chances for recovery depend less on their milieu than on the competence of their therapist.

However, the non-affirmed priest who is frustrated in his psychological needs, or, as can happen, denied even further in his relationships with older priests, pastors, bishops, and superiors (who fail him because they too were *trained* for the priesthood, rather than *educated* to be sensitive, wise, and loving priests), that priest senses that there may be hope for him outside the priesthood.

That he often seeks this in the company of a woman is no proof that his is a frustrated sexual need and certainly no cause to rescind the obligation to celibacy. On the contrary, the relatively high failure rate of ex-priest marriages strongly suggests the non-affirmative character of their frustrated psychological needs. After all, the sexual experience is easily provided in these marriages, but not the affirmative one. It takes a woman of great emotional and spiritual maturity to affirm the non-affirmed ex-priest or the one with Emotional Deprivation Disorder and to endure the early years of marriage in which the yet-to-mature husband is incapable of loving her as a woman wants to be loved. Not too long ago I read of a woman who took her ex-priest husband back to his bishop with the words, "You can have him back again; I thought I had married a man two years ago, not a boy!" Seen in this light, it is not difficult to imagine why a large proportion of marriages of ex-priests to divorcees, ex-religious, or much younger women are doomed to fail and bring suffering to both parties. It rarely is the result of sexual incompatibility!

The non-affirmed priest is incapable of affirming others, just as the similarly afflicted married man is prevented from affirming his wife and children. In this sense it must be considered a self perpetuating emotional illness in spite of all attempts at arresting it by self-affirmation. To quote again from *Healing the Unaffirmed*:

> Some unaffirmed people seek to affirm themselves in sexual promiscuity and the pursuit of various sensate pleasures. Others try to *impress* the world with their importance by amassing material riches, by *excessive striving* for achievement in work and community affairs, or through the acquisition of status symbols ranging from cars to academic degrees. Some *seek power* over others in politics, or become aggressive, even homicidal, toward their fellow human beings, but all attempts at self-affirmation are futile.[2] Even attempts to escape from the psychic prison of non-affirmation by mind-altering drugs are doomed to fail. Self-affirmation, we believe, is one of the major factors contributing to the increasing unrest in the world, especially in our sensate occidental culture in which people rush headlong from one pleasure to the next without ever finding tranquility and peace. Only other human beings, not things or symbols, can unlock this prison, can disclose a person's goodness to him or her. Unaffirmed individuals, who doubt their self-worth and do not know who or what they

---

[2] Wholesome self-affirmation is possible only for the person whose emotional, intellectual, and spiritual integration is already well on its way to completion. See *Born Only Once* by Conrad W. Baars (*Born Only Once: The Miracle of Affirmation*. 1975, 1989. Preface by Suzanne M. Baars. Quincy, IL: Franciscan Press, Quincy University, 2001, pp. 76-80).

are, try to hide this from others by wearing a mask and playing a role. Many become expert at *pretending* to be what they are not. The more energy they spend in this way, the more fatigued they become, the more they isolate themselves from others and also from themselves.

Only when unaffirmed people are unselfishly loved by another will they dare to lower their mask little by little, to play their role less rigidly in the realization that they are allowed to be who they really are; in this way they will find new strength and energy, will breathe more easily in the enlarging psychic sphere they share with the other, and thus will find *joy in living.* Without the loving other, life has little significance for unaffirmed persons locked within themselves, and they can mean but little to others. The suffering of the unaffirmed person was well described by Jean-Paul Sartre, himself without a father and raised as an only child by a childlike mother, when he wrote, *My loneliness is my prison, my punishment for a crime I am not aware of* (pp. 192-193).

In my opinion, the Catholic Church is faced with a unique task and challenge of the utmost urgency. Always a champion of volitional love, she will need to teach in word and example the equal significance of emotional love — and the other emotions as well — for the human person's spiritual life. Familiar with the psychological aspects of mature authority, aimed as it is at the fulfillment of each subject as a unique human being, she will stimulate mature obedience eager to listen to and find strength in the goodness of the person in authority, the author or *auctor,* the originator or creator of something or someone. She faces the challenge of being truly a Church worthy of the name

"Mother," of having a hierarchy whose every member — bishop, superior, pastor, and priest — is worthy of the name "Father." Both Mother and Father because they love, not in the saccharine ways proclaimed by the love and peace banners surrounding the altars, but in the way of Christ — who turned the other cheek in love only once, on the cross, after having resisted evil with all the faculties of His perfect human nature, including hate and anger — and in the spirit of Ecclesiastes 3:8: "There is a time for loving, a time for hating; a time for war, a time for peace."

The image of a priest affirming God and Church through his fortitude to proclaim the message of the Gospel and uphold encyclical teachings, simultaneously affirming his people through his sympathetic understanding of human failures and with enlightened sensitivity helping them in their growth toward the maturity needed to obey in love Christ's word, such an image will constitute an irresistible attraction for young men to serve humanity in the noblest vocation of all — the priesthood.

CHAPTER XII

Anger and Forgiveness

I. THE HEALTHY USE OF ANGER

Introduction

Anger can be lifesaving. I experienced the lifesaving power of anger when I was captured by the Nazis and spent two years in the concentration camp of Buchenwald. I was in the French underground and was caught helping downed Allied flyers to escape. Of a thousand prisoners sent to Buchenwald with me, only six survived the ordeal. I attribute my survival partly to anger.

Let me explain. As a physician, I was put in the camp "hospital," which was not much more than a place for the mistreated and malnourished prisoners to die. My constant anger at the Nazis for their inhuman treatment of the prisoners and for robbing me of my freedom stimulated my determination to survive and deny the Nazis the satisfaction of defeating me in death. Many of the prisoners died from what were relatively minor infections. When they gave up hope, when they lost their will to fight, then their resistance and immunity were also down. It was difficult for me to continuously restrain all outward show of anger, even though to manifest anger to the guards would have meant certain death. This tension was so great that in my last year there I suffered several myocardial infarctions. My anger would not have been enough to keep me alive. God in His mercy saved me before I was broken: we were liberated from Buchenwald by the Third Army under General Patton. In my two years of prison, I experienced a deepening faith in God and a hunger for Christ in the Eucharist — which we received very rarely and in secret. It was faith and hope in God, a desire for freedom, and my anger at the Nazis, which kept me alive.

In another Nazi camp there was a priest who is now a canonized saint, Maximilian Kolbe, who, though he was surely angry at the evils the Nazis were doing, not only forgave his persecutors but also lovingly sacrificed himself to save another prisoner. I was an angry young man, and I had yet to learn how to forgive my enemies. I had yet to learn that anger is not enough. Both anger and the spiritual powers of mercy and forgiveness are necessary for a truly Christian response to evil, as I will explain.

When we are suffering we may be tempted to feel anger toward God. Sometimes we may feel angry at God because of what we think God is doing to us or to our loved ones, or because God does not remove our enemies. If we were to really know what God is doing, however, then we would never become angry at Him. If we could really understand His Providence and Plan, if we could see things as God sees them, then we would not become angry at God. Such a vision is not easily attained in this life, however, because of our limited intellect and imperfect love, so in our weakness we misdirect our anger to God against whom we rebel — instead of trusting in His care and obeying His Will. We need to discern the difference between healthy anger and a spirit of rebellion against God. People who are angry at the evil and suffering in the world sometimes let this turn into a revolt against God, or even a denial of God's existence. I will not address all of these spiritual matters, but will direct my reflections to the healthy use of anger, to the unhealthy responses to anger, and to the ultimate response to the evils done to us: forgiveness.

The Proper Role of Anger

God created human beings not only with a fundamental drive to procreation, but also with a fundamental drive to self-realization and self-defense. There is a common notion today that humans have an aggressive drive that makes them attack without provocation — but this is not true. Humans do have an *assertive* drive. Assertive means to be confident, to maintain and defend, to put oneself forward boldly and insistently. In scholastic philosophy, the emotions of the assertive drive (also known as the *utilitarian emotions*) were named the irascible passions — from the Latin *ira* for anger. Derivative English words are irate and irritate. Anger is one of the emotions which serves our assertive drive. When obstacles are placed in the way of our self-realization, we become angry. When this anger is properly used under the guidance of reason and will, it can make our lives more pleasant, successful and safe. Anger can be a tremendous stimulant to move us to overcome great obstacles. Anger can give us determination and endurance in the face of difficulties. As I have said above, anger can be lifesaving.

Although psychiatry and psychology have said helpful things about the role of anger, these professions also may have caused misconceptions about anger, and thus may have kept people from using anger to the best advantage of persons and society. Therapeutic directives to "get angry" and programs of assertiveness training often result in the repression of fear or the promotion of a selfish self-affirmation. Sometimes professionals have not taught the distinction between *feeling* the emotion of anger and subsequent *behavioral expressions* of anger. Sometimes they have not taught the difference between the neurotic repression of anger and its rational direction. Furthermore, there has been an indiscriminate use of the word anger in association with terms like aggression, hostility, and immaturity.

That we fail to appreciate the goodness of anger is betrayed by our euphemisms for anger. We speak of anger as permissible only when it becomes "justifiable wrath." The nonsense of speaking about an emotion in this way can be grasped by comparing it to the expression "a justifiable arm." Every part of our nature, emotions included, is a God-given good; no part of our nature needs to be justified. What we need to do is recognize its natural function. Sometimes we say someone is "touchy" — by which we criticize the other for being sensitive to injury — and thus we deny the goodness of that person's anger. We speak of "losing our temper," but do we ever speak of "temper" as good? Additionally, we seem to say "exasperated" (a loss of hope for improvement in the other; an impatience with the other), rather than to simply say "angered." The words "huffy" and "upset" are often used by those who view themselves as having "hurt feelings." When we have such attitudes toward anger, our anger can be stifled and turn into resentment and even revenge. Resentment is more of an inner feeling due to a real or fancied personal affront; revenge is more of an outward expression of a grudge.

The human emotion of anger is misunderstood, maligned and condemned, as well as mishandled, repressed, distorted or twisted. One misconception is that any show of anger is equivalent to loss of control. Yet anger is rarely uncontrollable; if it is, it is probably the result of repression or personality disorder.[1] A

---

[1]   Editors' Note: The original text read "psychopathic personality," a term which is no longer used for diagnostic purposes. Please consult *Feeling and Healing Your Emotions* by Conrad W. Baars, M.D. (Rev. ed. Suzanne M. Baars and Bonnie N.

loss of control is suggested by the term "mad," by which anger is confused with madness (insanity). Yet to feel anger and to express it healthily is the antithesis of madness. Other mistaken ideas about anger are: one must get rid of anger because it is evil, a sin and a sign of immaturity; anger is destructive and hurts people's feelings; anger is a privilege of people in authority; nothing good comes of anger; and one blows off steam in order to get rid of anger.

The truth is that anger serves the God-given purpose of arousing me to do something in response to an injury and its perpetrator. This psychological arousal is always accompanied by a variety of physiological reactions in my body, internal as well as external ones, which prepare and enable my body to fully participate in whatever action I choose. Whatever action I decide to take will be prompted primarily by my concern for my own wellbeing, and also that of my loved ones, and will generally consist of an attempt to protect myself from further injury, or to seek restitution for the wrong already inflicted upon me. Of course, as a Christian, I will also be mindful of the ultimate goal of reconciliation. In making my decision, my intellect has to play the most important role, for it should be my reason, not my anger, which decides what to do in this or that situation.

The proper function of anger as a God-given emotion is to energize us, to arouse us to overcome obstacles to our survival and obtain basic human goods; to defend against and throw off an evil directed either at oneself or a loved one, or to one's community or beliefs; and to demand restitution as a means of restoring the order which is required for justice.

Shayne, eds., Gainesville, FL: Bridge-Logos, 2003) and *Psychic Wholeness and Healing: Using All the Powers of the Human Psyche* by Anna A. Terruwe, M.D. and Conrad W. Baars, M.D. (Staten Island, NY: Alba House, 1981) for a more complete understanding and explanation of this term.

Anger is a basic emotion of what may be called our "assertive drive," a warning bell built into our nature which is stimulated by a threat to our well-being. It can be stimulated by hunger or frustration, injury or pain, criticism or insult, physical or moral blows, or by obstacles and threats. Anger may be better understood by distinguishing it from fear. Anger is experienced as a tendency to fight or to strike back, with a feeling of increased strength (or of tears during a tantrum). Fear, on the other hand, is experienced as cowering or a tendency to flee, with feelings of pallor, flushing, and weakness.

The emotion of anger is simply the motor, the "psychic" or "psychological motor," that energizes us to do in a given situation what seems to be the most reasonable and effective way to deal with the wrongdoer. Human reason may be compared to the driver of a car whose motor or engine constitutes its driving force. If the car is driven recklessly and irresponsibly, it is the driver, not the motor, who is to blame. It is the person who has not learned the proper use of anger or chooses not to act responsibly when angry who is to blame. If the person has not been given opportunities during his or her growing years to learn responsible ways of behavior when angered by others, then, if anyone should be blamed, it should be the parents and educators who failed to teach that person about the appropriate use of anger.

When somebody causes me a bodily injury, I feel the pain of hurt. When I am offended, insulted, betrayed, taken advantage of, done an injustice, or wronged in some other way, I experience a psychological injury. In an emotionally mature person, these hurts are followed by a feeling of anger, annoyance or irritation. These emotions are aroused by our perceptions and thoughts about the various aspects of the injury inflicted on us, for instance, the particular reason why somebody has hurt us, our discovery of who this person is, or the extent and severity of the hurt and its consequences to our health, good name, reputation, and so on. For example, when someone steps on my toes, and I realize that it was a stranger who did it accidentally, I'll probably only feel a slight annoyance. However, when it is evident to me that the stranger did it on purpose, for whatever reason, I will feel very irritated. Or, in another case, when I am betrayed and discover that it is my best friend who betrayed me, I will experience intense anger. These are normal, healthy emotional reactions that every emotionally mature person will experience when injured.

Thus anger functions to protect us: it is a warning bell through the bodily changes it stimulates; it prompts our estimative power and mind to evaluate the cause and degree of threatening evil; it prompts our power of memory to compare the present with previous situations and the outcomes of our reactions in the past. So informed and motivated, our will can now choose to respond by direct action, postponement of action, or no action. We then express through our anger a behavior best suited to the circumstances: a response that can either be appropriate or inappropriate, calm or excited, verbal or nonverbal, effective or ineffective, mature or immature.

A Christian Learns About Anger

Responses to anger are learned in childhood at home and school through approval or disapproval, observation of the actions of others, and the results of one's own expressions of anger. In an ideal environment, all the emotions are accepted as having their proper role; there are no "good" or "bad" emotions. In a healthy environment, there is the freedom to feel and express feelings in increasingly constructive and mature ways. One can be honest about one's feelings. There is no pressure to stifle any emotion in order to please others. There is no climate of fear of the emotions. In a healthy home and school the adults lead children to the appropriate use of anger.

Mistaken attitudes and practices are learned from the parents' example of sinful expressions of anger, the improper use of anger, and attempts to stifle anger. Some parents withhold love and approval of the angry child. Some spank the child for having a temper tantrum — for visibly showing the frustration and anger he or she feels for being punished or not getting his or her way. For example, the little boy who is yelling and pounding on the floor does no harm to himself or the house by the tantrum; eventually he quiets down if he is ignored and his attempt to scare his parents gets him nowhere. If he is punished for the tantrum, however, for a display of his angry feelings, and made to feel guilty and ashamed for feeling angry, then he first learns to repress the outward show of feeling and eventually the feeling itself. This will spread to all his emotions in time. Some parents forbid anger by telling a child who reveals anger in facial expressions and tone of voice that the child has "lost his temper" and has "no self-control." This is tantamount to demanding that the child repress the feeling itself. It expects from the child a premature, adult degree of control in the use of anger. Yet, just as our physical muscles require many years of exercise to become coordinated, so too do our emotions, which can only grow gradually.

The proper development of our assertive drive with its emotion of anger requires guidance and exercise in childhood and youth. When our assertive drive has been allowed to grow under the guidance of reason and will, then we can become capable of a freely chosen surrender to God and healthy interpersonal surrender. Therefore, in teaching obedience, parents should not interfere with the natural development of this drive or try to break the child's assertiveness; if they do, the child might become servile or rebellious. When a person learns to properly use anger, however, it is a wonderful instrument for the perfection of human nature and virtue. In fact, our capacity for anger should be fully developed for the ultimate purpose of enabling us to become genuinely meek — like Christ. Meekness channels the power of wrath in order to serve the good. All of our emotions should be allowed to develop, for when they become integrated under our spiritual faculties, we are more capable of living up to Christian ideals.

Anger used in the service of Christian living can be an expression of love. When we let another person see our anger, it means that we care enough about that person to reveal how we feel. It means that we feel sure in our relationship with the other person, for we are not afraid that being angry will destroy the friendship. It means that we want to improve the relationship by helping the other to improve how he or she treats us. It means that we as their parent or teacher, friend or pastor, care enough to point out how their vice will deform their character if it is not opposed. The example of Jesus in this regard is most instructive. In Matthew 16:23, we read how Jesus got angry at St. Peter for judging by human standards, when Jesus pointed out to Peter — who needed to be strengthened in his spiritual judgment — that he must learn to evaluate all things, including the cross, in the way God judges them. We should also note here that Jesus had emotionally affirmed Peter in many ways before intellectually affirming him through this correction in the form of teaching him about the value of the cross.

In teaching children a Christian attitude toward anger, our instruction should first be based on a sound exegesis of Holy Scripture. Josef Pieper reminds us (in his essay on Fortitude) of a *principle of exegesis* from St. Thomas Aquinas (following St. Augustine): *we should interpret the words of Jesus in the context of Jesus' actions.* Thus, when we read in Matthew 5:39 that if we are injured we should "turn the other cheek," this should be taken in light of how Jesus himself acted. When Jesus was struck on the face during his trial, he did not turn the other cheek, but he challenged the soldier (John 18:23). St. Paul likewise responded assertively when he was struck on several occasions (Acts 23:3). In this way we teach children that the imitation of Christ and the Saints means an assertive effort to resist evil and rectify wrongs, but also to endure those evils we cannot change. We teach them that even suffering injustice is redemptive if it is united to Jesus on the Cross — who forgave His enemies as He died. The children thus learn not servility, but true Christian meekness: the power of wrath moderated to serve the good and oppose the evil — as God declares in Isaiah 63:5, "… my own wrath lent me its support."

Second, parents and religious educators should explain the role of anger as serving our defense of the good. Emotions are sources of (principles of) moral action, and participate in the moral value of an act. To oppose evil with wrath is more effective than a mere intellectual attack. In this context, Pieper cites St. Gregory, who writes that "Justice ministers more effectively with anger at her side." When the emotions, including anger and hate, are seen as integral parts of virtuous acts, instead of as enemies, the whole process of growing in holiness is less painful and frustrating, and more fruitful and rewarding. Parents cause the child to repress anger when they train the child to stifle all annoyance and irritation, with the mistaken idea that the feeling of anger is a capital sin and unchristian. If we cripple the child by stifling the development of his or her use of anger, then how will the child be able to oppose evil effectively as an adult? Does not the historic repression of anger by Christians explain the inability of so many Christians to be angry at the evil of abortion and strenuously oppose it?

Third, parents and teachers should make the child's *be-*

havior (actions and words) the object of moral evaluation — not the child's *feelings*. They should make a distinction between the feeling of anger itself and the behaviors that have followed, in word or deed. This is in accord with Ephesians 4:26: "If you are angry, let it be without sin." One does not commit the capital sin of anger simply by feeling angry. A sin which is not in word or deed, but only in thought, may be explained to children when they are older. A young child can confuse sinful thoughts with the feeling of anger. Parents and teachers should always make it clear to the child that it is OK to feel angry, that they understand the child's feelings, and that they too would feel angry in his or her situation, but also that they do not approve or tolerate when in anger the child throws food, breaks another's toy, or damages the house or furniture. The child has to make up for such bad behaviors; for such action he or she can be punished. Sometimes the parents will want to affirm the child's manner of acting-with-feeling: "that was a wonderful way of expressing your anger; it really helped and was effective." Gradually the child learns that behavioral reactions to injury and anger depend on many factors, the chief ones being the guidance of reason and faith.

One of the reasons that I became an emotionally mature adult was the fact that during the first eighteen years of my life I was fortunate to have parents and educators who allowed and helped me to learn what were effective and ineffective ways of expressing my anger. I learned this by trial and error, by trial and success, by being punished or praised and by observation of other people. As a consequence, now that I am an adult, I possess a storehouse of remembered experiences which help me to decide quickly upon a course of action that is likely to prove effective in having the wrongdoer make up for the injury he or she has caused me. If and when I get a satisfactory response from that person, my anger will subside, and its accompanying physiological reactions in my body will return to normal. All will be well, because my anger, under the guidance of reason and assisted by many years of experience in dealing with persons who have injured me, has served me well. I have been able to deal successfully with a threat or harm to my health, my peace of mind, my honor, my self-esteem, my good name, or whatever I hold dear and consider a good for myself and those I love.

The mature person thus has learned that there are infinite ways of expressing anger. One draws upon experience, memory, and creative imagination to find the most effective way in which anger may try to obtain a satisfactory response from the wrongdoer. The effective response will be quite different from situation to situation. In any anger-provoking situation, the mature person is able to choose from an unlimited number of possible responses — unique responses because each situation is different and calls for a different response. One can never expect to obtain satisfaction by routinely employing the same stereotyped tactic in every situation. The variety of responses range from the most primitive ones (and usually most ineffective ones) like screaming, swearing and physical abuse, to a mature and dignified reaction which leaves the wrongdoer no choice but to apologize and make restitution.

One of the mature responses may be to make no show of anger: to be silent. A mature person who has been injured and feels angry can decide to remain silent for two basic reasons: first, because reason or common sense tells that person that any action other than silence on his or her part is likely to make matters worse. For instance, if your employer is in a foul mood and offends you, it would be unwise for you in your anger to confront the employer then and there. If the boss will fire you for expressing any feelings, then the effective and reasonable way to respond is to be silent — all the while internally accepting your anger. You are not afraid of your anger, but you realize that to express it would risk losing your job that you need for a livelihood. You feel no guilt for being angry, and you will wait for an opportunity to find a way to clarify the issue with the boss so it can be corrected. In this you have given rational guidance to your anger. You have remained silent, but you have not repressed your anger. Your aim was to be moved by your anger to do what was effective and acceptable in that particular situation without being offensive in a way that would risk your job.

Second, one can choose to remain silent for higher motives, higher than those which play a role in the various ordinary situations, such as the one mentioned above. For example, a mature person may want to grow in the virtue of humility or meekness, and for these spiritual reasons chooses in a given instance to remain silent and suffer the injustice or whatever injury has been inflicted upon him. Another person may do the same for the sake of the good of his family, or of the community in which he lives. With his silence he does not seek peace at all costs. He is silent because he has learned from earlier experiences with certain members of the community, when he applied the general principles for showing anger, that it is futile with these members to try and obtain justice.

It should be evident that silence for the sake of higher spiritual motives and silence for the good of the community requires an emotionally mature and integrated person, that is, a person who has the well-developed capacity to confront his or her wrongdoer when angry according to the principles set forth above. When such a person decides to remain silent, it is not out of fear, cowardice, or an emotional affliction. This person withholds the outward expressions of anger without interfering with the emotion itself. In this way, the person provides the emotion of anger, and for that matter every emotion, with the very thing it needs and desires: namely, rational guidance. It is precisely because the emotion of anger is guided respectfully and without doing it violence in the decision to remain silent that the feeling will subside and thus allow the person to live in peace, without tension or resentment.

The examples we have given illustrate how emotionally mature persons of good will react when their feelings of anger are aroused by a wrong done to them. The fact that I, as a mature and integrated adult, feel at ease with my emotion of anger — not afraid or guilty — enables my intellect to fully face the task at hand: to obtain justice by deciding upon an effective response to the wrongdoer.

II. UNHEALTHY RESPONSES TO ANGER

The Pseudo-Christian Attitude Toward Anger

Persons who are not comfortable with their feelings of anger — who use much of their psychological energy to stifle the motor of their anger — are handicapped in trying to come up with a reasonable and effective way to deal with a wrong-doer. Their courage to act accordingly is diminished. Actually, most of these handicapped people do not see their anger as a call to obtain justice by dealing with the wrongdoer in the most effective way. Rather, they see their anger as a threat to their pseudo-Christian ideal of never hurting people's feelings; a threat to the external peace they want to preserve at any price, even at the cost of lacking inner peace and calm; a threat to their need to be true to mistaken childhood teachings about the sinfulness of anger; a threat to their need to be liked and loved by everyone; or a threat that risks repeating personal experiences which made them fear angry people.

People handicapped by an inadequate use of anger will be ineffective and immature and resort to childish temper tantrums or adolescent violence. They might slam the door, which often is not very effective because when each party is on the other side of a closed door they cannot resolve their problem. There are those who curse and act with a fury that makes the situation worse. Such persons seem to derive a kind of perverse pleasure from holding on to their feelings of resentment and bitterness, and are likely to seek revenge. There are people who stifle anger and then displace it elsewhere, transferring it by taking it out on persons other than the wrongdoer. I shift my anger to the least threatening person or situation: the boss is mean to me and I take it out on my wife and children. I am nice at the wrong time, and angry at the wrong time. When this is chronic it destroys relationships.

Persons not comfortable with their emotion of anger, who feel guilty for feeling angry, or are in the habit of suppressing this emotion for fear of hurting the feelings of the person who hurt them — feel only hurt, not angry. We will see that these persons who are stuck, so to speak, in the hurt phase, who cannot do anything but feel hurt, are handicapped in a way that not even forgiving the wrongdoer can remedy. Such persons have not been allowed to accept and integrate their anger under the guidance of reason and will, and so they find it hard to express and control it in situations. They often stifle anger until it builds up so much tension that from time to time it explodes in an angry outburst, usually at the most inappropriate time or when something small sets off the already great tension of weeks and months and years of repression. Of course, such persons have a lesser degree of guilt for their faulty behavior than would mature persons who are integrated and in control and who are therefore held responsible for all that they do with their anger.

Factors which cause interference of the normal course of anger are: an attitude that "civilized persons don't get angry";

a fear of feelings and of expressing emotions; distinguishing emotions into acceptable and unacceptable emotions; affective shallowness — no deep, rich, intense and vital emotional life; a tendency to feel one way but act another (smiling sweetly while hating); a habit of withdrawing love when faced with anger (you hurt my feelings); an attitude of "you don't get anywhere by being angry"; and an unhealthy home environment where parental roles are reversed, with a passive father and a domineering mother.

Persons with *Emotional Deprivation Disorder* cannot allow anger to take its normal course because they have a pathological need to be universally liked, to be nice all the time, to want peace at any price, and to avoid making waves or hurting feelings. They are likely to do nothing, or to try to forget the hurtful episode. The tragedy of this approach is that it doesn't work.

Self-affirming persons have no time for anger. They mind their own business and attend to their ambitions. They are "cool" and don't get involved in emotional and personal relations, for this would involve caring about others.

Persons with an *energy-based repressive disorder* have need for control and mastery; they use anger in a dishonest way, or use it to control, manipulate and bully people, or for vindictiveness.

There are those who *suppress* anger. Persons who suppress anger are stifling it on a conscious level, for motives such as fear, or for ideas such as a faulty notion of Christian virtue. They may also have a vested interest in not showing anger. One hears from them: "So I'm angry; that doesn't mean I have to give into it"; "I just control it — I forget about it"; "So I'm a little irritated, I'll take a drink and forget about it" — and the tension increases.

There are persons who have been trained since childhood to *repress* anger in an automatic, conditioned and subconscious way. This insidious and malignant repression spreads and deepens in their emotional dimension. One hears such persons saying, "Me, I just never get angry," "I can't be bothered," and "I could care less."

There is a *combination of suppression and repression*, whereby persons delay their response to situations, hoping the anger will go away. They put off decisions, responsibility, and problems, because they want to wait until it is safe to feel and express and act: "I can never think of what to say when I'm angry — until later, and then it's too late," "When I think about it now, it really gets me angry," "I didn't feel angry when it happened, and I still don't, but I have this terrible headache."

Anger may be *rationalized* — a mechanism by which we act in response to unrecognized motives, then afterward we offer various supposed "reasons" for our conduct. One who rationalizes why he or she can't be or act angry might say: "civilized people don't get angry"; "It isn't Christian"; "One must turn the other cheek"; "Anger is disrespectful"; or, "Only fools get angry."

General Consequences of Repression of Anger

All of the above processes, usually combined, harm not only anger but also interfere with the normal course of the other emotions, including love. God made human nature in such a way that persons cannot pick and choose and say, "I like this emotion," and "I don't like that one." Or, "I'm going to use some emotions, but not that one." If people try to do that, the emotions they approve of will suffer in the process of suppressing or repressing the emotions they forbid.

The repressive process shuts down our psychological motors — our emotions — and cripples us, just like the physical motors of our body — our muscles — can be paralyzed. The consequence of repressing anger is that we adversely affect our whole emotional life. The other emotions are submerged, deadened, anesthetized. This state of being kills our spontaneity and sensitivity, our creativity and our very self-identity and human relatedness. We also become tense and restless, due to the fact that the repressed emotions cannot be guided by reason because they are *buried alive* — out of reach of reason. So I won't be able to sit still; I'll have to be on the move. I'll try to be busy all the time in order to be distracted from my true state of being. Anxiety and even panic states may result. Physical symptoms and psychosomatic disorders may develop. The increase in tension will usually seek relief in drugs or alcohol, or hopefully, in a beneficial therapy.

Particular Consequences of Repression of Anger

1. Depression

It is depressing to be a doormat — an unassertive person — whom people walk all over. When you do not assert yourself, you cannot make others respect or obey you, and you must always give in. You are exploited. You realize what you are doing, and hate yourself for it. Persons who hate themselves or consider themselves unlovable may even try to punish themselves for being unlovable, so they become accident-prone, fail in their job, or resort to drugs or alcohol.

When you do not use your anger to make life better, to protect yourself from unpleasant, harmful, or painful situations; when you cannot help other people treat you better; when you do not develop real friends, because repressing anger interferes with your relating to others; when for whatever reason you do not use your anger, then life becomes miserable and one even considers escaping this by attempting suicide.

2. Eating Disorders

Perhaps the next most common consequence of avoiding anger is to overeat. If people are not nice to you — because they know they can take advantage of your lack of assertiveness — what is easier than to go to the refrigerator and be nice to yourself? The opposite is true as well: you can starve yourself under the same circumstances, a form of suicidal self-punishment whereby you refuse to eat and become anorexic.

3. Sleep Disorders

Repressing anger can lead to difficulty in falling asleep or to fitful sleep. If you are irritated many times during the day and you don't do anything about it, then lying in bed at night is the ideal time to re-live and go over the situations and wish and think of what you would like to have done or said, if you had dared to. Then you become so angry that you imagine all the terrible things you would like to do to the wrongdoer. One may also indulge in too much sleeping as a form of escape.

4. Obsessions

Some people develop obsessions of killing and injuring others, often the ones they love most, such as their children. A mother who suffers this symptom will think she is going insane because of her obsession with killing the children. She will remove all of the knives from the house. There is no reason for her to want to hurt the children; they are normal and lovable — but the obsession may be occurring because the woman cannot handle her anger toward her husband. Once she learns to be angry, her fears disappear by themselves.

5. Fear of Losing Control and Phobias

People who are afraid of feeling angry often like to be in control of situations so they can arrange everything as much as possible in such a way that there will not be any irritating things that arise. They must be prepared for any eventuality in order to avoid the unexpected: so they won't have to get angry; so they won't have to make a "fool" of themselves. This fear of being made a "fool" — should they be caught off guard and expose their immature use of anger or inability to be angry — is likely to be found in persons raised without objective morality and ruled by subjective human respect — fear of what others think.

A variety of phobias are connected with the need to be in control. For example, a man with a phobia of flying or riding in cars may be fine as long as he is flying the plane or driving the car, but if he has to be the passenger, then he is phobic. Or, he may have a phobia of sitting in the barber's chair, where he has no control.

6. Psychosomatic Disorders

Psychosomatic disorders are real illnesses, not imagined ones, chronically disturbing any organ or system of the body. Every emotion is accompanied by physiological changes in the body. For instance, in fear there is a secretion of hydrochloric acid in the stomach. If the source of the fear is removed, the secretion stops. If you are chronically fearful because you cannot be angry and dare not deal with the causes of the fear, however, the physiological effects occur continuously day and night, so that the secreted acid eventually burns an ulcer in the stomach.

High blood pressure, myocardial infarction, strokes, ulcer and colitis, skin disorders and psoriasis, migraine, and backache are all common consequences of chronically repressed anger.

Bronchial asthma may develop early in the life of a child who senses that to be angry is not acceptable to his or her parents, so the child expresses tension in an asthmatic attack. Such a child can be helped if circumstances are favorable, but it requires that the therapist make the child angry, for when the child is angry the asthmatic attacks stop because the anger produces adrenalin which is otherwise obtained as medicine during the former asthmatic attacks. Psychogenic asthma may often be relieved when the child is able to weep with rage.

Once a man came to me who had been diagnosed elsewhere as lazy and a malingerer because physical examinations showed there was nothing wrong with him, although he complained of paralyzing back pain. He was bigger and stronger than I am, yet unable to work. He wanted to work and needed to for a living, but his backaches were severe from the moment he woke until he went to sleep. One morning he came in and told me that for three hours that day he had been free of backache — the first time in a long time. During the night he dreamt of his mother and for the first time in his life — even in a dream — he dared to express his anger at her. This of course is what brought relief the next day. The somatic consequences of his anger went away for a while, but they came back because in his conscious state he felt very fearful and guilty for feeling angry at his mother.

As long as repression succeeds, these persons may not suffer any disturbing consequences — but they will be full of resentment and complaints about others who have injured them. They are never angry; only "upset." If they are alcoholics, they may use Alcoholics Anonymous as a means to control their main symptom of repression — drinking. Thus they misuse A.A. to continue to repress their anger.

Learning To Be Assertive and To Use Anger

What can we do when we are so unfortunate as to have become emotionally crippled as a result of faulty "training" and circumstances in our early life whereby we repressed our anger, or when we are in so much need of being loved by others that we dare not assert ourselves? How can we change this state of being?

The first thing is to know the truth, which is that God created our emotions, they are good, and they are meant to be integrated under the guidance of reason and will. This order, however, has suffered a degree of disintegration due to original sin, whose effects have touched everyone's person.

If one of the effects of this disordering is that you have not learned how to use anger, then the second thing to do is discover how this has happened in your life. If it is a case of repression of anger, healing may not necessarily require long-term and expensive psychoanalysis. The cause of repression was probably the general atmosphere in your home, perhaps aggravated by a few traumatic incidents. If it is necessary for healing that you identify the particular episodes in life that have caused or contributed to your repression of anger, then this knowledge will emerge in time in good therapy without probing on the part of the therapist.

Third, you must gradually begin to accept your feeling of anger without doing anything about it, without yet expressing it. Internally, you use every opportunity, when you feel irritated or annoyed, to reassure yourself repeatedly that it is good and permitted to feel the anger. You say to yourself, "I may feel angry," "Thank God I'm feeling angry." Just leave it at that for a time — just internally receive the anger. Don't make the mistake of an "assertiveness training" program which expects instant emotional growth and change, and which relies on an energetic repression of your fear of being angry. By internally receiving your anger for a time, you gradually lose the conditioned reaction of "anger is bad," and "I must not have feelings of anger." The opposite directive is followed: "I welcome my anger," "I'm beginning to grow now as a result of feeling anger." When you are alone, practice expressing your anger — on audio or video tape — and while driving in the car and annoyed by other motorists. Remember that it is not so much a method for being angry that you need, but to change your attitude to one of "my anger is good." When this stage of receiving anger has gone on internally for a time — and this may take weeks or months depending on how alert you are to irritating situations so you can practice it — only then gradually start the fourth step, which is to attempt to express anger outwardly to others.

Learning to be assertive by using your anger is not really a matter of learning to "express your anger;" rather, it is learning to do something effective when you are moved by anger. That "something" is whatever is most likely to be effective in removing the source of the anger.

If you are resolved to go through the process of learning to be angry and assertive, then you should be prepared to be very startled when you first hear yourself cuss someone out, or use an uncharitable expression in your anger. In general, be honest with all of your feelings. Don't wear a mask. Let your features and gestures show what you feel. Learn to talk with feeling. As much as possible, express yourself with feeling. This may mean that at times you will start speaking before you think.

Learning to use one's anger in a mature way means that you have to start living dangerously. It feels dangerous to change from a "safe" way of living. Start to risk living assertively; dare to differ with people. Sometimes it is necessary to do something drastic to get people's attention. I'm not saying be violent, but now you must start to listen to your angry feelings. You must begin to use them for your own good, for the good of the persons you love, and for the values you believe in and should stand up for and which you can now defend with feeling, not merely with words. Many people limit their disagreements and anger to just talking it out, but this has no effect because they argue only on the intellectual level. They may insist on calling it debating — but it is not presenting their feelings. This may be the case if you are a very intelligent person who has lived almost entirely on an intellectual level and have not given your emotions a chance. Now you will have to start speaking before thinking — but a lot of people do that anyway. You will have to think less and be more emotional.

In this learning process, you should expect to make mistakes. You will learn from them. You can say afterward, "That didn't work; I reacted in that way and look what happened." One must accept the mistakes and continue to experiment, learning by trial and error and trial and success, as to what ways are appropriate and effective.

It helps throughout this process to stop using the phrase, "My feelings were hurt." When you use this expression you create a mental image of yourself lying on the floor, bleeding and helpless. How inspiring for others to come to your aid. This is not helping you to learn to take care of yourself, however. When you say, "I feel so angry," then you imagine yourself standing up, even trembling with rage. Now you are alive and not bleeding to death. Now you are being assertive and doing something about the situation.

Your change in behavior will be felt most by those close to you. If you are smart, you can teach them to adjust to you and show them that your new way of living is healthier than the old way. Chances are you live in an environment where others have some of the same unhealthy attitudes about anger that have afflicted you. The ideal solution is to get everyone involved in the new and healthy way. If it is all up to one person who now has the insight to start living in an emotionally healthy way, and he or she must do so without help from others, it can be very difficult. However, if you know this is healthy, then as a Christian you have an obligation to find ways and means to make it possible to invite others to grow as well. Before you get that far, however, you already should have spent several months practicing using the anger on strangers.

Start with strangers because they are less threatening than the persons you are close to or have to live with and are most afraid of offending. This is not uncharitable advice; it is simply a fact that it will be easier within you and outside of you. The goal is to feel all your emotions and to be moved by truth, goodness and beauty. It means that you will also be moved by anger when the situation calls for it.

The goal of maturity is to feel all your emotions. Jesus felt deeply under all circumstances; He felt the intensity of love and joy, of hate and anger. He was fully integrated and in complete control of His feelings and their expression. In your full integration you will be able to imitate Christ, and say "Now I am fulfilled," "Now I am ready to die to self," "Now I can start to become truly meek and pass over this offense — not because I'm afraid of what the other person will think of me if I get angry, or because I'm afraid of my anger — but because I have now become really tolerant in a Christian way and not in a pseudo-Christian way of avoiding anger for my own convenience."

Pseudo-Christians find it convenient to be ready to forgive so that they may hide their anger. Premature forgiving is really pseudo-meekness. Such people quickly forgive the wrongdoer who has injured them, so they won't have to get angry, or so they won't have to be consciously aware of their anger. Whether they realize it or not, they do this because they think it is wrong to be angry, or are afraid of not being loved if they get angry at others.

They have never learned to respond to their feeling of anger in the manner and for the purpose that God made this emotion part of their nature. Instead, they were taught to repress and forgive the wrongdoer immediately, before they had a chance to be in touch with their angry feelings. Being of good-will they forced themselves to do what they were taught.

It is tragic that these persons, desiring to be Christ-like, must suffer doubly later in life. First they will suffer the psychological and somatic effects of repressing their anger. Second, they will discover sooner or later that, for them, to forgive and to forget is a myth. Their repressed anger will not allow them to forget the injustice done to them. They may hope their anger will go away, but that is nearly impossible. In fact, in their frustrating situation, the anger is likely to grow, to become resentment and bitterness. When this happens, these feelings will keep them preoccupied with the injury they sustained, cause them to re-live the injustice, and make them entertain thoughts of revenge. Moreover, these psychological effects resulting from their unresolved anger can be expected to interfere with daily work and duties, with recreation and even with sleep. No matter how hard they try to forget the whole unfortunate incident, it won't go away. Furthermore, as long as their anger remains alive, its accompanying physiological reactions will become permanent and develop into the aforementioned psychosomatic disorders: migraine, backache, ulcer, high blood pressure, heart attacks, etc.

Their premature forgiving may even cause them to doubt whether God Himself forgives and forgets. This threat to their faith can become a serious matter indeed, for anger has blocked the way to peace of heart.

The Ultimate Remedy is Forgiveness

How do we protect ourselves against these adverse effects of unresolved anger, when we have left nothing reasonable undone to obtain recompense for the injustice, even to the point of trying to effect a reconciliation? What happens when all of our reasonable reactions to the wrongdoer fail to obtain the hoped for satisfaction? There are only two choices left: to hold on to the anger, or to let go of it by forgiving the persons responsible for the injury. For the Christian the proper choice is to forgive the wrongdoer. Only the freely willed act of forgiving will set one free of bondage to the wrongdoer. The captivity of sin includes the chains of unresolved feelings of resentment and anger.

Our liberator, Jesus, must have had this in mind when He taught us to pray the Our Father. If we want to be forgiven by God and have His love flow into us, then we must first clear our channel of His love toward others by forgiving: "Be compassionate, as your Father is compassionate" (Luke 6:36). Jesus knew that all of us would find ourselves repeatedly in situations in which the purpose of our emotion of anger, namely of stimulating us to defend ourselves and our loved ones against any threat or actual harm, would be frustrated. He knew that in such situations we would suffer even more if we were not able or willing to forgive the wrongdoer.

Both physical and emotional illness in our lives may have been caused or aggravated by chronic anger and resentment. Frequently these illnesses resist all forms of therapy because our anger is a block to healing. These illnesses are not redemptive blessings which the Lord wants us to suffer; rather, they are signs that we are not redeemed, not whole, because we have not integrated our emotions and because we lack forgiveness. After we forgive, however, many healings do happen: "I give you my word, if you are ready to believe that you will receive whatever you ask for in prayer, it shall be done for you. When you stand to pray, forgive anyone against whom you have a grievance so that your heavenly Father may in turn forgive you your faults" (Mark 11:24-25).

It may be that we need to practice *self-forgiveness*. Carl Jung once noted that although we may be willing to forgive others, even for most heinous crimes; when it comes to ourselves, we can be unmerciful and unrelenting toward our own person in need of self-forgiveness.

Preparing To Forgive

As there are persons who do not know how to forgive, I will close with an instruction on the *manner of forgiveness* that culminates in an *act of forgiveness* which is a *prayer of forgiveness*.

First, a word of advice is in order. We must remember that *forgiveness takes time*; it should not be done prematurely. When sufficient time has passed for our initial rage to calm, when efforts to rectify the situation have failed, or when the other has offered an apology, then it may be the right moment to forgive. I have heard people accuse themselves of not having forgiven properly because they find that their feelings of anger and resentment continue to be felt after they have forgiven the injury. Because they expected these feelings to disappear when they forgave, they doubt their sincerity in forgiving. There is no need to accuse themselves of this, however. They do not realize that it always takes longer for these feelings to subside and disappear because these feelings do not know, so to speak, what has taken place on the intellectual and moral level. Therefore it is necessary to remind these emotions, any number of times, often for weeks or months, whenever they make themselves felt, that the person has indeed been forgiven. This is done in the second part of the prayer that follows, a part which you should repeat as often as necessary when the feelings of anger and resentment well up in you.

Thus the manner of forgiveness includes the gradual process over time of having accepted one's anger in an interior way, and sometimes having expressed it outwardly in appropriate and effective ways. These precede the act of forgiveness in usual circumstances, although in the saints who have achieved a perfect harmony of feelings and will, anger and forgiveness may occur together within the first response to injury. There is no denial, suppression or repression of anger in this case; rather, the sequence of response is fully integrated. As we grow toward that virtuous harmony, the experience of an injury will be followed by a period of time during which anger is fully felt. There comes a time when we realize that the ultimate remedy for the situation is to forgive — not to seek revenge. We accept that in this life there is no perfect justice and that mercy is the way to reconciliation and peace. We realize that in some cases the person is sorry for the wrong they did to us, but in other cases they may not regret it or apologize to us for it. In either case, we need to be released from unyielding anger which can grow into resentment and hatred.

For this liberation, and for the ultimate overcoming of the evil and the anger it caused, and for reconciliation and peace with our neighbor and God, *we pray for the Grace to forgive the offender unconditionally — from our heart*. It may well take time to pray for this Grace, but eventually it will be given because it is in accord with God's will that we be merciful and forgive others as we ask God to forgive us. When the anger has subsided because of the passing of time and through prayer for deliverance from hatred, we sense an interior spiritual readiness to forgive. Then we rely on the power of Jesus Christ to set us free and bring us a peace the world cannot give.

Do not repeat the act and prayer of forgiveness itself. Once is enough for each person and each offense done against you.

Forgiving is not an act aimed at "doing away with" what some people consider uncomfortable or bad emotions. *Forgiving is an act of the will informed by reason, a spiritual act aimed at setting yourself and the wrongdoer free, so you will be reconciled before God.* Forgiving imitates what God in Christ did on the Cross; *it participates in the Divine Mercy.*

The Act and Prayer of Forgiveness

Think of a person you are ready to forgive. This person may be alive or already deceased. The person may also be yourself. Placing yourself before Jesus, and imploring the power of His *Divine Mercy,* pray:

"Lord God, I thank You for this moment of quiet, for this opportunity to put myself in Your presence."

"Lord, it is good to meditate on the reality of Your loving presence. I praise You and I glorify You."

"Thank You Lord, for helping me to be still and know that You are a merciful God."

"Thank You for the Grace of being comfortable with the anger that I feel toward the person who has wronged me."

"Thank You for having taken away the guilt and fear I used to feel whenever I felt angry."

"You know, Jesus, that I have exhausted every reasonable effort to make peace with the person who has wronged me. You know that these efforts have been in vain because of this person's refusal to right the wrong, or because he (or she) is no longer alive, or because I waited so long before resolving my anger. I believe that You want me to be free of unresolved anger and resentment, for You desire my happiness and wholeness more than I could ever desire these for myself."

"Thank You for having taught us that it is by forgiving the wrongdoer at the right moment that we will be set free from resentment, so that we can go on living without bitterness and tension and their inescapable ill effects on our body and psyche."

"I ask You, Jesus, to increase Your life-giving power of Mercy in me. The power that flows from You is ever-present to me. I need this power to give me strength to do what You want me to do, for it is no easy matter to forgive when one feels so injured and so angry."

"Thank You Lord for giving me the strength of Your Divine Mercy at this difficult moment for the time when I *will* be able to say from my heart, 'Jesus, in Your name and in Your presence I forgive so-and-so (by name).'"

When you reach the time of spiritual readiness, pray:

"My Jesus, I visualize this person who has wronged me; I visualize him (or her) in Your merciful presence, and I say: *'I forgive you_____ in the name of Jesus Christ. I also ask Jesus to forgive you for the wrong you have done to me. I give thanks to God because you are now forgiven. Amen.'*"

In the next few days, whenever you become aware of the past pain and anger — which now gradually or almost totally subsides — give thanks for the act of forgiveness and its power to deliver us from evil:

"Lord, it is now several days later, and I again feel some stirring of the past anger and resentment toward this person. I

thank You that You have forgiven _____, and that You gave
me the strength and good will to forgive him (or her). I now
Bless _____ (name the wrongdoer I have forgiven) in the
Name of the Lord. I see _____ as a child of God, for through
my intercessory prayers God's healing love is entering into him
(or her). Amen."

APPENDIX A

The Essays of Conrad W. Baars, M.D.
in Chronological Order

1965   Periodic Abstinence — An Expression of Marital Love *

1965   Psychological Aspects of Obedience

1965   Moral Education of Children and Adolescents *

1971   The Psychiatrist — Friend or Foe of the Pregnant
       Woman? *

1971   The Alcoholic Priest

1971   How to Treat and Prevent the Crisis in the Priesthood

1972   A Priest for All Seasons: Masculine and Celibate

1974   Morality and the Christian Anthropology of Thomas
       Aquinas

1974   The Homosexual's Search for Happiness

1977   A Critique of Permissive Sexual Morality *

1977   Whatever Happened to Religious Life? "I Will Give
       Them a New Heart"

1978   The Secret of Affirmation (interview by Jack Wintz,
       OFM)

1978   Abortion and a World Split Apart *

1979   Psychic Causes and Consequences of the Abortion
       Mentality *

1979   Anger and Forgiveness

1979   Mature and Affirming Bishops

1980   The Affirming Power of Love

1981   Philosophy as Intellectual Affirmation of the
       Seminarian
1982   Psychic Wholeness and Healing for the Family *

* These articles will be contained in another volume.

APPENDIX B

Acknowledgments

"How to Treat and Prevent the Crisis in the Priesthood," "A Priest for All Seasons: Masculine and Celibate," and "The Homosexual's Search for Happiness," all published by Franciscan Herald Press as pamphlets in the Synthesis Series.

"Whatever Happened to Religious Life — I Will Give Them a New Heart," delivered to Consortium Perfectae Caritas convention, St. Louis, Missouri, 1978. Included are passages from an article by Conrad Baars: "Jesus, Perfect in His Way of Loving Us," first published as "Superhuman," in *Today's Catholic*, April 15, 1977. Excerpts from *The Peasant of the Garonne*, Jacques Maritain, Holt, Rinehart and Winston, 1968, are used with their permission.

"The Secret of Affirmation," first published in *St. Anthony Messenger*, Vol. 85, No. 9, Feb. 1978, interview of C.W. Baars by Fr. Jack Wintz, OFM. Reprinted with permission.

"Morality and the Christian Anthropology of Thomas Aquinas," first published as "The Christian Anthropology of Thomas Aquinas" in *The Priest*, Vol. 30, No. 10, pp. 29-33.

"Philosophy as Intellectual Affirmation of the Seminarian," first published as "Your Seminary: Right or Wrong?" in the *Homiletic and Pastoral Review*, Vol. LXXXII, No. 4, January 1982. Reprinted with permission of the *Homiletic and Pastoral Review*.

"The Affirming Bishop," private communication, reprinted with permission.

"The Psychology of Obedience," first published in *Cross and Crown*,
Vol. XVII, Nos. 1, 2, and 3, 1965. Reprinted with permission
of Tan Books and Publishers.

"The Alcoholic Priest," first published in *The Priest*, vol. 27, No. 6,
pp. 49-55.

"Anger and Forgiveness," is a transcription of a recorded lecture on
"Premature Forgiving" edited with other lecture notes.

Glossary

actus humanus — a human act

affectivity — the capacity to be affected or moved by the humane emotions of love, desire and joy

affirmation — a three part process of being present, moved by and revealing to another one's feelings of love or liking, which strengthen the other to be himself

agere contra — to act or fight against

aggiornamento — update

alter Christus — refers to a priest as "another Christ"

amor amicitiae — the love between friends

anthropology — study of the human being

appetitus sensitivus — the sensitive appetite or the emotions (also called the *animalis*)

assertive drive — drive toward self-realization and self-preservation

assertive emotions — hope, despair, courage, fear, anger

auctor — author

bonum naturale — the natural good

caelebs — not married, celibate

concupiscence — desiring

condition sine qua non — an indispensable and essential action

deprivation neurosis — original term for Emotional Deprivation Disorder (in English)

DSM — *Diagnostic and Statistical Manual of Mental Disorders*

effectivity — our readiness to think and act effectively

estimative power — ability to perceive abstract concepts

frustration neurosis — original term for deprivation neurosis or Emotional Deprivation Disorder (in Dutch)

humane emotions — love, hate, desire, aversion, joy, sadness

ira — anger

irascible — easily provoked to anger

natural law — moral or eternal law that can be known by reason

lower nature — the "passions" or emotions

Magisterium — teaching authority of the Roman Catholic Church

malingerer — feigning physical or psychological symptoms to avoid something or for secondary gain

social mores — norms, customs and unspoken rules of a society

mortification — practice of disciplining the emotions

neurosis — a disorder in the emotional life

novitiate — probationary time in a religious order

passio — passions

passions — emotions

phobia — irrational fear of something

pleasure appetite — humane emotions: love, hate, desire, aversion, joy, sadness

premature forgiving — forgiving before allowing the healthy emotional process, including anger, to take place

psychic incarnation (psychological) — one's second or psychological birth

psychological birth — sense of identity and confidence arising from another's unconditional love (affirmation)

psychosomatic — the inseparable connection between psyche (soul) and soma (body)

ratio — reason

repression — conflict between two emotions, one of which is pushed into the subconscious by the other

sadomasochistic — obtaining pleasure from inflicting mental or physical pain on oneself or others

scrupulosity — morbid sensitiveness in matters of conscience

self-affirmation — unhealthy and futile process of attempting to convince oneself and others that one is worthwhile

sensus fidei — supernatural appreciation or sense of faith

sublimation — redirecting unacceptable desires into acceptable actions

utilitarian emotions — assertive emotions; hope, despair, courage, fear, anger

utility appetite — assertive drive

voluntaristic — the idea that the will is supreme and that everything can be accomplished through sheer willpower

voluntas — the will

Bibliography

Adler, Mortimer J. *The Time of Our Lives: The Ethics of Common Sense*. New York: Fordham University Press, 1996.

_____. *The Idea of Freedom*. Westport, CT: Greenwood Press, 1973.

American Psychiatric Association: *Diagnostic and Statistical Manual of Mental Disorders*. Fourth Edition, Text Revision. Washington, DC, American Psychiatric Association, 2000 (2nd ed., 1968; 3rd ed., 1980; 4th ed., 1994).

Aquinas, Thomas. *Commentary on Nicomachean Ethics*. Trans. C.I. Litzinger. Chicago: Regnery, 1964.

_____. *Summa Theologica: St. Thomas Aquinas*. Trans. Fathers of the English Dominican Province. Westminster, MD: Christian Classics, 1981.

Aristotle. *Nicomachean Ethics*. Mineola, NY: Dover Publications, 1998.

Arnold, Magda B. *Emotion and Personality*. 2 vols. New York: Columbia University Press, 1960.

Aumann, Jordan & Conrad Baars. *The Unquiet Heart: Reflections on Love and Sexuality*. Staten Island, NY: Alba House, 1991.

Baars, Conrad W. *Born Only Once: The Miracle of Affirmation*. 1975, 1989. Preface Suzanne M. Baars. Quincy, IL: Franciscan Press, Quincy University, 2001.

_____. *Doctor of the Heart*. Staten Island, NY: Alba House, 1996.

_____. *Feeling & Healing Your Emotions*. Rev. ed. Suzanne M. Baars and Bonnie N. Shayne, eds., Gainesville, FL: Bridge-Logos, 2003.

_____ and Anna A.Terruwe. *Healing the Unaffirmed: Recognizing Emotional Deprivation Disorder*. Rev. ed. Suzanne M. Baars and Bonnie N. Shayne, eds. Staten Island, NY: Alba House, 2002.

Boekel, C.W. Van. *Katharsis*. Utrecht: DeFontein, 1957.

Boxtel, J.P. Van. "Moraal en Affectiviteit" in *De Menselyke Persoon in de christelyke moraal*, 1958.

_____. "Moraal en Gevoelsleven volgens Thomas van Aquino" in *Tydschrift voor Philosophie*, June, 1959.

Brennan, Robert E. *General Psychology*. New York: Macmillan, 1937.

_____. *Thomistic Psychology*. New York: Macmillan, 1941.

Calon, P.J.A. *De Jongen*. Haarlem: De Toorts, 1969.

_____. "Ontwikkeling van de menselyke persoon. Consequenties voor de christelyke moraal." *Voordracht gehouden op studie-dagen voor de priesters van het aartsbisdom Utrecht en bisdom Groningen*. August, 1958.

_____ and J.J.G. Prick. *Psychologische Grondbegrippen*. Salzburg: O. Müller, 1969.

Donceel, J.F. *Philosophical Psychology*. New York: Sheed and Ward, 1961.

Duynstee, W.J.A.J. *Verspreide Opstellen*. Roermond: Romen, 1963.

Ford, John C. *Depth Psychology, Morality and Alcoholism*. Weston, MA: Weston College, 1951.

_____ and Gerald Kelly, S.J. *Contemporary Moral Theology*. Vols. I and II, Westminster, MD: Newman Press, 1958-63.

Freud, Sigmund. *A General Introduction to Psychoanalysis*. Garden City, NY: Garden City Publishing Co., 1943.

Gerets, J.P. *Psychasthenie en frustratie neurose*.

Graauw, H.J.M. de. *Een Academische Opleiding in De Pedagogiek*. Nymegen, 1972.

Guardini, Romano. *The End of the Modern World*. Wilmington, DE: ISI Books, 2001.

_____. *Das Gute, das Gewissen understand die Sammlung*. Mainz: Matthias-Grunewald-Verlag.

Harvey, John F. *The Homosexual Person: New Thinking in Pastoral Care*. San Francisco: Ignatius Press, 1987.

John Paul II. *The Theology of the Body: Human Love in the Divine Plan.* Boston, MA: Daughters of St. Paul, 1997.

Journet, Charles. *The Meaning of Evil.* New York: P.J. Kenedy & Sons, 1963.

Joyce, Mary Rosera. *Love Responds to Life – The Challenge of Humanae Vitae.* Kenosha, WI: Prow, 1971.

_____ and Robert E. Joyce. *New Dynamics in Sexual Love.* Collegeville, MN: St. John's University Press, 1970.

Kelsey, Morton T. *Healing and Christianity: A Classic Study.* Minneapolis, MN: Augsburg, 1995.

_____. *Caring: How Can We Love One Another?* New York: Paulist Press, 1981.

Kolb, Lawrence C. and Keith H. Brodie. *Modern Clinical Psychiatry* (10th ed.).

Kreeft, Peter. *Summa of the Summa.* San Francisco: Ignatius Press, 1990. Philadelphia, PA: W.B. Saunders Co., 1982.

May, William E. (ed.). *Principles of Catholic Moral Life.* Chicago, IL: Franciscan Herald Press, 1981.

Meany, John. "Reflections on Thomism and Client-Centered Psychotherapy." Paper presented at the 16th Annual Scientific Session, Guild of Catholic Psychiatrists. Los Angeles, 1964.

Montagu, Ashley. *Touching: The Human Significance of the Skin* (3rd ed.). New York: Perennial Library, 1986.

Nicolosi, Joseph. *A Parent's Guide to Preventing Homosexuality.* Downers Grove, IL: InterVarsity Press, 2002.

_____. *Reparative Therapy of Male Homosexuality: A New Clinical Approach.* Northvale, NJ: J. Aronson, 1997.

_____ with the assistance of Lucy Freeman. *Healing homosexuality: Case Stories of Reparative Therapy.* Northvale, NJ: J. Aronson, 1993.

Pfürtner, Stephanus. *Triebleben und Sittliche Vollendung.* Freiburg, Schweiz: Universitätsverlag, 1958.

Pieper, Josef. *A Brief Reader on the Virtues of the Human Heart.* Trans. Paul C. Duggan. San Francisco: Ignatius Press, 1991.

_____. *The Four Cardinal Virtues: Prudence, Justice, Fortitude, Temperance.* New York: Harcourt, Brace & World, 1965.

_____. *Happiness and Contemplation.* Trans. Richard and Clara Winston. South Bend, IN: St. Augustine's Press, 1998.

_____. *Leisure – The Basis of Culture.* Trans. Alexander Dru. Indianapolis, IN: Liberty Fund, 1999.

Rahner, Hugo. *Man at Play.* Trans. Brian Battershaw and Edward Quinn. New York: Herder and Herder, 1967.

Royo, Antonio, and Jordan Aumann. *The Theology of Christian Perfection.* New York: Foundation for a Christian Civilization, 1987.

Rzadkiewicz, Arnold L. *The Philosophical Bases of Human Liberty According to Thomas Aquinas.* Washington, DC: Catholic University Press, 1949.

Smith, Vincent Edward. *The General Science of Nature.* Milwaukee, WI: Bruce Books, 1958.

Terruwe, Anna A. *The Abode of Love.* St. Meinrad, IN: Abbey Press, 1970.

_____. *Affectiviteit – effectiviteit : breekpunt van menselijk leven : over waarde-overdracht in het onderwijs.* Lochem: De Tijdstroom, 1988.

_____. *De frustratie neurose.* Amsterdam: Anthos, 1998.

_____. *De liefde bouwt een woning.* Bussum: Romen, 1978.

_____. *De toename van agressie, suïcide en druggebruik binnen de consumptiemaatschappij.* Lochem - Gent: De Tijdstroom, 1986.

_____. *Emotional Growth in Marriage.* Glen Rock, NJ: Paulist Press, 1968.

_____. *Geloven zonder angst en vrees.* Roermond: J.J. Romen, 1969.

_____. *Give Me Your Hand.* Trans. Martin Van Buuren. Croydon, Victoria: Spectrum Publications, 1973.

_____. *The Neurosis in the Light of Rational Psychology.* Trans. by Conrad W. Baars. New York: P.J. Kenedy & Sons, 1960.

_____. *Aopening van zaken.* In Usum privatum. Nymegen, 1964.

————. *Ouders en kinderen op weg naar de toekomst.* Lochem: De Tijdstroom, 1976.

————. *Psychopathic Personality and Neurosis.* Trans. Conrad W. Baars. New York: P.J. Kenedy & Sons, 1958.

————. and Conrad W. Baars. *Loving and Curing the Neurotic: A New Look at Emotional Illness.* New Rochelle, NY: Arlington House, 1972.

————. *Psychic Wholeness and Healing.* Staten Island, NY: Alba House, 1981.

———— and A.L. Kroft. *De stap over de drempel: moderne visies op hulpverlening bij menswording van mentaal gehandicapte mensen.* Baarn: Arbor, 1993.

———— and H.P. Van Cranenburgh. *Hooglied van de nieuwe liefde : antropologie van de weerhoudende liefde.* Baarn: Gooi en Sticht, 1996.

Tournier, Paul. *The Gift of Feeling.* Atlanta, GA: John Knox Press, 1981.

————. *The Person Reborn* in *The Best of Paul Tournier: Four Volumes in One.* New York: Iversen Norman, 1977.

Vanier, Jean. *Man and Woman He Made Them.* Mahwah, NJ: Paulist Press, 1985.

Vann, Gerald. *The Heart of Man.* New York: Longmans, Green & Co., 1945.

————. *Morals and Man* (rev.). New York: Sheed and Ward, 1960.

Veldman, Frans. *Haptonomie: science de l'affectivité: redécouvrir l'humain.* Paris: Presses universitaires de France, 1998.

Virtue, William D. *Mother and Infant: The Moral Theology of Motherhood.* Pontificia Studiorum Universitas: Romae, 1995.

Wilhelmsen, Frederick D. *The Metaphysics of Love.* New York: Sheed & Ward, 1962.

Index

A

abnormal 6, 26, 113, 132, 165, 178, 218, 219, 220, 234, 257
abortion xi, xxx, 14, 65, 167, 224, 247
abstinence xix, 196, 211, 216, 257
abuse xxiv, 106, 140, 149, 226
achievement 208, 212
act, human xiii, xx, 44, 73, 76, 77, 136, 157, 251
act, moral xiii, xx, 75, 76
act of the will 121, 133, 136, 244
actus externus 77
actus humanus 75, 251
actus internus 77
Adam 39, 49, 143, 162
addiction xxiv, 148, 209
adolescent 5, 210, 229
affective xviii, xxvi, 42, 44, 47, 81, 82, 121, 133, 134, 230
affectivity xv, xxx, 44, 47, 56, 81, 251. *See also* effectivity
affirmation, authentic xxix, xxx, 14, 16, 193, 198, 200, 203. *See also* non-affirmation, pseudo-affirmation, self-affirmation
affirmation, emotional xvii, xviii, 102
affirmation, false 55
affirmation, intellectual xix, 87, 102, 195, 197, 248, 249
affirmation, lack of xvii, 63, 174, 202, 210
affirmation, misinterpretation of the word 46
affirmation, opposite of 14, 51, 101, 181. *See also* denial
affirmation, process of 56, 197
affirmation therapy 194, 196, 198, 203
affirmed ix, xix, xx, xxvi, 10, 23, 48, 49, 50, 51, 52, 53, 56, 58, 63, 69, 70, 71, 72, 95, 98, 100, 101, 102, 116, 151, 158, 189, 190, 191, 193, 195, 196, 200, 202, 223, *See also* unaffirmed
affirmer, first 45, 48, 70
affirming life 45, 46, 47, 48, 56, 57, 67, 72, 102
affirming living ix, 46
affirming love ix, xi, xv, xvi, xxv, 15, 41, 48, 100, 121
affirming presence 48, 49, 50, 69, 103
agere contra 85, 251
aggression 16, 169, 212, 217, 218

Alcoholics Anonymous 202, 208, 209, 210, 235
alcoholism 3, 17, 18, 24, 184, 205, 207, 209, 256
alter Christus 176, 181, 251
American Psychiatric Association xiv, xxx, 185, 186, 255
amor amicitiae 165, 251
anger, accepting your 226
anger, appropriate use of 220, 222
anger as a capital sin 8
anger, emotion of 60, 61, 176
anger, express xxviii, 218, 221, 222, 225, 227, 237
anger, forbid 222
anger, goodness of 218
anger, healthy 216
anger, holding in 71
anger, identifying our hurt as 61
anger, outbursts of 174, 229
anger, proper function of 219, 223
anger, repression of 169, 218, 224, 231, 232, 233, 236, 243
anger, sinfulness of 228
anger, suppress 230
anger, unresolved 240, 241, 245
angry, I may feel 236
animal 43, 78, 114, 155, 156, 157, 158, 164, 251
anorexic 233
anthropology vii, xii, xxi, xxiii, 4, 33, 43, 45, 73, 74, 75, 81, 85, 87, 88, 95, 133, 176, 177, 178, 184, 247, 249, 251
anxiety xiv, 7, 8, 10, 26, 142, 148, 198, 205, 208, 209, 232. *See also* tension
aphrodisiac society 153
apostles xxv, 50, 100, 103
appetite, pleasure xiv, xv, xviii, xxi, xxiii, 6, 9, 25, 84, 130, 252
appetite, sensitive 78, 81, 82, 251
appetite, utility 6, 25, 253
appetitus sensitivus 76, 80, 251
approval xviii, 127, 128, 129, 130, 183, 221, 222
Aquinas, St. Thomas vii, x, xii, xiii, xvii, xx, xxi, xxvii, 33, 43, 44, 45, 73, 74, 76, 77, 79, 80, 81, 82, 83, 84, 85, 88, 95, 112, 134, 146, 175, 176, 177, 178, 223, 247, 249, 255, 258
aridity, spiritual 5, 148

Aristotle 154, 155, 255
arousal, emotional 171
arousal, psychological 219
Art of Loving, The 173
asceticism xxi, xxiii, 9, 10, 22, 45, 84
assertive vii, 62, 67, 71, 84, 168, 170, 197, 199, 200, 217, 222, 236, 237, 238, 253
assertive drive xii, xiv, xv, xviii, xxi, xxiii, 45, 84, 115, 217, 220, 222, 251
assertive emotions 6, 9, 10, 22, 23, 25, 47, 84, 251, 253
assertiveness training 217, 236
assimilation 150, 152, 156, 157
asthma 234, 235
atheism 95, 167
attitude 5, 8, 16, 27, 29, 31, 34, 35, 36, 39, 44, 45, 61, 65, 74, 78, 79, 80, 109, 114, 139, 140, 141, 149, 180, 183, 184, 196, 198, 199, 223, 228, 230, 237
auctor 97, 180, 213, 251
Aumann, Jordan x, 126, 255, 258
authoritarian xxii, 9, 16, 109, 118, 124
authority, abdication of 120
authority, divine 137
authority, fraternal 119
authority, mature 45, 180, 213
authority, paternal 119
authority, resistance to 123
authority, respect for 110, 123
authority, submission to 114

B

beatings 131
beatitude 41
behavior 54, 98, 100, 109, 110, 111, 115, 129, 132, 152, 155, 156, 158, 169, 183, 189, 192, 198, 200, 220, 221, 224, 229, 238
behaviorism 155
belittle 53, 54. *See also* criticize
Benedict, St. 122
benevolent 121
birth, psychological 69, 190, 252
bitterness 30, 42, 229, 240, 245
bonum fundamentale 12
bonum naturale 4, 251
bonum rationis 79, 81
Born Only Once 52, 69, 190, 191, 202, 212, 255

brainwashed 115, 171
bridalmother 49
Bride of Christ xxv, 50
Buchenwald xxvii, xxviii, 52, 57, 60, 215, 216
buried alive 232

C

caeleb 145, 146, 150, 151, 165, 181, 251
Cajetan 136
Calvin 34, 65, 137
canon law 124
capital sin 8, 224, 225
cardinal virtues 83, 257
Catholic Church vii, 2, 65, 78, 88, 92, 101, 102, 129, 213, 252
Catholic school 35, 91, 126
Catholics, fallen-away 126
celibate xxv, 5, 19, 20, 21, 26, 37, 74, 88, 145, 146, 147, 148, 149, 150, 151, 152, 153, 155, 156, 157, 159, 161, 162, 163, 165, 167, 169, 171, 173, 175, 177, 179, 181, 182, 190, 191, 196, 197, 211, 247, 249, 251
childhood, perpetual 116
Christ, bride of 48, 50
Christianity 28, 29, 30, 31, 37, 167, 257
Christology 40, 41
co-creator 47, 57, 70, 97
cold 23, 51, 54, 99, 115, 125
command 20, 105, 106, 107, 108, 109, 110, 112, 114, 119, 122, 123, 125, 141
commandment 20, 39, 116, 136, 138, 172
communication 8, 47, 120, 125, 160, 249
communion 47, 126, 160, 162
Communism xxvii, 167
community xxix, 8, 50, 89, 92, 103, 106, 122, 133, 139, 140, 166, 176, 180, 182, 212, 219, 227
compassion 37, 47, 67, 102, 164, 181
compliance 81, 118, 120
compulsion 36, 47, 146, 151, 153, 189, 193, 195, 196, 198, 205
concentration camp xxvii, 52, 215
concupiscence 78, 251
concupiscible xii, xxi, 8, 23, 83, 84, 121

conditio sine qua non 12
confession 124, 126
confessor 25, 201
conflicts 17, 124, 149, 197, 206
conscience xiii, xvi, xxiv, 6, 25, 30, 38, 124, 131, 140, 189, 252
contemplative 47, 67
continence 20, 83, 151
contraception 24, 152, 167, 192
control xxvii, 6, 77, 80, 84, 124, 127, 218, 219, 222, 229, 230, 234, 235, 239
courage xiv, xxi, 6, 8, 34, 36, 38, 43, 71, 84, 102, 115, 129, 152, 166, 167, 168, 169, 170, 175, 200, 228, 251, 253
creation x, xiii, xxvi, 12, 28, 46, 57, 67, 68, 136, 175, 190
Creator 9, 12, 175, 180, 190, 198, 213
crisis, vocation 87, 88, 89, 91, 92
criticism 10, 14, 40, 53, 54, 113, 181, 200, 218, 220
curriculum xix, 74, 94

D

delight xviii, 19, 46, 55, 56, 57, 68, 70, 78, 102, 117, 126
delinquency 124, 132
denial xi, xv, 14, 15, 29, 32, 51, 53, 54, 55, 56, 57, 58, 78, 79, 101, 102, 120, 164, 191, 216, 243
dependence 110, 114, 141, 142
depression 7, 38, 65, 71, 171, 176, 184, 191, 232
desensitization 90
despair xxviii, 6, 22, 60, 115, 251, 253
Diagnostic and Statistical Manual of Mental Disorders xiv, 185, 186, 251, 255
disapproval 127, 130, 131, 221
discipline xv, xviii, xxi, 75, 84, 118, 124, 125
discursive mind 67
divorce 8, 154, 211
docility 114, 124
doormat 232
drugs 16, 24, 65, 212, 232
duty 19, 20, 98, 120, 129, 131, 135, 177
Duynstee, W.J.A.J. xiii, xxxiii, 6, 33, 74, 75, 84, 133, 256

E

eating disorders 233
ecology of the emotions xxx
educator 5, 7, 14, 23, 65, 113, 124, 127, 128, 129, 130, 131, 132, 143, 158, 179, 181, 210, 220, 224, 225
educator, sensitive 55
effectivity 251. *See also* affectivity
egocentric 107, 109
Emotional Deprivation Disorder xii, xiv, xv, 7, 10, 11, 12, 17, 25, 37, 40, 66, 154, 168, 175, 188, 189, 194, 198, 200, 206, 207, 208, 210, 211, 230, 251, 252, 255
emotional illness xii, xiii, 3, 22, 36, 37, 41, 66, 148, 149, 187, 210, 211, 212, 241, 259
emotions are good 20, 60
emotions, assertive 6, 9, 10, 22, 23, 25, 47, 84, 251, 253
emotions, "bad" 60, 221, 244
emotions, feel all your 60, 239
emotions, humane 47, 67, 115, 121, 251, 252
emotions, "positive" 171, 173
emotions, sexual 90
emotions, the goodness of our 45, 172
emotions, unacceptable 173, 188, 230
enemy 15, 28, 30, 58, 59, 62, 63, 64, 71, 76, 102, 172, 173, 216, 224
energy-based repressive disorder 36, 41, 66, 115, 142, 230
equilibrium 43, 117, 118
estimative power 221, 251
euthanasia 152, 167
evil, Christian response to 216
evil, moral 173, 181
evil, oppose 38, 74, 145, 150, 168, 169, 172, 175, 177, 224
ex-priest 211
exploitation 71, 100, 160, 162, 164, 172, 200, 232
extramarital 146, 148, 154

F

fear, existential 7
fear, irrational 7, 252
fear of asserting oneself 114
fear of being angry 237
fear of hurting other people's feelings 61, 176, 181
fear of "lower nature" 35

fear of not being loved 200, 234
fear of one's emotions 80, 84, 176,
  229
fear of others 101, 195
fear of our "lower nature" 44, 65, 180
fear-based repression 66, 217, 237
Feeling and Healing Your Emotions xii,
  xxvi, 17, 36, 52, 147, 218
feelings are pathological 34
feelings, be honest with your 59, 62
feelings cannot be commanded 172
feelings, experience your 60
feelings, express your 62
feelings, fear of 230
feelings, hurt 131, 218
feelings, "negative" 173
feelings, rise above their 37
feminine 150, 159, 160, 164, 165,
  167, 175, 199
flesh and the spirit 37, 80
forgiveness 62, 111, 215, 216, 217,
  227, 229, 231, 233, 235, 237, 239,
  241, 242, 243, 245, 247, 250
Forgiveness, Prayer of 242, 244
forgiving, premature 239, 240, 250,
  252
fortitude 45, 69, 74, 83, 166, 167, 168,
  169, 175, 214, 223, 257
"fraternité" approach 120
free will 73, 131, 143, 170, 190
freedom 23, 57, 76, 77, 78, 120, 138,
  141, 142, 143, 144, 146, 151, 158,
  159, 160, 215, 216, 221, 255
Freud, Sigmund 155, 158, 159, 256
friendship 68, 71, 121, 160, 171, 223
frigidity 11, 152
Fromm, Erich 173
frustration 5, 30, 72, 115, 116, 188,
  192, 193, 194, 220, 222
frustration neurosis 7, 252

G

gay 189, 192, 196, 199, 202, 203
Gay Liberation Movement 183, 184
gay militant 185
gender identification 197
genital 47, 146, 147, 152, 159, 189,
  193, 194, 198, 199, 200
goad, kick against the 102
government 15, 166, 167, 171, 174
grace 32, 39, 43, 44, 45, 129, 150,
  243, 244
Gregory the Great 112

guilt 40, 166, 185, 196, 208, 227, 229,
  244
Guitton, Jean 153

H

habit 126, 130, 143, 196, 229, 230
hands and intellect 161
happiness 5, 9, 17, 19, 21, 41, 44, 48,
  50, 53, 65, 75, 82, 98, 121, 130, 141,
  149, 150, 154, 163, 172, 174, 183,
  185, 187, 189, 190, 191, 193, 194,
  195, 196, 197, 199, 201, 203, 245,
  247, 249, 258
harmony 39, 42, 43, 79, 82, 83, 150,
  243
hate 6, 22, 42, 60, 62, 63, 115, 135,
  169, 170, 171, 172, 173, 174, 176,
  177, 197, 214, 224, 232, 239, 252
healing 42, 45, 58, 102, 198, 203,
  236, 241, 246, 255, 257
Healing the Unaffirmed xii, 7, 52, 154,
  169, 188, 207, 212, 255
health, emotional 133, 176
health, psychological 52
health, spiritual 42
heart ix, x, xv, xxv, xxvi, xxxi, 42, 43,
  44, 49, 99, 106, 122, 163, 167, 240,
  243, 245, 247, 249, 259
heart, stony 62
heterosexual 90, 148, 186, 189, 193,
  194, 195, 198, 200, 201, 203
Holy Spirit xvi, xxii, xxv, xxx, 47, 101,
  119, 120
homosexual acts 183, 184
horse and rider analogy 9
House of Affirmation xxiii, xxix, xxx
"Human Growth in the Priesthood" 3
human nature ix, xi, xx, xxi, xxiii, xxix,
  25, 34, 35, 42, 43, 48, 65, 67, 75,
  84, 132, 143, 151, 152, 154, 155,
  156, 158, 159, 161, 173, 180, 214,
  223, 231
human nature, goodness of 44, 143,
  179
Humanae Vitae 39, 45, 257
humane emotions 47, 67, 115, 121,
  251, 252
humanity xxvi, 5, 40, 45, 48, 143, 151,
  167, 173, 182, 214
humiliate 124, 131
hurt 54, 55, 61, 71, 145, 166, 171,
  176, 181, 192, 199, 220, 228, 229,
  230, 233, 238
hysterical 188, 209

I

identification 113, 114
identity 2, 3, 5, 10, 16, 18, 20, 22, 53, 145, 159, 160, 174, 178, 190, 194, 195, 252
imagination 8, 47, 62, 98, 165, 211, 226, 233, 238
imagining, positive 62
immature 2, 14, 21, 26, 116, 124, 149, 153, 168, 186, 21, 229, 234
immaturity, emotional 3, 16, 18, 150
immaturity, psychosexual 11
immoral 25, 189
impotence 11, 17, 114, 152
inadequacy 7, 10, 110, 113, 191, 208
independence 100, 105, 113, 119
inferiority 7, 10, 26, 110, 174, 191
injustice xxiv, 29, 220, 224, 227, 240, 241
insecurity 10, 26, 191
integration vii, xi, xxx, 26, 79, 82, 83, 85, 149, 171, 212, 239
intellect and will 19, 26, 133, 134, 150, 152
intellectualistic 85, 133, 136, 139, 140, 141
intuitive 47, 67, 161, 162, 164

J

Joyce, Mary and Robert xxv, xxx, 155, 156, 257
judgment 81, 87, 91, 116, 119, 122, 123, 148, 183, 223
Jung, Carl 63, 64, 242
justice xxii, xxiv, xxv, 44, 74, 80, 83, 145, 219, 227, 228, 243

K

Kant, Immanuel 77, 137
Kolbe, Maximilian 216

L

laicization 26
laity 30, 35, 37, 43, 69, 89, 91, 92, 180
law, moral 137
law, natural 133, 136, 154, 252
law of gradual development 125
lesbian 189, 196, 202, 203
liberation 65, 95, 243
liberté, égalité, and fraternité 105
libido 79

listen 44, 67, 68, 70, 76, 80, 81, 84, 106, 122, 213, 237
Little Way 50
living dangerously 237
loneliness 7, 10, 15, 46, 69, 174, 191, 213
love, authentic 198, 199
love, being 159
love, emotional xv, 7, 11, 16, 20, 22, 23, 37, 121, 213
love, possessive 54
love, self-restraining xv, xix, 22, 25, 41, 49, 98, 99, 100
love, spiritual 7
love, unselfish xv, 13, 41, 143
love, volitional 11, 20, 22, 23, 121, 172, 213
Loving and Curing the Neurotic xii, 154, 259
lower nature 35, 40, 44, 65, 252
Lumen Gentium 4
lust 32, 35, 78
Luther, Martin 137

M

Magisterium xxii, 147, 179, 181, 184, 252
malingerer 235
man and woman xxv, 136, 156, 159, 160, 161, 162, 163, 167
Manichaeism 28, 29, 30
Mary xxv, 40, 48, 49, 50
masculine xxv, 73, 74, 145, 150, 159, 160, 164, 165, 167, 175, 178, 179, 181, 197, 199
mask 3, 171, 212, 213, 237
Mass xxviii, 101, 126, 179
masturbation 11, 148, 154
maturity, emotional xxiv, 17, 100, 127
maturity, intellectual 127, 150
maturity, spiritual 127, 150, 211
Me-generation 88
meekness 113, 114, 171, 224, 227, 239
memory 221, 226
mental health 155, 176, 185
migraine 234, 240
Montessori 57, 157
moral judgment 60, 183, 195
moral law 137
moral norm 147
moral obligation 134

moral order 61, 68, 70, 83, 168
moral theology xxii, 73, 75, 85, 177,
    184
moral value 44, 77, 78, 136, 224
morality xiii, xviii, 35, 66, 77, 136, 151,
    154, 183, 234
mortification xxi, 11, 25, 32, 75, 78,
    79, 84, 252
Mother Teresa 2
motor 8, 9, 170, 220, 228
"moved mover," will is a 81

N

natural law 133, 136, 154, 252
neglect 11, 26, 100, 106, 131, 153,
    180
neurosis xiii, xiv, xv, xxi, xxiii, 5, 7, 65,
    203, 209, 251, 252, 258, 259
neurotic repression 20, 24, 38, 39, 66,
    74, 85, 115, 153, 169, 218
New Dynamics in Sexual Love 156,
    257
non-affirmed 3, 10, 17, 18, 19, 25, 99,
    173, 174, 175, 202, 206, 207, 210,
    211
novitiate 36, 114, 116, 252

O

obedience, blind 9, 118, 119, 120, 122
obedience training 140
obedience, vow of 119
obligation, moral 134
obsession 36, 146, 147, 153, 233
obsessive-compulsive xxiii, xxiv, 17,
    18, 25, 35, 36, 142, 146, 147, 152,
    188, 211
Ockham 135
openness 14, 20, 21, 107
orbit 52, 69
ordinatio rationis 134
orientation, change in 196
orientation, heterosexual 186, 187,
    189
orientation, homosexual 183, 185,
    187, 194, 195, 196, 197, 198, 201,
    203
original sin ix, xx, xxi, 9, 28, 34, 65,
    143, 236
other, significant 12, 13, 188, 191
Our Father 241
outburst 229

P

parental role reversal 197
parents, overprotective 54
passio 78, 252
passio nata est obedire rationi 76
passion 78, 79
personality development 24, 74, 148,
    149, 176, 201
personality disorder 153, 187, 218
Philosophy Serving Contemporary
    Needs of the Church: The Experience
    of Poland 92
phobia 234, 252
physiological reactions 219, 226, 240
Pieper, Josef 165, 166, 223, 224, 257
Plato 83
pleasure appetite xii, xiv, xv, xviii, xxi,
    xxiii, 6, 9, 25, 94, 130, 252. See also
    humane emotions, utility appetite
pornography 11, 167
power, estimative 221, 251
practical judgment 81
pretend 59, 71, 200
pride 32, 41, 130, 131
promiscuity 65, 193, 212
prout substat rationi 6, 19, 76
pseudo-affirmation 55
pseudo-Christian 61, 171, 228, 239
pseudo-obedience 113, 115, 116,
    117, 143
psyche xii, 13, 34, 38, 56, 115, 153,
    245, 252
psychic 13
Psychic Wholeness and Healing xii,
    xxiii, 6, 17, 36, 115, 153, 154, 219,
    259
psychoanalysis 25, 35, 197, 209, 236,
    256
psychological birth 69, 190, 252
psychomotor reactions 82
psychopathic 209, 210, 218, 259
psychosomatic 37, 148, 232, 234,
    240, 252
puberty 109, 147, 210

Q

quicksand, psycho-theological xviii, 39
Quixote, Don 15

R

rapport 10, 171
ratio and passio 78

rational good 44, 134, 138, 139, 140, 141, 143
reactions, physiological 219, 226, 240
reason and will xv, xxiv, 6, 9, 44, 67, 75, 76, 77, 78, 80, 82, 84, 151, 195, 217, 222, 229, 236
reason, guidance by 195
rebellion 115, 120, 123, 125, 164, 216
receptivity xxv, 107
reconciliation 219, 241, 243
religion 30, 34, 35, 65, 126, 127, 179
repressed anger 234, 240
repressed emotion 6, 153
repressing emotion 77
repression, energy-based 45
repression, fear-based 217, 237
repression, neurotic 20, 24, 38, 39, 66, 74, 85, 95, 115, 153, 169, 218
repression, obsessive-compulsive 17, 18, 25, 35, 152, 211
repression of anger 169, 218, 224, 231, 232, 236, 243
repressive mechanism 155
repressive process 38, 206, 231
resentment 30, 120, 171, 176, 218, 228, 229, 235, 240, 241, 242, 243, 245
restlessness 7, 10, 22, 148, 197, 232
restraint 20, 26, 39, 61, 68, 70, 151, 154, 165, 200
revenge 218, 229, 240, 243
risk 72, 108, 122, 129, 166, 181, 199, 227, 237

S

sadomasochistic 117, 252
salvation 9, 41, 116, 130
same-sex attraction 183, 187
Scotus, Duns 135
scrupulosity xxiii, 10, 17, 25, 36, 45, 66, 80, 142, 152, 211, 252
self-affirmation 59, 72, 100, 168, 174, 192, 202, 210, 212, 217, 253
self-control 77, 100, 124, 222
self-forgiveness 242
self-restraining love xv, xix, 13, 22, 25, 41, 49, 98, 99, 100
self-worth 2, 10, 12, 18, 58, 59, 150, 173, 195, 200, 212
senses 8, 31, 35, 47, 57, 67, 116, 172, 193, 211, 235
sensitive appetite 81, 82, 251
sensuality 78

Serra 90, 91
servility 114, 141, 143, 224
sex drive 147, 152
sex, genital 146, 193
sex, oral 192, 199
sexual appetite 153
sexual feelings xxiv, 39, 152, 193, 196
sexual gratification 88, 153, 189, 199
sexual intercourse 20, 201
sexual need 152, 153, 211
sexual orientation 185, 194, 201, 202. *See also* homosexual orientation, heterosexual orientation
sexual orientation disturbance 185
shame 40, 117
shy 51, 52
silence 15, 105, 226, 227
sin, capital 224, 225
sin, fear of 8
sin lies in the will 172
sin, original ix, xx, xxi, 9, 28, 34, 65, 143, 236
situation ethics 24, 39
sleep 233, 235, 240
spiritual life xxii, 6, 11, 13, 22, 32, 33, 39, 42, 45, 48, 72, 122, 133, 148, 150, 159, 191, 213
spiritual maturity 127, 150, 211
spoiled 127, 153, 178
status 59, 91, 98, 191, 212
Stein, Edith 163, 164
stony heart 42
strengthen your brothers 101
striving 7, 22, 34, 59, 79, 83, 90, 128, 147, 148, 152, 153, 181, 193, 197, 212
Suarez, Francisco 136, 177
sublimation 79, 155, 158, 253
submissive 23, 35, 108, 113, 115, 116, 117, 123, 164, 176, 197
suicide 15, 233
superego xiii, 6, 25, 38, 155
suppression xv, 40, 43, 79, 84, 122, 183, 196, 229, 230, 231, 243
surrender 8, 39, 43, 45, 82, 108, 113, 116, 127, 143, 222
Synod of Bishops 4

T

tantrum 220, 222
technique 46, 56
temperance xxiii, xxiv, 45, 69, 83, 166, 257

tension xxiii, 6, 7, 10, 78, 148, 171,
205, 206, 209, 216, 228, 229, 230,
232, 235, 245. *See also* anxiety
Terruwe, Anna A. vii, ix, x, xii, xiii, xiv,
xv, xvi, xviii, xix, xx, xxi, xxii, xxiii,
xxiv, xxv, xxix, 3, 5, 6, 7, 10, 11, 13,
33, 36, 52, 74, 77, 84, 115, 153, 154,
156, 188, 194, 207, 219, 255, 258
theology x, xxii, xxiii, 9, 33, 34, 73, 75,
85, 89, 90, 92, 93, 94, 126, 177, 180,
184, 256, 258, 259
therapy, affirmation 194, 196, 198,
203
Thérèse of Lisieux 50, 116
touch xv, 17, 57, 110, 166, 199, 240
Toynbee, Arnold 106
trained 7, 8, 16, 24, 32, 36, 39, 44, 59,
82, 85, 88, 94, 114, 130, 131, 140,
149, 151, 155, 158, 170, 171, 206,
211, 217, 230, 236
training vs. education 157
truth, possessing the 47
turn the other cheek 224, 231

U

unaffirmed xv, xvii, 38, 41, 53, 58, 60,
62, 66, 70, 71, 72, 98, 188, 189, 190,
191, 192, 193, 194, 195, 196, 197,
198, 199, 200, 202, 203, 207, 209,
210, 212, 213. *See also* non-affirmed,
affirmed
unassertive 232
unconscious 28, 29, 30, 79, 155, 158

unselfish xv, 7, 13, 20, 41, 143, 188,
192, 199
utilitarian 23, 47, 67, 74, 112, 114,
122, 217, 253
utility appetite 6, 25, 253. *See also*
pleasure appetite

V

Victorian 34, 66
violence 45, 76, 83, 109, 125, 142,
174, 176, 228, 229, 237
virtue of obedience 106, 119, 142,
143
virtues, cardinal 83, 257
vocation crisis 87, 88, 89, 91, 92
voluntaristic xxi, xxii, 24, 75, 76, 80,
81, 85, 133, 135, 136, 137, 139, 140,
141, 177, 253
vows 48, 147, 148, 149

W

weakness 35, 66, 162, 164, 216, 220
will, free 73, 131, 143, 170, 190
will informed by reason 9, 21, 176,
244
will is a "moved mover" 81
will must first be moved 44, 81
will power xxi, 10, 37, 142
will, supremacy of the 137
will, training of the 80, 82
work ethic 34
wrath 218, 223, 224